Interprofessional Practice in Health and Social Care

CHALLENGING THE SHARED LEARNING AGENDA

Interprofessional Practice in Health and Social Care

CHALLENGING THE SHARED LEARNING AGENDA

Carolyn Miller BA (Hons) DPhil

Professor of Health Studies and Head of the Centre for Nursing and Midwifery Research, University of Brighton, Brighton, UK

Marnie Freeman SRN HV BA (Hons) DPhil Ch Psych

Senior Research Fellow, Centre for Nursing and Midwifery Research, University of Brighton, Brighton, UK

Nick Ross BA RGN Dip. N (Lond) Cert. Ed. (FE) MA (CDHFE)

Senior Lecturer in Medical Education, University of Birmingham School of Education, Birmingham, UK

A member of the Hodder Headline Group

LONDON

First published as *Interprofessional Practice in Health and Social Care* by Arnold
A member of the Hodder Headline Group
338 Euston Road, London NW1 3BH

British Library Cataloguing in Publication Data
A catalogue record for this book is available from the British Library

ISBN 0 340 76256 X (pb)

1 2 3 4 5 6 7 8 9 10

Commissioning Editor: Aileen Parlane
Production Editor: Anke Ueberberg
Production Controller: Martin Kerans

Typeset in 10 on 12 pt Palatino by Cambrian Typesetters, Frimley, Surrey
Printed and bound in Great Britain by Redwood Books, Trowbridge

Contents

Acknowledgements

This book is based on the findings of a 3-year research study of multiprofessional working and shared learning, commissioned by the English National Board for Nursing, Midwifery and Health Visiting. We are grateful to the Board for its support, and in particular to Dr Sonia Crow, Assistant Director of Policy, who was unfailingly helpful and facilitative.

The research benefited from exploration of emerging ideas at all stages with the following individuals: Professor Richard Vincent, cardiac physician and former Director of the Trafford Centre for Research and Postgraduate Medical Education, Sussex University (now Head of Postgraduate Medical Education, University of Brighton); three colleagues from the School of Health Care Professions at the University of Brighton, namely Professor Ann Moore (Head of the Clinical Research Unit, Physiotherapy), Dr Philip Mandy (Head of Podiatry) and Marion Martin (Senior Lecturer, Occupational Therapy); and also Shona Brown, Director of Nursing, Surrey and Sussex NHS Trust (formerly at Brighton Health Care NHS Trust).

The authors are also very grateful for the support, encouragement and stimulating discussion fostered by members of the research project's Steering Group, and would like to thank John Brown (Senior Lecturer, University of York), Andrea Hughes (Senior Lecturer, Middlesex University), Helena Low (Education Officer, English National Board for Nursing, Midwifery and Health Visiting), Ian Stronach (Professor of Education, Manchester Metropolitan University), Sue Studdy (former Dean of Nursing, St Bartholomew's School of Nursing, City University) and Lonica Vanclay (former Director of the Centre for the Advancement of Interprofessional Education).

The research evidence has been gathered from clinical teams, higher education lecturers, NHS trust managers and representatives of professional bodies in health and social care. The team would like to thank all those who contributed to the research by giving up their time to complete surveys and to be interviewed and observed. Without their considerable help, research such as this would be impossible to undertake. We are most appreciative of their contribution.

The agenda for multiprofessional practice and education

1

WHAT THIS BOOK IS ABOUT

This book explores and brings together two significant concerns which impact on the well-being of patients who are being cared for in hospitals and the community. First, how well do the different health and social care professionals work together in the team that is caring for a patient? Secondly, are they being adequately prepared by their education to work effectively in a team?

These questions are particularly relevant because, over the past decade, there have been increasing calls from successive governments for health and social care professionals to *work more closely together* for the benefit of the patients or clients who use the National Health Service (NHS). Emphasis has been placed on the importance of a multiprofessional approach to health care, in which all the professionals who are contributing to the care of an NHS patient or client work not just alongside each other, but 'inter-professionally', as a team. The aim is to provide a 'seamless service' for patients and clients of the Service (Griffiths, 1988; Department of Health, 1989). This means that they can move between hospital and community without gaps in or barriers to communication about their needs. Thus the different people caring for the patients or clients, whether at home or in hospital, are well informed about what other carers' interventions have been, and there is an agreed plan for their future care.

To underpin this approach to care, the government's education and training directives have highlighted the need for more *shared learning*, both between the different health professions and between the health professions and social care professions. The argument is that those who learn together will be able to work together more readily than if they had learned in separate professional groups, and consequently they will deliver better total care for patients or clients. In response to this, shared learning initiatives[1] for health care and social care students in higher education have been increasing over

[1] We use the term 'initiative' as a broad term to include a course, module, seminar series or practical workshops (i.e. any of a range of learning activities in the curriculum in which more than one health and social care profession is involved).

the past five years, and there are many long-standing advocates of shared learning who strongly believe that it represents the way forward. The meaning of the term 'shared learning' requires clarification. Health and social care students follow monoprofessional programmes of education (e.g. nursing, radiography, medicine, physiotherapy, social work, etc.), but may come together to share a part of their learning with students who are studying for other professional qualifications.[2] If professionals are already qualified, all or part of their continuing education may be shared with other professions. If shared learning is set to expand further in future, then this is an opportune time to consider what the initiatives in higher education offer, and to determine whether they are helping the different professionals to work together.

The extensive research study on which this book is based reveals a fascinating and complex variety of teamworking problems and issues. These are illustrated by examples of highly collaborative teamworking as well as teams that are fragmented in various ways. Different professionals in the same team can have dissimilar and conflicting understandings of the nature of 'effective teamwork'. In collaborative teamwork, many issues arise concerning the way in which clinicians communicate with each other, their understanding of different roles and their awareness of the impact of management and organisational policies on the team. The benefits to patients of collaborative strategies and practices also emerge clearly. Looking at these results from an educational viewpoint, there are clear lessons to be learned about what can be done at all levels to prepare students for effective teamwork by developing their skills and their understanding of these issues. The views of NHS managers on shared learning and teamwork confirm this.

However, a second strand of the research, consisting of a national survey of higher education, followed up by interviews and visits to universities, showed that little of the multiprofessional education on offer follows the pattern suggested by the NHS multiprofessional teamworking agenda. The evidence suggests that a gulf may be developing between the reality of current practice in the NHS and the multiprofessional education which is evolving to prepare students to meet that reality. Although there have been a number of initiatives in higher education to bring professionals together so they can learn together, analysis of the research conducted on shared learning courses and programmes, and of the views and experiences of education course leaders and university curriculum developers, has revealed a divergence between education provision and the health service teamworking agenda. It was found that the higher education agenda taking forward shared learning was based on other priorities.

In the light of the lack of consistency between the knowledge and skills needed to function effectively in a multiprofessional team and the majority of the current education provision, the book will argue that new models of shared learning education are urgently needed. One such model is proposed,

[2] There is a small number of 'joint training' programmes in which the education of (usually two) different professionals is carried out jointly throughout their learning provision, leading to a single qualification; these were not included in this research.

based on clinical case studies of teams. The implications for health service managers for creating and fostering environments in which teamworking can flourish and where students have effective role models are discussed in the context of the real constraints of staff shortages and fragmentation of services.

The picture is complicated by the use of different terminology – the terms 'multiprofessional', 'multidisciplinary', 'interdisciplinary' and 'interprofessional' are frequently used interchangeably. In the literature, the same terms may be given different definitions (Temkin-Greener, 1983; Leathard, 1994). A distinction has been made between 'multi', as being composed of many who may not interact, and 'inter', which implies an interaction between team members (e.g. Luszki, 1958; Petrie, 1976). Different 'disciplines' (meaning different branches or specialisms) may also be referred to within the same profession.

In the research study, we decided to refer to 'multiprofessional teams' as being composed of members of different health and social care professions. The nature of their 'interaction' was for us to establish before we could describe them as 'inter-professional'. Then there is the question of what distinguishes a team from a group of individuals. One apparently straightforward definition is '*a group of people working together towards a common goal*'. However, this is not clear-cut. Some people work together towards the same goal but do not describe themselves as a team, while others are clearly identified both by themselves and by other professionals (but perhaps not by patients) as teams, (e.g. theatre teams and diabetic teams). We shall explore the nature of teams further in Chapter 2.

THE STAKEHOLDERS

The 3-year research study on which the book is based began by recognising that several different groups have an interest in multiprofessional work and shared learning. These include patients, carers, clinicians, educators, managers, professional bodies and the Department of Health (DoH). These stakeholders each have their own areas of expertise, their own 'language' and their own understanding of the problems. One of the first questions to be addressed was the extent to which individuals within these interest groups would agree or differ in how they perceived the issues surrounding multiprofessional teamwork and shared learning.

The stakeholders in multiprofessional work and education have all been influenced by a range of factors, including Government changes to the organisation of health care and higher education, changes in some professional roles, advances in treatments, and the needs of an ageing population. The various interest groups will view the advantages and disadvantages of enhancing multiprofessional work, and underpinning it with shared learning, both from their own perspectives and within the context of their own organisational, financial and professional constraints. For example, some of the factors which contribute to current consideration of the role of multiprofessional teamwork in the NHS (e.g. continuity of care) differ from those which affect educational institutions (e.g. greater flexibility of education provision to a wider field of students).

COLLECTING INFORMATION

Given the potential for differences in the driving forces behind shared learning initiatives and the rapid rate of change in both sectors, it is clear that the developments in the NHS could easily become out of tune with those in education. From the student's perspective, a new kind of theory–practice gap could be created, particularly as more developments in multiprofessional education move towards pre-qualifying level. This would be a gap between the reality of multiprofessional teamwork in different types of teams and shared learning education.

We concluded that a key element of the research should be to study a variety of teams in which students (both pre- and post-qualification) could find themselves working, and to define and analyse key aspects of multiprofessional team functioning. This would be done alongside an examination of the content and organisation of shared learning initiatives. Thus, rather than attempting to evaluate the outcomes of specific higher education initiatives in clinical practice, the research would direct attention to the prior question of what was happening in multiprofessional teamwork about which students might need to learn.

As part of this, the research team expected to throw some light on how teamwork affected patient care. This is because, although teamwork in health care has a long history, it cannot simply be assumed that multiprofessional teamwork improves care. Research evidence has been slow to accumulate, as Leathard (1994) has pointed out. Although interprofessional co-ordination is generally accepted as a valuable goal, can it be shown to have improved the well-being of patients? West and Slater (1996) believe that this is a difficult question to answer because of the problems in devising effective methods for assessing the outcomes of teamworking. However, evidence is gradually accumulating, as is illustrated, for example, in Tope's review (1998). Yet if pre- and post-qualification students and staff are to be educated to enhance their interprofessional abilities, they will need to view the results in terms of their *value to patient care.*

The research questions that we asked were as follows.

- What qualities and skills are needed by practitioners in order to work effectively in a multiprofessional context?
- How do people interpret 'shared learning' in the curriculum?
- If shared learning involves preparing practitioners to work effectively in a multiprofessional context, do shared learning programmes address what students need to understand in order to function effectively in a multiprofessional team?
- What is the *fit* between the qualities and skills needed in practice, and the teaching and learning which actually take place?
- What is the influence of learning to work together *outside* the formal curriculum?
- Professional roles have been evolving, particularly in nursing, but also in other professions. How are the changes in the boundaries between roles viewed by the bodies which oversee professional standards?

In order to obtain information on these questions, we collected material from four sources.

1. *Clinical teams.* Intensive studies of six multiprofessional teams that were caring for patients with different needs, both in hospitals and in the community, were conducted. Each team was observed and its members were interviewed over a 3-month period.
2. *Higher education institutions.* All UK universities offering health and social care programmes were surveyed to determine whether there was any shared learning between students in their curricula. The initiatives reported were followed up by means of a questionnaire in order to find out more about them, telephone interviews with programme leaders of a sample of initiatives, and visits to observe and interview staff and students in a further sample.
3. *NHS trust managers.* A sample of managers was interviewed in order to discuss their views of multiprofessional work and education to support it.
4. *Professional bodies.* Representatives of a sample of professional bodies were interviewed about developments in professional roles and learning between different professions. Some bodies that were approached for an interview preferred to provide documents setting out their position on multiprofessional education.

Before discussing the outcomes of the research in more detail, we shall examine the background context which has contributed to raising the profile of multiprofessional working and shared learning in recent years. There have been several key changes and developments in the NHS and in higher education which have had a significant influence on multiprofessional practice and educational developments.

THE CONTEXT FOR MULTIPROFESSIONAL PRACTICE AND SHARED LEARNING

> The changes in the health service over the last ten years have stimulated reassessments and re-evaluations of professional roles and core values. They have also led to a growing emphasis upon an improved capacity for teamwork. Those trends can be expected to increase, as tasks are redistributed within and between professions, and overlapping skills and responsibilities are identified and reassigned, depending upon patient and client need.
>
> (United Kingdom Central Council for Nursing, Midwifery and Health Visiting, 1999, p. 15, 2.18)

The enhancement of multiprofessional teamwork and the development of multiprofessional education have risen up the agendas of NHS management and universities in the last decade. The main reasons for this can be attributed to the effects of the recent changes in the delivery of care in the NHS, and the implications of those changes for education and the professions.

Changes in the NHS

The growth and increasing complexity of health and welfare services in recent years, and the escalating costs and increasing demands for services as the population ages, provided the impetus for the previous Government to urge rationalisation of resources, reduction of duplication and the provision of a more effectively integrated service. The legislation (Department of Health, 1990a) which created independent hospital trusts, general practitioner (GP) fundholders and community trusts, each responsible for working within fixed (and increasingly overdrawn) budgets and, more recently, the introduction of one-tier practice led by primary care groups (Department of Health, 1997), have produced radical changes in the organisation and delivery of care, including the following:

- moves to reduce the number of different health care professionals in contact with patients. These can be seen in initiatives such as 'integrated patient care' or 'patient-focused care' (e.g. Garside, 1993), which aim to give patients a more efficient service, with increased continuity through delivery of care by smaller teams of professionals. Consequently, within the reduced team, knowledge of each other's role and function becomes even more important;
- emphasis on evidence-based care has encouraged the development and implementation of guidelines for good practice in managing a wide range of conditions in primary and secondary health care. The effective use of the guidelines and the development of 'patient pathways' require co-ordination and communication between the health and social care professionals who draw up and operate the pathways;
- the Patient's Charter, which contributes to raised patient expectations about the quality of service that they can expect from the professionals who care for them;
- the introduction by some trusts of multi-skilling of health care workers, with a consequent overlap of interprofessional boundaries. This creates both opportunities for professional development and threats to professional integrity;
- the changing role of nurses, including the delegation of some work to health care assistants, the take-up of some work that was formerly carried out by junior doctors, and the advent of nurse practitioners;
- new surgical techniques and the emphasis on care in the community, which have both resulted in earlier discharge of patients from hospital. This places even more emphasis on good liaison between primary and secondary health carers. A number of these patients continue to require specialised care from a range of professionals, so the development of skills, including good teamworking and communication, is considered to be essential.

The moves to increase care in the community and the greater emphasis on inter-professional and inter-agency working have considerable implications for the integrated management of services, as well as for the roles of practitioners. For example, the report of the Sainsbury Centre for Mental Health states that:

> We believe that the transition from hospital based to community based services needs comprehensive changes in staff roles as well as in the structure and organisation of services.
>
> (Onyett, 1997, p. 23)

The report indicated some of the disquiet accompanying role changes:

> Other submissions to the review provided further evidence of the preoccupation with multidisciplinary working by the professions and high levels of professional disquiet about changing roles are evident from all of the evidence considered. In many submissions, role blurring was linked to fears of de-skilling.
>
> (Onyett, 1997, p. 55)

Concerns about de-skilling, and the fear that multi-skilling also means *dilution* of skills, are being expressed in the context of chronic shortages of staff, particularly nurses, but also of professionals allied to medicine (PAMs) and GPs. Current problems of staff recruitment and retention have brought multi-skilling even closer to the fore over the last 3 years. Managers in the NHS are having to consider how to meet a range of patient needs with fewer staff. Issues of role flexibility thus become a necessity rather than a virtue, with all of the associated professional concerns. This is happening at a time when NHS trusts are being asked to be more accountable for their actions, with the introduction of clinical governance (Department of Health, 1997, 1998a, b). This is associated with the higher expectations of patients who are increasingly resorting to legal redress for mistakes, leading to a climate of defensive medicine. In this context, lack of communication and co-ordination between members of the clinical team and their patients or clients and relatives is seen to be a potentially serious factor in compromising good care. The Government White Paper entitled *The Health of the Nation* (Department of Health, 1992) highlighted the need for partnerships between individuals and organisations for the improvement of health care. Most recently, the recommendations on clinical governance have stressed the need for good multi-professional practice.

NHS requirements for education to support effective multiprofessional practice

These were highlighted by the Department of Health (1993) in *Targeting Practice: The Contribution of Nurses, Midwives and Health Visitors*, which focused on alliances to provide multidisciplinary solutions, supported by multidisciplinary education. Since then, the NHS Executive's education and training planning guidelines have consistently emphasised the importance of multidisciplinary teamwork, supported by shared learning. For example, its 1995 planning guidelines stated that:

> Education commissioners should actively explore opportunities to commission multidisciplinary education and training programmes which provide opportunities for shared learning.
>
> (NHS Executive, 1995, Priority 5 [non-medical education and training])

The following year, Priority 5 remained an important medium-term goal, and the guidelines acknowledged that progress was being made in primary care and mental health, but also commented that:

> Reports from the Health Service Commissioner about team-working, especially around the boundaries of health and social care but also elsewhere, point to the need for further work to improve collaborative team-working and mutual understanding of roles, responsibilities and expertise amongst health professionals.
>
> (NHS Executive, 1996, Annex B, p. 6)

The responsibility for planning and commissioning education and training in the NHS began to be devolved from regional health authorities to local education consortia from 1996. The NHS Executive (1997) further defined the future work of the consortia to include promoting:

> shared learning to support team-working across professional and organisational boundaries, preparing the health care workforce to provide a coherent service within a primary care led NHS and across health and social care boundaries.
>
> (NHS Executive, 1997, Point 19)

The NHS Executive's planning guidelines also contributed two other points of relevance to shared learning, which appear to be directed at professional bodies. These concern professional qualifications and the use of a common language across occupational standards. First, there was the assurance that in advocating shared learning, no 'threat to existing professional qualifications or to independent self-regulation' was implied. Secondly, it was stated that the NHS Executive:

> encourages statutory and professional bodies to explore the integration and use of occupational standards within new and existing health professional educational programmes. This approach can assist in creating an explicit 'common language' for the expression of individual and multiprofessional competencies; improving links between academic, vocational and professional structures and enhancing access routes into professional education.
>
> (NHS Executive, 1996, Annex B, p. 6)

These guidelines were not directed at dental and medical education.

The messages are therefore clear – commission shared learning, improve and support multiprofessional teamwork, and create a common language to facilitate the integration of standards and transfer across qualification boundaries.

A whole constellation of factors is leading to the delivery of these messages at this particular time. One factor is greater cost-efficiency in work-force planning as the NHS struggles to meet the demands that are being made on it. Associated with this is growing flexibility, both in working across boundaries and in reducing the control of the professions over the ring-fencing of their territory.

NHS managers' views about a multiprofessional approach

In our research study, we sought the views of trust managers and senior NHS executives across the professions. Of those who were invited to take part, it was mainly nurse managers who responded, and they dominate the sample of 14 respondents, together with two physiotherapy managers. This provides a rather uneven picture of management perspectives, but nevertheless a number of important issues were raised.

NHS managers' thinking about multiprofessional working was clearly influenced by the impact of staff shortages, financial imperatives and government directives about delivering care based on evidence of clinical effectiveness. With fewer professionals in post and greater demands on stretched resources, trusts were having to explore the concept of greater role fluidity, in order to find alternatives to traditional professional practice and to address the way in which those roles combined.

Resource shortage has been a fact of life in the NHS for years, and this was perceived as a major driving force with regard to thinking about service delivery:

> I suppose when you look at the philosophy that has developed over the last ten years in terms of the quantitative approach to care management, particularly the targets, waiting times, Patient's Charter standards, the drive to look at reduction in the length of stay – [these are] very much financially driven agendas. I think for us as a trust I think it is important because we, like every other trust, are going to have to accommodate the waiting-list initiative. We are going to have to look very much more explicitly at our services. The financial arrangements are going to continue for quite some time and the year-on-year cost improvement programmes for efficiency just continue to force us to look at areas in a very different way.
>
> (Manager 3)[3]

However, the response to the Government drive for professionals to deliver services effectively, while at the same time being efficient by cutting back on expenditure each year, has been complicated by work-force shortages. More than half of the acute care managers commented on the adverse effects of falling nurse recruitment rates and the high attrition rate of recently qualified nurses, and there were similar shortages in the therapy professions.

[3] In this and subsequent extracts, the numbers of the managers refer to the 14 managers who were interviewed.

Work-force planning is therefore a vital part of the management role. The shortages had focused the mind of one manager on the need for *multiprofessional* work-force planning, which was currently achieved as a monoprofessional exercise. She felt that this situation impeded flexibility and posed a barrier to multiprofessional education:

> because you are doing this by professional group for existing professional courses, and that seems to be an endless bureaucratic nightmare we go through every year. Because actually we have to train at risk a lot of the time, because we don't know what we are going to be doing in three years' time.
>
> (Manager 7)

The availability of less money and fewer professionals had necessitated radical thinking in terms of how to deliver effective services. Some managers recognised that future health workers might bear little resemblance to current traditional roles, as these were simply not proving to be effective for the continuity of care:

> That is because there are professional boundaries that are becoming more and more counter-productive; roles overlap and who does what for the patient has arisen from professional territorial reasons and for historic reasons. It is now becoming detrimental to patient care. And the time has come to stop and ask the patient what they need, and then decide who is going to do it.
>
> (Manager 6)

Managers talked about the drive to provide evidence of clinical effectiveness as well as efficiency. In some trusts, audit as a method of examining clinical practice had evolved into a research and development programme, and a vast array of initiatives, both monoprofessional and multiprofessional, had developed to reshape practice. Where multiprofessional initiatives had developed, managers felt that they had led to more 'integrated multiprofessional working'. Several trusts had introduced integrated care pathways (ICPs) related to specific conditions such as colorectal cancer and breast cancer, and to acute medical conditions such as asthma and stroke. Again, the pathways required professionals to reflect on their input to the care process. In a similar way, the development of guidelines and protocols was compelling them to think about how they related to other members of the multiprofessional team:

> There are lights coming on like that all the time as we get those groups together. So I think that is forcing the groups to recognise that they need to get together to begin to do that.
>
> (Manager 1)

However, the way in which some of these changes to practice were introduced and promoted had a profound impact on their outcome. Several managers felt that some impetus for change in terms of clinical effectiveness had arisen from those working *'at the coal-face'*. This had in turn occurred as a result of an evolving change in culture. Although other professionals were seen to contribute, it was perceived that nurses were more prepared to question approaches to patient care:

> We are getting more people who are doing the PRDN course, so they are already diplomates. All of those groups are very much focused on reflective practice, 'why are we doing it this way', questioning.
>
> (Manager 12)

This increase in reflection on practice led to the realisation that there were ways *to restructure service delivery*, which included professionals taking on wider aspects of care, and negotiating more comprehensively in the various stages of patients' progress. In effect, professionals were prepared to look beyond their perspective and to embrace an integrated multiprofessional approach.

For some managers, the introduction of ICPs was an example of the importance of grass-roots support. Three of them spoke about the lack of initial success in the development of pathways, and one commented that these pathways were originally imposed by the clinical audit department – an approach which had not been successful. This manager and others recognised the need for professionals to determine for themselves where their practice would benefit from a pathway approach:

> What nursing did with its other colleagues, like OTs, chiropodists and pharmacists, we all got together in a room and thrashed it out over a period of about 3 months, and came out with something we were all prepared to sign up to.
>
> (Manager 3)

It seems likely that the *inclusion of all relevant professionals* is fundamental to the success of such an initiative. In this context, several managers talked about the difficulties they had experienced in *'getting the docs on board'*. Some managers noted that there was still a difference in perception between health work as a science and as an art, and hence a split between doctors and other professionals, and to some degree between pharmacists and other professionals, about how skills and knowledge were learned and what it was deemed important to learn. This division was also perceived by several managers to apply to the medical profession's view that their training needed to be separate:

> Partly I think because they feel they don't need to attend; they already know. Partly because they perceive that they are not going to get anything out of it.
>
> (Manager 8)

> People like me have got all excited and talked about multiprofessional education and this has really gone down like a lead balloon with the consultants. There is very much this elitist thing, there's a big culture thing. There's no doubt but that the culture of medical training is just so different . . . I don't know that they would necessarily articulate this, but this repulsion that they feel about joint education is very much tied to

> the strange adversarial upbringing you have when you are a medical student.
>
> (Manager 6)

Some of the managers were frustrated by the attitude of the medical profession towards shared learning. It was noted that medical staff were frequently absent where there were mechanisms for multiprofessional educational development, as for example in the sessions held around the development of ICPs. Not surprisingly, this gave rise to negative perceptions of the potential success of particular strategies:

> I was only talking today about the organisation tackling the medical staff on the basis of a strategic development, and all you need is one medic to say 'I'm not playing ball', and the whole thing folds. But they get away with it time and time again.
>
> (Manager 11)

Where ICP introduction had failed, the lack of ownership at grass-roots level was perceived to have been fuelled by the fact that doctors not only did not participate in the development of the pathway, but also would not contribute when it was in operation. Instead they 'opted out', leaving others (nurses in many cases) to bear the brunt of the work.

Despite such difficulties, and to help to ameliorate them, there was a clear message from many managers that there was a need to develop more informal learning processes and more shared learning programmes, at both pre- and post-qualification level. For several trusts the latter process was in its infancy. However, the need to reshape professional roles as part of the education process was acknowledged; future professionals would be required to share a wider knowledge base and more common skills. While recognising the core of each specialist role, managers foresaw far larger areas of overlap (more integrated working), with professional roles becoming dictated by patient need (i.e. away from specific professional role territory towards a more 'dynamic responsive multi-skilled work-force'.

There were differences in how strongly the trusts were promoting multiprofessional learning, and whether this was to support multiprofessional initiatives or to create developed nursing roles. Some trusts had recognised that their clinical research and audit had raised an awareness of the need for professionals to learn both together as professionals and from each other. For example, it was noted by three managers that the process of working together on various projects and writing multiprofessional protocols and guidelines had initiated multiprofessional learning. This was not as a formal procedure but as part of the project process:

> Because they are working together more closely in terms of reviewing their roles to meet that need, the commonalities of learning are bubbling up, and beginning to be seen. . . . For example, we have developed a common policy for expansion of the roles of nursing and professions allied to medicine.
>
> (Manager 7)

Comments from managers demonstrated an acceptance that some skills – both interpersonal and technical – could be learned together or from each other. There was also evidence that learning needed to be formal – that is, there was a desire for a common foundation for all health professionals. Three managers put forward the view that core curricula would be viable at foundation and post-qualification levels. For example:

> A lot of the core elements of training are the same across all the professions; so it is wasteful to teach them in isolation. . . . Also as, increasingly, health care focuses on team approaches to delivery of care, it makes sense to get these teams together right at the time that they are learning their jobs, if you like.
>
> (Manager 12)

Despite this belief in educating professionals together, it would seem from the interviews that little systematic work on shared learning is being done in, or on behalf of, any of the trusts. In cases where ICPs had been developed or research projects undertaken, there was some specific shared learning (i.e. it had come out of the process of exploring a new approach). Discussions that focused on the writing of guidelines or protocols were seen to have led to a greater understanding of others' contributions to care, and they consequently improved multiprofessional teamworking. Furthermore, one trust had developed the minor injury nurse role. In the early part of this development process the manager acknowledged that learning was 'one-way', from the radiographer or pharmacist to the nurses. The radiographer would teach the nurses how to identify fractures, and the pharmacist would advise on prescribing. However, it was later identified that radiographers could save other professionals' time if they could cannulate patients prior to X-rays. This procedure was taught by the nurse practitioners.

As well as teaching technical skills, some practitioners used multiprofessional situations to teach interpersonal skills such as assessment and communication. For example, some trusts had developed common policies on role development. One such trust's manager again commented on the slow dawning of awareness that the learning could be reciprocal:

> the way we developed a common policy was, for instance, in prescribing within protocols, both our nurses and our pharmacists prescribed within protocol. Now the nurses need the pharmacological development, the pharmacists, although they didn't recognise it to begin with, needed the assessment skills. I said 'well, OK, I'm a patient in bed with a pain in my leg, what would you do?'. And the pharmacist immediately said 'well, I would look at what drugs you were on and I would think about paracetamol, etc., etc.' He hadn't thought to look at the leg, and that brought it home very graphically to them that they needed skills in actually assessing the patient.
>
> (Manager 7)

A second example of skills teaching was a situation where there had been co-ordinating or facilitating roles, such as the team support sister. This role also provided opportunities for greater discussion with medical staff, and led to some teaching sessions with the ward nurses and junior doctors on the subject of breaking bad news.

In order to promote better understanding of how professionals could work together and what this would mean for their roles, one trust had introduced preparatory change management training:

> There's lots of impact analysis so that people choose projects that are relevant, and all that training is always multiprofessional. We invite [independent firm of consultants], very expensive, to come in and run training days . . . it is such a good day that word gets around. So the first one there was stick, carrot, anything you like, in order to get people on to this course, and they got a cracking good lunch, etc. Then they spend the afternoon working up a real proposal that they present. And they do that in teams, they have to work in teams.
>
> (Manager 6)

One final aspect of in-house shared learning was the development of team training in terms of exploring common processes of service delivery. This was only spoken about by managers in community trusts, particularly with regard to helping the community mental health teams to grasp new concepts such as the care programme approach (CPA). Only one manager spoke of this approach as a whole team process. Others spoke about community psychiatric nurses (CPNs) and social workers (SWs) being involved with their managers. (However, a national primary health care team training programme has for the past few years been run by multiprofessional 'local organising teams'. This had been available in the region and had trained a number of general practice teams.)

Where post-registration programmes were available, several managers commented that they encouraged staff from across the professions to attend. Those that were mentioned were MScs on communication and information technology, and management programmes. However, some managers mentioned that only certain professions applied for certain programmes, so that while a multiprofessional input was hoped for, it rarely occurred in practice. For example, counselling programmes were open to all professions, but were mainly taken up by occupational therapists (OTs) in one trust, so that they could instigate group work. Some managers recognised the need to promote the multiprofessional appeal of some programmes to more professionals, but were aware of the inhibiting effect of some professional management:

> maybe they are not moving with the times as much as we would wish. It is not all of them by any means, but we do have some people, and the problem is that they have influence on their PAMs and scientist colleagues as well to maintain the status quo . . . I think [that is] part of the reason why, although courses are open to all professions, they tend not to be nominated.
>
> (Manager 12)

Managers acknowledged that, in order to support the development of multiprofessional shared learning, they have had to become creative in acquiring funding. For example, some of them spoke about using traditionally monoprofessional funding and person training days in a multiprofessional fashion. (However, this only applied to nurses and PAMs, since medical training had its own 'vast amounts of money' from the Council for Medical Education.) One manager commented that, in her view, one of the main reasons for multiprofessional learning was financial:

> that it is actually cheaper and more cost-effective to train physios, OTs, nurses and radiographers together.
>
> (Manager 7)

Several of the managers who were interviewed also sat on local education consortia, and there was widespread recognition of the role of these bodies in promoting multiprofessional shared learning, particularly since many of them had acquired devolved budgets. The consortia appeared to facilitate the development of a wider perspective for trust managers, enabling them to see more clearly the links between what is learned and what culture develops in the workplace. Several of these managers recognised the need for congruence in terms of pre- and post-registration education, in-house learning, and organisational structure and process.

The consortia, as purchasers of education from the universities, are an important forum for the discussion of multiprofessional learning. Potentially, developments in NHS trusts and their relationship with shared learning initiatives in higher education curricula can be discussed and mutually influenced. It is the trusts which provide students with the contexts and role models for multiprofessional working, and they can have a considerable influence on the higher education agenda, as we shall discuss below.

Changes in the provision of shared learning education

Before the NHS Executive's guidelines for purchasers and providers of education were published, educational institutions and health and local authorities were increasingly offering shared learning initiatives in primary and community care for the health and social care professions. A report from the Centre for the Advancement of Interprofessional Education (Barr and Waterton, 1996) indicated an increase from 1990 in the number of such initiatives. The numbers rose rapidly from 1992, and 75% of them were post-qualifying initiatives (see Figure 1.1).

During this period of development, all schools of nursing have been integrated into universities to join other health and social care professions, such as social work, health visiting, physiotherapy, occupational therapy and podiatry. The role of consortia in purchasing education has implications for quality, relevance and cost. As in the NHS, much of the impetus for change in these educational institutions has been related to financial efficiency. In a competitive market, the higher number of students resulting from the addition of

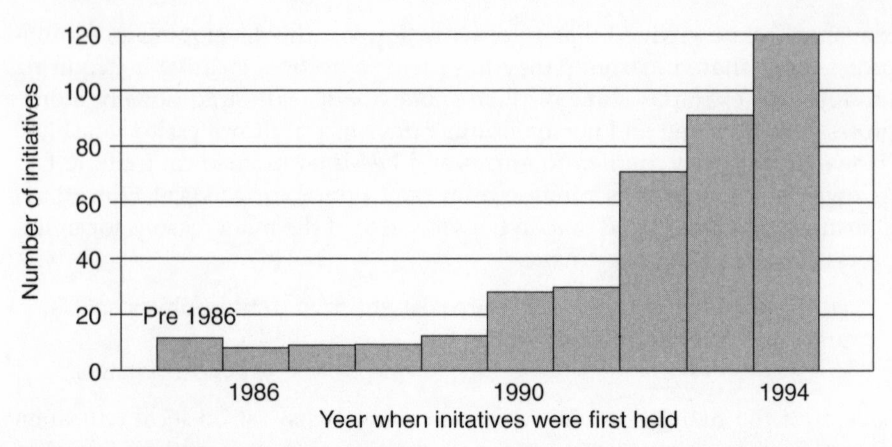

Figure 1.1 Rise in shared learning courses in primary and community care during the period 1986–1994 (Barr and Waterton, 1996).

nursing has increased the concern to avoid unnecessary duplication of the planning and provision of teaching, and to make cost savings. With the potential for yearly fluctuations in contracted student numbers, educational institutions have identified the value of a flexible, modular system that enables programme components to be shared between health care disciplines. This has the advantage that dips in local need for students in one profession may be compensated for by increased numbers in another. Teaching staff can be employed to provide input on a range of modules, rather than depending on one main programme or contract. If offering multiprofessional education modules can provide the flexibility and efficiency that the educational institutions need to achieve, while still attracting students and meeting the NHS Executive's directives, this would *appear* to provide a good solution.

However, the driving forces in programme development to promote shared learning which might meet strategic planning targets, may not match the interests of the NHS. Curriculum developers need to be convinced of the necessity for giving a central place to knowledge about multiprofessional practice in their curriculum design, in preference to offering elements of existing academic programmes or modules which are deemed, by their apparent generalisability, to be suitable for sharing.

The teaching of larger groups together can also mean that there is little interaction between them, and that their learning experience might more appropriately be called 'common learning' rather than 'shared' learning. In pre-qualification shared learning, Shaw (1995) argues that unless learning is purposively interactive, changes in students' attitudes to other professions will not occur. For example, if shared learning aims to provide a common knowledge base, this does not necessarily enable different professions to work together or to understand how others see their roles. Gill and Ling (1995) distinguish between the following different types of knowledge that are involved in shared learning:

- the interactive experience of learning with others (the process);
- knowledge about the work, roles and responsibilities of others;
- knowledge focused on the skills and strategies for collaboration.

They also discuss the following ways in which these may be combined:

- models of learning in which students learn separately about what other professions do;
- models in which there is a shared learning process but no focus on strategies for interprofessional collaboration;
- models in which learning is interactive and includes methods of collaboration in practice.

The question of what is being 'shared' by students who are learning together, in a variety of contexts was a key element of our research. We examined both the impetus behind the development of shared learning initiatives and the content and teaching methods for students from different health care disciplines in their shared learning curriculum. As with all curricula, the stated intentions must not be confused with what actually happens.

Professional bodies and shared learning

There are over 40 professional bodies in health and social care. The sample who gave us information represented nursing, medicine, professions allied to medicine, and social work, and all of them had positive views about the value of shared learning. A statement in support of 'multidisciplinary education and training' was issued in 1983 by the national bodies responsible for training district nurses, general practitioners, health visitors and social workers.[4] The United Kingdom Central Council for Nursing, Midwifery and Health Visiting (UKCC), endorsed the term 'shared learning', supporting it in principle within the context of professional practice (UKCC, 1992). Such learning was seen to increase the scope for collaboration and co-operation in care, the level of understanding between members of the care team, and cost-effectiveness in the development of skills common to more than one discipline. In their 1999 document, *Fitness for Practice*, the UKCC state that:

> The health care professions should be actively encouraged to learn with and from each other by:
>
> - purchasers of education including interprofessional teaching and learning – as appropriate – as a criterion for evaluating the quality of the education;
> - explicit encouragement for interprofessional learning in the planning

[4] Statement on the development of interprofessional education and training for members of primary health care teams (1983), CETHV, PADNT, RCGP, CCETSW, as cited in English National Board for Nursing, Midwifery and Health Visiting and Central Council for Education and Training in Social Work (1994).

of all pre-registration curricula;
- the development of shared use of learning resources and technology in practice placements;
- the UKCC leading joint initiatives with relevant regulatory bodies.

(United Kingdom Central Council for Nursing, Midwifery and Health Visiting, 1999, Recommendation 32, p. 52, 5.44).

The English National Board for Nursing, Midwifery and Health Visiting and the Central Council for Education and Training in Social Work published a joint strategy for shared learning which highlighted the desire of health care consumers to receive integrated services to meet their needs, rather than being prey to professional boundary maintenance (English National Board for Nursing, Midwifery and Health Visiting and Central Council for Education and Training in Social Work, 1994). The two bodies also published a joint set of guidelines in 1995 (the York and Coventry conferences outcomes) which stated that shared learning can:

- increase practitioners' understanding and develop the skills required to work in multidisciplinary teams, across professional boundaries and in extending networks;
- provide practitioners with an understanding of the roles, cultures and values of different professions, leading to benefits for service users as a result of increased co-operation and collaboration;
- help to address the perceptions and stereotypes that impede inter-professional work.

The English National Board's guidelines for revising the pre-registration programmes for nurses and midwives, *Education in Focus: Strengthening Pre-Registration Nursing and Midwifery Education* (English National Board for Nursing, Midwifery and Health Visiting, 2000) emphasise the importance of collaborative working within the care team, and state that:

> Interprofessional, interdisciplinary teaching and learning which aims to encourage integration and collaboration in learning should be an integral part of pre-registration nursing and midwifery programmes.
>
> (English National Board for Nursing, Midwifery and Health Visiting, Section 1, 4.3, p. 13)

Although some of the NHS managers whom we interviewed talked of their difficulties in persuading some of the medical profession to participate in activities such as IPC development, which required input from the whole care team, the guidance from their professional bodies is clear. The Standing Committee on Postgraduate Medical and Dental Education (1997) produced a working paper for consultation on multiprofessional working and learning, and a final report with recommendations in 1999. The working paper was based on consultations and written evidence across a number of health professions. It presented views on organisational and education contexts for multiprofessional learning, which it stated had:

> entered a new phase which is about preparing practitioners to operate within a multiprofessional context in the clinical environment. This approach requires a new set of skills centering on how professionals interact with one another in the clinical environment . . . how professionals form teams, how they plan together and make decisions together within the clinical context.
>
> (Standing Committee on Postgraduate Medical and Dental Education, 1997, p. 15)

This paper made a specific point about the skills required to operate in a multiprofessional team, citing 'forming, planning and decision-making' as distinct from theoretical knowledge. It concluded with the view that:

> the time is now right for some principles to embed a multiprofessional approach into systems for health care delivery and medical and dental education.
>
> (Standing Committee on Postgraduate Medical and Dental Education, 1997, p. 17)

In their final report, *Equity and Interchange: Multiprofessional Learning and Working* (Standing Committee on Postgraduate Medical and Dental Education, 1999) it is interesting to note, in view of these earlier statements, that a statement is made (based on slim evidence in the Report) that skills training is not needed:

> A skills training approach in team-working is neither necessary nor appropriate. *If individuals are provided with autonomy and a climate of equity and mutual respect between different professions is created*, then a multiprofessional group will develop its own ways of working and learning effectively together.
>
> (Standing Committee on Postgraduate Medical and Dental Education, 1999, p. 11) (our emphasis)

Some would argue that individuals cannot be 'provided with' a climate of equity and mutual respect, but that it has to be developed. Even where it exists, such a climate may be insufficient in itself to bring about changes in working practice without further training or facilitation.

The General Medical Council in successive documents for doctors (General Medical Council, 1993, 1995, 1997, 1998) advocates the importance of teamworking and multiprofessional practice. However, the commitment of professional bodies to the preparation of professionals for more integrated practice was called into question by some trust managers we spoke to who sat on the consortia responsible for purchasing education. They were concerned that ultimately professional bodies would protect their own specific bodies of knowledge. In the debate about the need for greater role fluidity between professionals, with one possible end-point being the creation of more generic working, they felt that the professional bodies would 'pull up the drawbridge' around their role and the knowledge and skills required for that role:

> In its widest context they will talk about how valuable it is, provided that it doesn't impinge too much on their separate status. The danger of course is that people end up talking about it and never doing it. And . . . some professional bodies' vested interests in the status quo will mean that we have a fight on our hands.
>
> (Manager 12)

It is difficult to know how widespread these views were. Among the managers who were interviewed, only those who had started to think about developing multiprofessional learning and who had an active role in the education consortia expressed concern. If the general concept of multiprofessional learning is accepted, but interpretations of role fluidity differ widely across the professions, then even though common core modules may be developed, there may still be little change at the point of service delivery – the artificial barrier described by some managers would remain. The representation of a broad range of professions on education consortia is important here if they are to develop a multiprofessional approach to education.

Interestingly, the trust managers' concerns that professional bodies would support the rhetoric of shared learning but resist it in practice were not borne out by the experiences of curriculum leaders in higher education. In our survey, the majority of these leaders made no comment about the professional bodies, and certainly did not identify them as putting up barriers to shared learning. The remainder reported that the professional bodies had raised no objection, or were even enthusiastic.

Our interviews with a sample of professional bodies and the documentation provided by others supported this view; initiatives were mostly welcomed. For example:

> The [professional body] is not comfortable any longer with universities which do not have any multiprofessional element in their programmes. That's the advice we give to the education purchasing consortia, and the Joint Validating Committee gives to universities. . . . [University] suffered because they were unable to offer any shared learning in their programme.
>
> (Education and Practice Officer, professional body)

A representative from another professional body had a caveat:

> We encourage multidisciplinary working . . . we encourage [our professionals] to be part of the team, but I haven't seen any evidence to suggest that multiprofessional education makes for better multiprofessional working. We look towards making sure that, where it occurs, it doesn't do any harm. I've seen no evidence that it can do any good.
>
> (Officer representing professional body)

Professional body representatives commented on the economic driving factors for shared learning and its resulting interpretation:

> I can't think of any post-registration professional development programmes which have come through recently which function on a

> monoprofessional basis. People are thinking along the lines of income generation and that pushes them towards a multiprofessional cohort.
>
> (Professional body's Education and Practice Officer)

This officer went on to comment on the interpretation of shared learning:

> In the universities . . . I am sure the culture is there for people to own shared learning which is designed to benefit the workplace. [Region] have been problematic, because there is a lack of understanding of what shared learning really means. They see it as revolving around generic issues . . . common learning . . . although this is changing. . . . There is no discrimination in the [professional body] advice about the types of shared learning which a university may offer. But there is much more support for the real shared learning of case work, problem-based learning, etc.
>
> (Professional body's Education and Practice Officer)

The intentions stated in formal documents and by representatives may not be experienced in the validation processes conducted at grass-roots level. However, if there were any difficulties in gaining acceptance of shared learning on the part of the representatives of professional bodies, they were not flagged up by programme leaders in the way that other problems were (for a discussion of these see Chapter 7).

One representative of a PAM raised a point which had implications for education about the variation in alliances between different professions at various levels:

> There has been a huge effort to improve the links between ourselves, physiotherapy and speech and language therapy. They are our closest political links . . . links at my level. But [our professionals] on the ground would say that nurses, doctors, clinical psychologists and social workers were closer working colleagues. There is a huge impetus to improve links with these professions.
>
> (Professional body representative)

The question of which professions are allied during purchasing of education by the consortia depends upon what is available in their location. For example, if there is no medical school or radiography training, the mix in shared learning programmes purchased from higher education would not reflect a grass-roots professional mix. With a handful of exceptions, doctors and dentists are educated in the old universities and nurses and PAMs in the new ones, which adds to the planning and logistic feat of their learning together, as some programme leaders had already found. These problems could be overcome through inter-university alliances, but this adds to the tariff in developing shared learning between professions which work together in practice.

OVERVIEW OF THE FOLLOWING CHAPTERS

We shall now consider in detail what is involved in multiprofessional teamworking. Chapter 2 discusses three different types of teamwork identified in our research, and the implications for learning. The next three chapters focus on an analysis of the work of clinical teams, illustrating the impact on them of organisational policies (Chapter 3), the effects of the different beliefs about teamworking held by individuals (Chapter 4), and the influence of group processes on the team (Chapter 5). The implications for education are identified in each chapter. These implications are then considered further in terms of shared learning, from 'novice to expert', in Chapter 6.

Chapter 7 presents an analysis of data from higher education about shared learning initiatives, examines the barriers and levers, and questions whether the initiatives are meeting the needs identified in the analysis of multiprofessional practice. Chapter 8 makes proposals for the direction that shared learning curricula might take in order to enhance their fit with the needs of practice. It offers a new model, outlining a suggested content for the different stages of student development. Finally, Chapter 9 considers some of the gaps between the rhetoric and reality of multiprofessional practice and education to support it, and discusses the implications for the future development of shared learning.

Patterns of clinical teamworking

2

INTRODUCTION

We have argued that if education is to support clinicians to enable them to work more effectively with other professionals in the clinical setting, it is important to understand the exact nature of the real issues in working as a multiprofessional team member in the NHS.

In this chapter, we identify three different types of working in the teams we studied, and we then describe their key features. The working of some teams had identifiable benefits for their patients or clients that were not evident in other types of working. Some of the terms used in the literature to describe 'effective teamworking' are seen to be far more complex when examined in the reality of practice.

Then, in Chapters 3, 4 and 5, we shall explore the ways in which professionals work together by looking at examples of patterns of practice and interaction among team members. We shall do this at three levels of analysis – *organisational, individual* and *group* – in order to understand more clearly how these influence the ability of professionals to work collaboratively.

Some of the six teams we examined were officially and structurally recognised as teams. However, not all members of these groups regarded themselves as part of a 'team', nor did they feel they were necessarily engaged in 'teamwork'. This applied equally in other clinical settings, where there was a looser definition of the term 'team'. Only in one team did members hold the almost unanimous view that they were part of a highly collaborative team and that their patterns of working reflected this. In other teams there was varying understanding of the level of collaboration that was possible. Whatever people felt about being in these teams, and their practice as team members, there was a multitude of underlying reasons for the way in which these patterns developed. We shall examine the nature of these teams' practice (i.e. how they worked together) and explore how these patterns of working came about.

However, before we begin to look at the teams in our study, it is important to examine in more detail the terms 'teamwork' and 'working together'.

Teamwork

A great deal has been written about teams and teamworking. Much of this applies to teams set up to focus on a specific problem or task, rather than the ongoing and less clear-cut nature of teamwork in the NHS, and can therefore ficult to apply to current clinical work. Teamwork in primary care has extensively documented (e.g. Øvretveit, 1990, 1993, 1995; Pritchard and chard, 1994; West and Pillinger, 1996; West and Slater, 1996).

Mandy (1996), reviewing the characteristics of 'successful interdisciplinary teams', draws on Clark *et al.* (1986) to select five main attributes:

- *goal-directedness: a central purpose, a clear, recognisable idea which serves as a central focus for the work (Petrie, 1976), which is embodied in a concept or model that transcends disciplinary boundaries.* In a health care team, members come together to promote patients' health. However, different team members may have widely differing views of the role of care, so that evolving a model that transcends disciplinary boundaries, the patient and their problems can be challenging;
- *disciplinary articulation: all members understanding each other's role and recognising areas of overlap within the traditional disciplines.* Hilton (1995) suggests that this is one of the main areas that education needs to address in order to combat fragmentation and isolation within interprofessional work;
- *communication: appreciating how other disciplines understand knowledge and the methods by which it is gained and used.* If members do not understand each other's 'cognitive map' they will not understand how others interpret the same phenomenon differently. In addition to the differences in language used by different professions, the same terms may be interpreted differently (Pietroni, 1991);
- *flexibility: to include valuing different perspectives, accepting changes in authority and status and being willing to take on challenges.* The influence of differences in status between nurses and doctors has long been recognised, and the management of such differences can be crucial to productive teamwork;
- *conflict resolution: this can include understanding the difference between accountability and responsibility of different team members and knowing what is expected of them (McKenna, 1981).* Sands *et al.* (1990) argue that when a common value base, language and conceptual framework are established, the team may see conflict as an opportunity for growth and integration.

Such examples identify important characteristics of teams that have been seen to contribute to their 'success', but they do not address how they can be achieved. Reviewing teamwork in health care, Embling (1995) concluded that while 'multidisciplinary teamwork' is a well-accepted strategy, 'Recent management and health care literature presents a positive picture of teamwork, yet [this] often seems difficult to achieve in practice' (Embling, 1995, p. 144).

Embling identifies potential barriers to effective teamwork as problems of leadership, decision-making and team membership, concluding that 'Understanding key teamwork issues may be an important first step for health care teams who wish to improve their performance' (Embling, 1995, p. 144).

However, the measurement of improvements in performance is complex. West and Slater (1996) comment as follows on evaluating teamwork effectiveness in primary health care: 'Teams can be seen as more or less effective depending on the criteria adopted. Consequently, the assessment of team effectiveness has come to be seen as a political as much as an empirical process' (West and Slater, 1996, p. 26).

Views of teams' effectiveness relate to expectations about teamwork. These vary not only among individuals but also according to their professional role. For example, Temkin-Greener (1983) suggested that views and expectations differ between doctors and nurses because of the different values and norms of medicine and nursing: 'Team care, therefore, may be more accurately termed an intercultural rather than an interprofessional venture' (Temkin-Greener, 1983, p. 642).

Temkin-Greener interviewed senior heads of nursing and medicine in a teaching hospital, and concluded that:

> On the individual level, physicians see nurses as extenders of their roles and as helpers. Nurses, on the other hand, view a team as providing access to direct patient care, and as a means to gain status. On the overall professional level, medicine's goal is to maintain authority over health care delivery while relegating some tasks to other providers. . . . The overall professional goal of nursing is to gain a share of authority and to improve the status of the profession.
>
> (Temkin-Greener, 1983, pp. 654–5)

On the basis of this analysis, 'Teamwork is a political problem where nursing demands a share of professional authority and medicine will not relinquish it' (Temkin-Greener, 1983, p. 648).

Does this imply an ever-present dissonance or is this view outdated? Although the literature repeatedly reports that much about the situation remains the same, evidence of change has been identified. The nurse's role in the multiprofessional team has important historical and social antecedents, which some authors have argued are the key to understanding its development. The dominance of medicine over nursing has been traced through the history of women's and men's roles in health. For example, Colliere (1986) traced how cure and treatment became associated with written knowledge and the technical skills of medicine, whereas care, associated with women's work, depended on unwritten knowledge and was difficult to appraise and value financially. Corner (1997) argues that such dominance made much of nurses' therapeutic role invisible, and defined illness in terms of medical management. The rise in medical knowledge and technology led to the view that 'getting better' and maintaining good health are essentially dependent on the interventions of doctors, and that nurses simply 'carry out orders'.

Many studies seem to support that view (notwithstanding the role of senior nurses in guiding junior doctors). One line of enquiry has been the study of communication and decision-making during the ward round. The dominance of medical staff over nurses and other team members has been consistently demonstrated (Sanson-Fisher *et al.*, 1979; Fewtrell and Toms, 1985; Mallik, 1992; Whale, 1993). Busby and Gilchrist (1992) comment on nurses' lack of assertiveness and the 'dominance of medical staff who acted as the central focus for all discussion'. Social interaction between doctors and nurses in the working environment has been described as a 'game they play' to avoid confronting inequalities of power and status (Stein, 1967; Tellis-Nayak and Tellis-Nayak, 1984). Wicks (1998) explored the effects of hierarchy and power differences in Australian doctors and nurses, and found that nurses constructed methods of circumventing clashes with doctors by getting management on their side and obtaining nursing consensus. Stacey (1992) argued that doctors need to relinquish the one-to-one relationship with patients, recognise the contribution of others (including the patient), and adjust their notions of clinical autonomy, control over allied professions, and doctors' exclusive right to sit in judgement over other doctors.

However, recent research is beginning to signal a change (Stein *et al.*, 1990; Porter 1991). Nurses are now more questioning and are able to negotiate with doctors in decision-making (Svensson, 1996). Svensson's research was based on interviews in five hospitals with 45 nurses and ward sisters about their interaction with doctors. He points out how valuable it would have been to follow these with observation of their actual behaviour. Our own research study confirms the relevance of observing the whole multiprofessional team in action.

Social, educational and demographic changes have been cited as leading to a change in the doctor–nurse relationship (MacKay, 1993; Walby and Greenwell, 1994). Factors such as the emphasis in nurse education on autonomy and critical thinking may be significant, and holistic models of care are more appropriate to the care of the increasing proportion of elderly people with chronic illnesses, and emphasise social aspects of care. Organisational changes in hospitals, the nursing process, primary nursing and the advent of nurse specialists have all contributed to this changing climate. Our team research indicated that the climate may be changing, but that the balance of power in a team is rarely evenly distributed.

Working together

This term covers a multitude of different interpretations. For example, people may be designated as a team but work independently for some or all of the time. When they do work 'together' this may be one after the other, in parallel, interactively, or any combination of these.

A further dimension is the type of area in which they 'work together'. Is this in relation to tasks, decisions or both? If collaboration is in decision-making, what weight is given to the contributions of different members? These questions only begin to reveal the multidimensional nature of teamwork illustrated in Table 2.1.

Another area of complexity is the variety of different types of team. A clinical area may have a nursing team, medical team, ward team (which consists of nurses, nursing auxiliaries, domestics, housekeeping staff and ward clerks), clinical team, ward-round team, management team, community liaison team, student team and others such as a physiotherapy team or dietetics team. These teams have overlapping membership, and allegiances may be strained as members are 'expected' by different teams to be in two places at once.

Table 2.1 The multidimensional nature of teamwork

'Team' may mean:
Designated as a 'team' but may work as individuals or together
Not designated as a 'team' but may work together
'Work together' may mean:
Work independently in sequence
Work independently in parallel
Work collaboratively in sequence (i.e. separately, but each member feeds back to the next at the end of their input)
Work collaboratively in parallel (separately but providing feedback *en route*)
Work interactively for some of the time
Work interactively for all the time
'Collaborative work' may mean:
Tasks
Decision-making contribution (input of different members may have differing weight)

A further dimension concerns the definition of who is in the team. The answer to this depends on who is being asked. Perceptions of team membership and the perceived centrality of different members can vary considerably. For example, in research by Miller *et al.* (1997), 15 members of a diabetes team were asked to draw a map of the team, and every map was different with regard to both who was included and how they were arranged.

This preamble should alert us to the complex nature of teams and teamworking and the contexts in which they exist. Our study provided a clear demonstration of the different perceptions of these terms and different patterns of working, underpinned by influences ranging from the wider organisation to the beliefs of individual team members.

THE NATURE OF THE STUDY

The evidence on which this and the next three chapters are based was provided by in-depth case studies of six multiprofessional teams from the following specialisms: *neuro-rehabilitation, medicine, child development assessment, diabetes, general practice* and *community mental health*. These were chosen on the basis of the following criteria.

- *professional mix:* the team should have several different professionals contributing to patient/client care;
- *diversity of context*: settings were chosen to include examples from hospital and community and those which linked both contexts; there was a range of different types of patient/client including those in adult, paediatric, mental health and learning disability categories. Midwifery and health visiting were represented to some extent in the community-focused case studies;
- *national reputation*: the neuro-rehabilitation unit had a reputation for

multi-professional care, and was chosen in order to study what that meant in practice;
- *cross-organisation perspective*: to encompass evidence of team function across organisations in addition to that between professionals;
- *geographical spread*: all teams were based in southern England. Given the focus on interprofessional team activity, wider geographical spread was not considered to be a key variable.

We make no claims that the settings studied are representative. There may be no such thing as a 'typical' team; not only can the professional mix be different for different clinical problems, but teams represented by the same professions will vary in how they work together and where they work, whether in a hospital or in the community. Instead, the aim is to present a *recognisable reality* (Schatzman and Strauss, 1973) with which others in similar situations can identify. By studying a number of different teams, theoretical concepts may emerge which are shared by at least some of them. In addition, some of the contextual factors that contribute to a team's behaviour may be identified.

From an educational point of view, there were two points about the generalisability of the data in this context. First, the research illuminated problems and processes of current multiprofessional working to set alongside the aims and content of shared learning curricula. This contributed theoretical evidence to address the question of the match between multiprofessional practice and the preparation for it through shared learning initiatives.

Secondly, the findings were used as part of the evidence when considering what types of models of shared learning would be appropriate. The literature on teamwork identifies such aspects as roles, focus, communication and conflict as being significant. The research was likely to illustrate these in action, as well as possibly showing other dimensions from which further theoretical generalisations (Sharp, 1998) could be derived.

THE CASE-STUDY APPROACH

To investigate the working practices of the teams, we used a case-study approach (Miller and Parlett, 1974; Simons, 1980; Miller, 1983; Merriam, 1988). This approach is designed to take account of the context in which people learn and work, and individuals' experiences and perceptions within that context are central to the research. Individuals see their work from their own perspectives, and discovering these perspectives was a key concern. Further details of this methodology can be found in the Appendix.

All of the case-study sites were visited intensively for a period of up to 3 months, and similar methods were used to collect evidence, namely: *non-participant observation*, *semi-structured interviews* and *document analysis*. For observation, teams were visited on each day of the working week for several hours at a time (and at some weekends, where appropriate, in order to observe differences in patterns of working). All aspects of team function were observed. This included both formal and informal meetings among the various professionals, sessions in which they were working together with patients or clients, and telephone calls that they made to other team members. Some professionals in each team were 'shadowed' for part of the day, enabling us to explore patterns of individual practice and how these linked with other team members.

We interviewed all members of smaller teams, and in the case of large teams we used purposive sampling of all professional groups. Documents such as relevant case-notes, promotional literature, policies and guidelines were then used to reinforce our understanding of teamworking in each case study.

This in-depth approach allowed us to observe behaviours and events that could then be explored in interview with the relevant professionals. In addition, it enabled us to relate answers to interview questions to subsequent behaviours and events, and allowed team members to reflect on those later. The long-term nature of the case studies enabled us to detect trails of cause and effect with regard to team care and team relationships.

Team membership

In each case study, identifying who was 'in the team' formed an early part of the evidence gathering. Since this may have been defined differently depending on who was asked, it was an important point at which to begin. We wanted to establish how the idea of a team was understood by different people. This also included individuals who were considered to be outside the immediate team, but who might have had a considerable impact on team members' work (e.g. managers and senior clinicians).

During the initial interviews we enquired about team membership and asked individuals to draw diagrams of their team. These drawings helped us when asking further questions about team structure – for example, the people who were included, the 'shape' of the teams, and the 'distance' that some team members were perceived to be from others. From their identifications, other professionals were included in the 'case' as appropriate. Not all of the individuals in a team necessarily identified the same team members, nor were they in the same configurations. This enabled us to explore these different views and the nature of the whole team's relationships.

Roles

The initial interviews also included questions about the perceived roles of the interviewee and of other team members, how these roles worked to provide patient care, what the boundaries of the roles were, whether and where they overlapped, and what happened at the boundaries. The answers that individuals provided enabled us to focus our observations.

Teamworking – ideal and reality

A further aspect of the interviews was to ask professionals about their understanding of teamworking – both how they felt it *should* be practised and how it was *actually* practised in their team. We wanted to understand people's views about historical events and how those might have influenced current teamwork. People were also asked to identify how their ideas about teamworking had developed, and what experiences had shaped their beliefs, both negatively and positively. This gave individuals a further point of comparison for the way in which they currently experienced teamworking.

Building up patterns of teamworking

Comparing and contrasting the evidence that emerged from watching and interviewing different team members enabled us to build up a picture of the reality of teamwork for each team, and then to compare and contrast the findings across the teams. From this analysis, both common issues and issues specific to certain teams were identified.

Testing by feedback

At the end of each case study, an anonymised and abstracted account of the findings was fed back to the teams, who were asked to comment on the interpretations we had made. In all of the studies, despite being asked to confront what might have been uncomfortable issues, none of the teams disagreed with the findings.

THE PICTURE: THREE TYPES OF MULTIPROFESSIONAL WORKING

We are not suggesting that the following description of different types of working is necessarily representative of all teams, but simply stating that this was the nature of practice among the teams in our study, influenced by the particular circumstances in which they found themselves.

Some teams worked more closely than others, and we analysed three forms of multiprofessional working which we saw from the data across the six teams. We named these types: *'integrated'*, *'fragmented'* and *'core and periphery'* (see Figure 2.1).

First we shall give a brief description of each of these three types of working, accompanied by a description of the teams that fitted each category, and identifying the main issues that emerged. In Chapters 3, 4 and 5, the team issues will be discussed under three main areas, namely *organisational, individual* and *group*, with each chapter covering one area. We shall describe how teamworking was influenced by various factors within each of these areas. In this way we shall be able to see how the context within which teams work, individual thinking about teams and teamworking, and the subsequent nature of the dynamics which develop between team members all have a significant effect on the way in which teams operate. Within each of the three areas, aspects of teamworking such as *communication, role* and *focus* will be discussed. These components were deemed to be important by members of the teams.

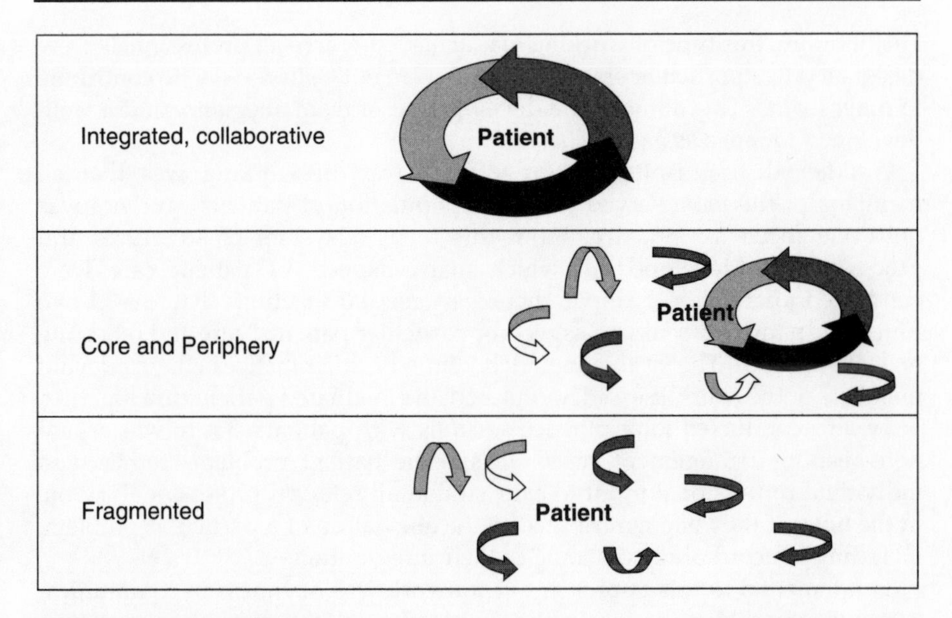

Figure 2.1 Different ways of working.

We shall argue that consideration of the ways in which these components are affected by the organisation, the individual and the group is therefore pertinent for all teams, and for all students learning about multiprofessional teamworking. Throughout the book we shall highlight specific issues which educators and therefore also students will need to consider when thinking about an education to provide a solid grounding in the skills and knowledge required to work effectively as a member of a multiprofessional team.

For the sake of brevity, the initials that professionals employ themselves are used for some of the main professional groups. For example:

Physiotherapist – PT
Occupational therapist – OT
Speech and language therapist – SLT
Health visitor – HV
General practitioner – GP
Community psychiatric nurse – CPN.

Integrated working

As a function of a whole team, this type of working was only seen in neuro-rehabilitation. In this context most members of this team displayed the highest degree of collaborative working among the teams studied. This type of working existed in an organisational context of stability and predictability, which enabled professionals to plan their work, and to develop in-depth knowledge both about their fellow team members and about their patients.

Furthermore, this type of working was achieved where all professionals were designated to a particular specialism, and were not 'called away' to contribute to other teams. This allowed the development of team allegiance and a well-developed identity as a group.

Another distinguishing feature of this way of working was that all members of the team served the same population of patients, so there was only one focus for practice. From this focus a system of structures and processes had developed in which many aspects of patient care were conducted jointly. For example, there were regular meetings that served two functions, namely discussing aspects of particular patients' care and reflecting on team practice. The system included joint working practices where relevant members of the team assessed, monitored and evaluated patient care together. They also conducted joint practice sessions with patients. There was a joint note-keeping arrangement based on specific patient problems rather than individual professional input to care, so that all relevant professionals wrote in the notes if they had contributed to the alleviation of a particular problem, including a record of the outcome of their intervention.

Fundamental to this approach to teamwork was openness in communication, with team members being encouraged to raise issues about patients, professional concerns and personal difficulties with patients. In order to ensure that team practice remained dynamic, challenge to the status quo was a cultural norm. As a result of the level of joint practices and the nature of communication, there was a strong and 'safe' learning environment. This was manifested by a high level of understanding about individual contributions to patient care, and of knowledge about where specific roles met or overlapped. This ability to learn about each other's work encouraged flexibility at professional role boundaries, and helped to create a pool of team knowledge and skills. Furthermore, implicit in the notion of team knowledge and skills was the development of professional skills and knowledge.

The system of structures and processes was developed and supported by facilitative leadership, and by joint management across the various professional heads of department. In this way strategies for patient care and the development of team practice suggested by those 'at the coal-face' could readily be put into operation. Teamworking was therefore seen to be an evolving and negotiated process.

Benefits to patients

We identified a variety of benefits to patients as a result of this type of working. These included continuity, consistency, a reduced number of ambiguous messages, appropriate and timely referrals, actions resulting from a holistic perspective, and problem-solving. These benefits were valued by team members and promoted a high level of commitment to the concept of such collaborative working.

Continuity Professionals learned skills and gained knowledge from each other, which they were then able to 'carry over' at times when the 'experts' were not around. Continuity could also be seen where a pattern of care needed to be followed with one professional performing an action with a patient which then enabled another professional to slot into the care with their own intervention.

Consistency Professionals learned about other team members' interpretations of patient difficulties, so that they were able to 'pick up' on patients' cues more readily in their own interventions, and act in a similar way to their colleagues when dealing with patients.

Reduction of ambiguity Because of joint practices there was also a high level of 'team knowledge', and therefore no conflict in the message being given to the patient about aspects of their diagnosis or care plan. Furthermore, the depth of role understanding within the team enabled individual professionals to explain each other's rationale for therapy to the patients, which increased the patients' perception of collaborative interaction.

Appropriate and timely referral Because each professional had a detailed and accurate knowledge of other professionals' roles, and also of their boundaries, they were better able to judge accurately when it was appropriate to refer to another member of the team for their assessment and treatment.

Actions and decisions based on a holistic perspective Through the use of in-depth discussion it was possible to develop a picture of the patient which encompassed all aspects of self – social, physical and psychological. These multiple perspectives enabled decisions to be made using a wider knowledge base, and allowed professionals to determine how aspects of that knowledge might combine to require professionals to take a different path of patient care.

Actions and decisions based on problem-solving Because of the nature of the structures for focused discussion around specific aspects of patient care, and the subsequent dissemination of shared knowledge among team members, this provided a wider source of ideas about possible causes and likely actions to be taken. It also encouraged the development of joint strategies for care and therapy.

The integrated team

The neuro-rehabilitation team worked in a purpose-built 20-bed unit which was isolated from the rest of the trust buildings due to its being located in a residential environment. Because of the nature of the unit, all professionals worked in close proximity to each other, which meant they had the opportunity to communicate freely and to see how each member of the team contributed to patient care.

The unit catered for medically stable patients who had recently suffered brain damage due to a variety of reasons (e.g. stroke and accident trauma). After multiprofessional assessment, patients were given a tailored course of therapy that was developed within a highly structured, problem-focused, goal-oriented programme. The collaborative note-keeping system that had been started was still in the process of development at the time of the case study. The team had actively chosen to work in the way described above, their rationale being that neurological damage created complex and wide-ranging problems, and unless the professions worked closely together, the necessary co-ordination of information and knowledge would not be achieved.

The team was led by a non-medical director, with medical cover being provided by a local group of GPs. The staff consisted of a large group of trained nurses and nursing assistants who operated a four-team nursing model, with five patients per team. Other professionals included groups of PTs, OTs and SLTs, a social worker and a clinical psychologist. The whole team was subdivided into two, each smaller team having responsibility for a specific group of patients. The nursing structure therefore enabled the nurses to provide two daytime shifts covering each of the two multiprofessional teams.

The team had recognised the need for, and to a large extent developed, a shared philosophy of care and a system of joint working practices based on a Bobath approach to therapy (Lennon, 1996). This approach aimed to secure the optimum quality of patient rehabilitation, rather than simply functional improvement, and relied on a system of 'carry-over' by all other team members. The shared nature of the approach to care helped to promote such 'carry-over' among all team members, including the nurses who, albeit less intensively, were able to provide continued therapeutic input over a 24-hour period.

This team had a culture that encouraged integration (as identified earlier), and this stemmed from and was actively supported by the director and the leaders of the professional groups. It was clear that there were expectations of 'how to be as a team member' which encompassed both professional and interpersonal practices, the beliefs and values that existed with regard to team membership and teamworking being very similar across most of the team.

However, the team was not without its areas of tension. One of these related to a rift between some of the nursing group and the therapy groups (although this was identified as being relative; team members' experience of therapist/nurse working in other settings was seen to be much less collaborative). The rift was partly related to organisational factors, but more importantly it related to perceptions of the nursing role in the rehabilitation team. The lack of medical direction had created the opportunity for a therapy model to become dominant, and some nurses had difficulty in determining their role within this framework. As a result, communication between the therapy and nursing groups was not always as efficient as it could have been. Furthermore, some nurses lacked confidence with regard to the perceived importance of their contribution to the team.

However, of potentially greater importance for teamworking was the arrival of a new professional – a clinical psychologist who had different ideas about working in a multiprofessional context, which were antithetical to the culture which had been established. The lack of integration of this professional into the team caused widespread consternation among other team members. As will be seen later, being a newcomer to a team with an enmeshed history can be very difficult. However, more significantly, this professional's lack of willingness to be involved as a team member created doubts about his clinical practice – a situation which made other team members very defensive for their patients.

Fragmented working

The second type of working was seen in three teams, namely the primary health care team (PHCT), the community mental health team (CMHT) and those in the medical ward. These teams worked in a more *fragmented* fashion. The teams were apparently dissimilar, the first two being community based and operating in relatively stable environments. Those based in hospital were working in a very fluid and unpredictable environment. The CMHT was recognised and designated in government policy, whereas the PHCT and those in the medical ward were more loosely defined.

Although many individual professionals in these teams may have identified that their own work with patients was effective, this was not part of a team focus. This was reinforced by the nature of the patients/clients who were served by these teams, as there were multiple populations of focus for all of the teams.

The working of these teams was characterised as follows. Although individuals may not necessarily have wanted to operate in this way, many aspects of patient management, including problem-solving, decision-making and responsibilities for actions, related to single-profession groups. Partly as a result of this, communication between team members was relatively brief and related more to the giving of information than to the sharing of professional perspectives. By the same token, role understanding was superficial, with team members being unable, or in some cases unwilling, to develop an in-depth understanding of others' roles. In this context, role boundaries were actively protected by many professionals, thus reinforcing the monoprofessional nature of practice.

Leadership was problematic in this type of working. Those in positions of power behaved in one of two ways with regard to clinical decisions. Either they employed autocratic decision-making without consultation, or they steered team decision-making without consensus. Other professionals perceived this as being unsupportive of multiprofessional collaboration, and indeed there was considered to be an unsafe environment for communication and learning. As a result, skills and knowledge remained within the individual professional groups.

Unlike the integrated team, there was mixed awareness among the team's members of the benefits to patients that could be achieved through collaborative practices. Because professionals did not come together to discuss how effective teamwork could be achieved, negotiated agreements on how to proceed as a team were rarely achieved, and thus the benefits of working in that way were not demonstrated.

The fragmented teams

Despite the fact that the term 'fragmented teams' appears to be a paradox (and this was reinforced by the perceptions of members of these teams), we shall retain the term 'team' because of the designated nature of two of them. The first of these teams, namely the PHCT, worked in an old, purpose-built health centre in a large town. It was generally agreed that the team consisted of two groups of professionals, one located on site and the other 'attached' to it. The former was the general practice group, which included a practice nurse, practice manager and administrative staff employed by four GPs. The second group consisted of satellite professionals, such as HVs, district nurses, midwives and counsellors, employed by the local community trust but 'attached' to the practice. Of this group, only the HVs had office space in the practice buildings. Because of the distance of some professionals' bases from the practice (and also even where the professional was on site) a system of books had been devised for all interprofessional communication.

Apart from the GP surgeries, professionals ran a variety of clinics. For example, there were clinics for antenatal care, child development, child health, and sessions relating to health education on diet and smoking. However, these sessions were generally monoprofessional. Professionals also (in various permutations) attended various business meetings on site, but there was no sense in which 'team' meetings were held.

As suggested by the term 'fragmented', there was no explicit cohesive purpose for this PHCT in terms of strategies for practice, nor was there any shared philosophy of care. In addition, there was no talk of allegiance to something called the PHCT. However, this did not indicate indifference to these issues on the part of all professionals. Some members of the 'attached' group would have actively pursued ways to change the situation, but this group's interaction was strongly influenced by traditional medical attitudes. There was an assumption that the GPs primarily decided patient care, while other professionals contributed as and when required (this hierarchical view did, however, engender security among the district nurses in terms of both patient care and professional support).

This perception of a medically headed hierarchy need not have resulted in a lack of cohesion and direction. However, most of the GPs did not display leadership, but only the use of power to shape interactions. For example, most GPs perceived a one-way passage of information or expertise from the top down to be sufficient, and considered that willingness to share information and ideas was their prerogative. As a result, communication from others was suppressed and therefore compromised. This concept of communication was perceived to influence the GPs' willingness to attend meetings at which their views or decisions could be challenged.

The apparent lack of interest in other professionals' views was not appreciated by other members within or associated with the practice. It also affected perceptions of patient management. Other professionals felt that patient care was managed individually on a day-to-day basis rather than by the development of an overall team strategy of care. However, some 'attached' professionals, such as the midwife and HV, had circumvented the 'system' and had worked hard to negotiate protocols across organisations, having set up forums for discussion about subjects such as antenatal referral and breastfeeding management.

The assumption of medical primacy also appeared to diminish the doctors' need to understand others' roles or to value others' input as autonomous practitioners with their own ideas about patient care or practice management. Other role input seemed to be valued only in so far as it 'soaked up' aspects of the GPs' work which they *could* do but had no time for. This seemed, in the view of other professionals, to lead to inappropriate referral and frustration at the lack of shared perspectives on care, and in particular it limited the practice manager's freedom to shape the practice as an effective business.

Despite its isolation as a semi-urban practice, the GPs themselves perceived pressure and interference from local health managers. In some ways the actions of the health managers reinforced the fragmentation of the team, since they were deemed to be counter-productive to the idea of PHCTs. The nature of professional attachment to the GPs was certainly inconsistent, and had undergone many changes to both structure and process. Furthermore, communication between these health managers and the GPs with regard to changes was felt to be meagre, and was observed to be so.

The second of the fragmented teams, namely the CMHT, was actually subdivided but was difficult to conceptualise as two separate teams. For example, the OT was shared, and a further complication was that some professionals moved across the teams during the time of the study. Therefore the designation of members to one 'team' or the other seemed to be very loose. However, staff were divided in the following way. Each team consisted of three community psychiatric nurses (CPNs), one full-time and one part-time social worker, one consultant psychiatrist and the shared OT.

The teams operated from two adjoining offices, and there had been a deliberate decision to bring professionals together under one roof in the hope of achieving greater co-ordination of service delivery. The overall remit of the teams, within a specific geographical location, was to manage the care of all people aged 18–65 years with severe or enduring mental health problems. This was done under the umbrella of a system of categorisation of the severity of mental illness, with its appropriate care protocols, known as the Care Programme Approach (CPA). Despite the fact that this system had supposedly been jointly developed between health and social services, the latter continued to use their own system, with which it conflicted.

In order to work with this client group, professionals liaised with various other mental health facilities such as a day hospital, in-patient and out-patient sites. Although there were interview rooms in the offices for professionals to conduct one-to one sessions with their clients, in general the work was domiciliary in nature, or took place at out-patient clinic sessions held in the psychiatrist's surgeries, or at the day centre. The use of their offices solely as an administrative base would have given team members the opportunity to talk with each other about various clients, and to learn about each other's practice.

However, because they did not share many clients, this did not occur as a *team* function.

Like the PHCT, professionals in these teams had retained a largely mono-professional approach to patient care. For example, referral and allocation of clients to particular professionals were conducted through single-profession recording systems and meetings. All business meetings were held in single professional groups, so that issues related to practice and professional concerns were discussed separately.

Two meetings were supposed to be multiprofessional. The first was held on a weekly basis at the in-patient facility where the discharge of clients was discussed. Together with the relevant in-patient staff members and the consultant, the appropriate CPNs and social workers were supposed to attend in order that an agreed discharge procedure could be decided and a key worker assigned. The social workers attended these meetings inconsistently, and the CPNs did not attend them at all.

The second multiprofessional meeting was a weekly case review. In one team this was in no way systematic, the clients for discussion being simply drawn from the most recent consultant out-patient clinic and the latest discharges from the in-patient facility. In the other team, review was organised around recent referrals and the monitoring of current problematic clients, giving it a wider base for discussion, but still without a comprehensive systematic review process. These meetings were also inconsistently attended, often for genuine reasons of prioritisation, but also as a deliberate expression of disagreement with the perceived suppression of some professionals' voices.

Structurally, the different professional groups' day-to-day practice was conducted in a largely unconnected fashion. This lack of day-to-day interaction resulted in a paucity of detailed communication, together with a lack of role understanding created by the degree of 'hidden role'. Part of the problem was the fact that professionals did not share case-loads. The different population groups that the various professionals had to manage made it difficult to find a team focus. This was particularly evident in CPN and social work practice, where there was an understanding that, if the population group did overlap, it was interpreted as a duplication of intervention. This issue of duplication was related to a shift in the CPN role towards a more psychosocial emphasis, similar to that of the social worker.

The CPNs had moved from working largely with relatively mildly ill people for whom short periods of therapy could be given, towards dealing with the more severely mentally ill. This meant that the CPN role had become more diffuse, requiring both psychotherapeutic and social care input. A further problem was then created as the CPNs generally felt that they were unprepared, and indeed not necessarily willing, to engage in managing both aspects of care. As a result, professional defensiveness between the CPN and social work groups was rife. This was exemplified in the hotly contested interpretation of the key-worker role, a fundamental aspect of the CPA. Did it mean one person co-ordinating care across the team and other professionals? Or did it mean case management where one person actually executed a care plan him- or herself? Agreement on this could not be reached in these CMHTs.

This area of conflict was reinforced by the fact that the CMHT brought together two different agencies, namely health and social services. There were differences in policy decisions, differences in the documentation used, and a lack of communication between the two management structures. These factors directly affected multiprofessional working by reinforcing the separation between the professional groups and creating resentments where decisions had been made unilaterally. Furthermore, cultural differences between the two agencies promoted discord with regard to role definition and communication styles.

A final issue for the CMHT was the way in which the communication style and actions of the consultant psychiatrists influenced team interaction. One psychiatrist was perceived as authoritarian and brusque, but also as inconsistently using his power to influence others' practice. The other psychiatrist appeared to be more open and friendly, but in fact frequently attempted to direct others' practice, and indeed whole team practice, by more subtle but no less undemocratic means. As a result, some professionals felt that their professional judgement and autonomy were being undermined.

To a large extent, the communication among the CPNs was non-challenging, keeping discussion to a minimum, and yet grumbling among themselves. Meanwhile, some of them continued to practise in a relatively autonomous fashion (i.e. they went ahead and did what they felt was important for their clients, despite direction by the consultants). The social workers and the OT perceived that the consultants' behaviour inhibited their contribution, but to some extent they did still challenge them. Particularly in the case of some social workers there were angry exchanges, which was one of the reasons that led to these professionals absenting themselves from team and discharge meetings.

The final 'team' that operated in a fragmented fashion was the group of professionals working in a 26-bed medical ward designated as a 'respiratory' ward. This ward was staffed by nurses working in two 'teams'. They were arranged geographically (i.e. each 'team' took an area of the ward to manage). There was also a four-bed high-dependency unit (HDU) within the ward, which was staffed by a semi-permanent group of nurses. Various consultants and their firms (doctors of all grades working under one consultant) visited the ward, as did PTs, OTs, SWs, a pharmacist and several specialist nurses.

In the medical ward, perceptions of 'teamwork' were essentially monoprofessional, and this was where primary allegiances were rooted. This perception was steered by the way in which organisational reality alienated professionals from each other. Bed management had created an unpredictable situation where patients with many different varieties of illness were placed together in order to maximise bed-filling. In tandem with increasing professional specialism, this meant that professionals other than the nurses attended many wards in order to see their patients. Because of the number of sites which professionals were expected to attend, the nurses were unable to predict when, or how often many of these professionals would come to the ward. As a result, nurses were often unable to attend consultants' ward rounds on a regular basis. The problem of uncertain timing and the perceived large number of visiting professionals was compounded by the fact that many of them were on short rotations through the hospital.

The effect of these organisational factors was that opportunities for forming sound relationships in which professionals could gauge the skills, competencies and knowledge base of other individuals serving the ward were greatly reduced. In addition to this lack of role understanding, it was both observed and perceived that ineffective communication and co-ordination of care were frequent outcomes with regard to patient care. This situation created frustration for all of the professionals involved, and resulted in the development of counter-productive defensive strategies.

Professional defensive behaviour was also seen in relation to the extension of certain roles (e.g. nurse specialist roles). In the uncertain environment created by the speed of organisational change, this was seen as a cause for concern, largely because of the hidden nature of these new roles. One might expect that new roles would of necessity take time to be assimilated into an organisation. However, if people do not have the opportunity to identify the exact nature of the role and how it impacts on other roles, especially when viewed as occupying the same stratum in the organisation, then suspicion would be a likely outcome. In this context, the ward nurses perceived the nurse specialists to be encroaching on their territory and interfering. This created resentment, and nurses were aware that it could compromise patient care through an unwillingness to refer. There was also an indication that defensive responses were being made by the medical profession as a result of the raising of the pharmacist's profile.

One final issue in this setting was the continuing dominance of the medical model and the subsequent emphasis on medical input to decision-making. Despite the fact that negotiated decision-making was observed between PTs and OTs, nurses and PTs, and nurses and junior doctors, at the level of consultant, where overall strategies for patient care were decided, other professionals had only a limited input. This was also related to consultant communication style, or attribution thereof, where nurses had at worst developed avoidance tactics, and at best offered information rather than ideas to the discussions.

Assertive communication by the nurses did make an impact on the amount and type of nurse input. This was particularly apparent within the HDU, where continuity of the nursing staff, the small number of patients, and consequently the small number of professionals who visited frequently, together created opportunities for better communication and role understanding. In these circumstances, nurses spoke about or were observed to be offering suggestions for care procedures that were listened to and acted upon.

Core and periphery working

The final type of working, which we called *'core and periphery'*, and combined both integrated and fragmented working within the team. This was observed in two teams, namely the diabetes team and the child development assessment team, both of which had a recognised and designated professional membership. However, despite this fact, part of each of these teams had formed an integrated multiprofessional core, the remainder of the team being peripheral to that core. This identification of peripheral working did not relate to those members of a team who would, by the nature of their involvement with a patient or client, expect or be expected to be peripheral. Rather, it related to those who could and possibly should have been closely collaborating with other members of the team.

Like the team which worked in an integrated fashion, these teams operated in relatively stable and predictable contexts whilst working within these specific teams. However, despite the fact that the teams had designated status, some professionals did not, being required to provide care for patients in other contexts as well. In one case, this was within a general hospital setting, and in the other with another community-based team. One might surmise that all those who were required to work outside the confines of the team would be peripheral, and all those who worked solely within the team would be core members. However, this was not the case, the situation being more complex than that.

Within the multiprofessional core, many practices identified in 'integrated working' were demonstrated. For example, there were multiprofessional assessment, monitoring and evaluation practices, and a communication system that encouraged in-depth discussion of both cases and strategies for the 'core' team. Within the core, a high level of role understanding had developed. Professionals were able to extend the boundaries of their roles, learn from each other, had developed 'team' knowledge and skills, and felt that they were able to offer greater continuity and consistency of care and therapy for their patients.

The dislocation of the peripheral group from the core meant that communication between the two groups was constrained. It also meant that there was a lack of understanding of others' roles and how such roles could come together to provide more comprehensive care. In one team that exhibited this type of working, detrimental outcomes for patients were observed to result from these issues.

Despite the existence of some apparent similarities between these two teams (e.g. they were both designated teams which sat at the boundary between primary and secondary care), the reasons for the dislocation of the core group from the peripheral group had a very different basis, as we shall see.

Core and periphery teams

The diabetes team was situated in a purpose-built Diabetes Centre in the grounds of a general hospital. It consisted of a consultant diabetologist, two diabetes specialist nurses, two dietitians, a podiatrist and two chiropodists. The team provided assessment, monitoring and education for patients with diabetes. Patients were referred to the centre by GPs and could be chiefly managed in the community, with input from the Centre. Alternatively, if patients were admitted to hospital, then staff from the Centre would maintain links with those patients while they were in secondary care. Like the members of the rehabilitation unit, all team members were established in one geographical location, thus giving them the opportunity, when on site, to communicate with each other and to develop an understanding of other team members' work with patients.

All members of this team espoused a particular philosophy of diabetes care that stressed an educative and enabling approach designed to encourage maximum self-care by the patients. To this end, two diabetes specialist nurses worked chiefly in the Diabetes Centre and were responsible for the ongoing monitoring and education of the patients in nurse-run clinics. Both of them offered outreach work – one maintaining links with in-patients, and the other helping to develop GP-run diabetes clinics in the community. Other team members, such as the consultant, podiatrist, chiropodists and dietitians visited regularly for clinic sessions. These sessions included review of the patient's physiological status, specific foot care and education with regard to foot care, and the identification and management of dietary problems. The team also ran review and initial assessment clinics in the out-patient department (where the original Centre had been situated). Weekly meetings were held for all team members where it was intended that all professionals should discuss patient care and new developments in diabetes care, and have presentations from outside speakers.

Despite there being an official, nationally recognised team membership, within the team itself there were perceptions of a core group which consisted of the consultant, one of the two diabetes specialist nurses and a podiatrist. This group of professionals exhibited all the aspects of 'integrated' working that were identified earlier.

One of the chief reasons for the perception of the existence of a core and a periphery in this team was the historical, group context. Together with a community dietitian (now promoted into management), the members of the core group had all been involved in improving the diabetes services. Enhanced by a stable situation, they had pioneered the development of the diabetes team, supported the establishment of the Diabetes Centre, and jointly, written professional education courses on diabetes management for others' professional development. Over time, they had developed great trust in each other's competence and judgement, and they had learned to deal effectively with interpersonal issues such as working with a consultant who had a difficult communication style. For all of these members, allegiance to the team was considered paramount, and there was a high level of motivation with regard to diabetes care. This historical context had created a situation in which incorporation of newcomers into the established group was difficult.

Newcomers were at a disadvantage for the following reasons. First, they did not all share the same overriding interest in the diabetic condition. Secondly, because of the organisational context, all of them except the second diabetes specialist nurse were obliged to provide professional input to many other areas of the hospital. This compromised their input to the team, and created difficulties in terms of prioritisation to the diabetes team – a factor that caused particular resentment among the core group. Thirdly, the exclusivity of the original team undermined newcomers' felt professional value, as they perceived that relevant input on patient care was sought from the core group in preference to their input. Finally, the non-facilitative communication style of the consultant diabetologist was problematic. Because of their standing with the core group, newcomers did not feel that they could challenge the consultant in the way that other core members did.

All of these issues created resentment on both sides. However, they had been ameliorated to some extent by the communication skills of the diabetes specialist nurses, one of whom acted as an intermediary between the consultant and the more junior diabetes specialist nurse. The latter then acted as an advocate for the hospital-based professionals.

The final team we shall consider is the child development assessment team. This also operated from a purpose-built Centre within the grounds of a hospital, and provided assessment and therapy mainly for very young children with special needs. It consisted of SLTs, HVs, OTs, a playroom teacher, a social worker, PTs, consultant paediatricians, clinical psychologists, nurses, nursery nurses and a centre co-ordinator. Again, working from one Centre gave team members the opportunity to communicate and develop an understanding of each other's work. However, as will be seen later, the need to actually do this was limited.

Apart from the PTs and the social worker, all other professionals were employed by the local community trust, and had an office and practised in the Centre. The PTs were employed by the acute sector trust and only visited the Centre when this was necessary. The social worker was employed by the local Social Services Department, and was available for one day a week at the Centre. Although the clinical psychologists were employed by the community trust, they belonged primarily to the child and adolescent mental health team, and were therefore only able to offer limited input to the child development team.

The team provided assessment, therapy and monitoring mainly for very young children with special needs – both physical and mental (some professionals also had responsibility for school-age children). Their work involved a large number of clinic and therapy sessions, and all children were seen by appointment except for a 'drop-in time' for children with sensory deprivation. This session offered therapeutic play for children who, for example, were blind or had cerebral palsy.

Several of the sessions were multiprofessional. For example, children who were new to the Centre had a series of three initial assessment sessions at which it was intended that all potentially relevant professionals should observe the children and draw up a multiprofessional care plan (despite the description, it was perceived that not all of the potentially involved professionals made this assessment). Another series of sessions, run by the playroom teacher, nursery nurse and an SLT, was offered to children with language and behavioural disorders. These included a wide range of disorders, from autism to more simple delayed speech development. The drop-in session had the playroom teacher in full-time attendance and a PT and OT coming in for brief periods of time.

As might be expected from the nature of professional involvement in the team described earlier, the team structure and interaction were complex and confusing. Many professionals had separate and different case-loads, operated with different foci, and had separate line management. As a result, the team had grappled for many years with the type of service it provided and the way in which that service was provided. Time was spent reflecting on these issues at 6-monthly 'away-days'. However, despite many attempts to define themselves and their practice, team members were confused. A major issue was the lack of a shared vision of practice and a sense of direction. This related not only to difficulties in giving time to regular reflection and discussion of the issues involved, but also to the lack of a common philosophy of teamwork. Given the various foci, separate line management and the persistence of different professional cultures, this was not surprising. However, the team also felt that it lacked a strong but facilitative leader.

Within this large team there was an acknowledged core consisting of an SLT, an HV, one of the four consultants and the playroom teacher. Apart from the playroom teacher, all of these professionals had commitments outside the work of the team. However, they were highly motivated to work collaboratively, and they shared similar ideas about how to achieve this. Two of these professionals could identify the influence of prior experience that led to these beliefs, and meeting those with similar ideas had enabled them to develop collaborative practices. For example, they had evolved joint working practices and to some extent a shared note system. They had been responsible for developing the highly structured initial assessment sessions, the language disorder sessions and specific case-review sessions. These case discussions were open to all professionals, and were intended to provide regular forums for debate on different aspects of the team's work. However, only the OT described earlier actually attended with the other core members.

Other professionals were peripheral to this group to varying degrees. For example, the one OT identified above was perceived, and saw herself, as almost a core member. The PTs were perceived as largely separate, and they felt excluded. The clinical psychologists were regarded as extremely marginal, and indeed towards the end of the study they actually removed themselves from their Centre offices. In general it did not seem possible for the core group to 'bring on board' most other team members to their type of working. This related to historical incidents, perceptions of a specific orientation to the work of the assessment centre (i.e. language disorder), and organisational issues.

This chapter has provided an overview of ways in which the evidence for reshaping shared learning programmes was collected. It has presented some of this evidence by describing three different types of multiprofessional working and the teams which demonstrated these types of working. The issues that were specific to each team, and the ways in which they impacted on aspects of teamwork such as communication and role understanding, have been briefly highlighted. Before we move on to the next three chapters, these aspects of teamwork require further elaboration.

Research on teamwork has identified the importance of communication and role understanding (e.g. Clark *et al.* 1986; Abramson, 1990; Iles and Auluck, 1990; Øvretveit, 1990, 1993, 1995; Gibbon, 1992; Poulton and West, 1993; Pritchard and Pritchard, 1994; Field and West, 1995; Onyett *et al.* 1996; West and Pillinger, 1996; West and Slater, 1996). They are seen as a prescription for 'effective multiprofessional teamwork', with the implicit expectation that these terms are comprehensively understood. In our study we identified the many shades of meaning that these terms subsume, and how these need to be addressed by teams in order to develop effective collaboration. On the basis of our findings, the following description will allow the reader to identify for him- or herself just how possible effective teamworking would be under the particular circumstances that will be described and discussed later.

Communication consists of a complex set of components in terms of how effectively teams collaborate. First, it relates to what is said. However, does the information that is given by one professional to another include mere sharing of information, or does it encompass professional opinion? Furthermore, does this imply a sharing of professional opinions? It also relates to the range of perspectives on patient care that are included, (e.g. physiological, psychological and social aspects of a particular patient that interact in the process of an illness). Secondly, it concerns the person to whom it is said. Fundamental to this is the extent to which information and opinion are shared as a team, rather than being kept within professional boundaries. Thirdly, it includes how it is said. Is communication given in a way that encourages other professional input, or does it inhibit other people from saying all that they feel they would like to say? Finally, it relates to why it is said. On what basis are people deciding to give a piece of information or an opinion?

Role understanding is similarly complex. First, it relates to understanding the tasks and responsibilities which are undertaken by professionals in a team. Secondly, it relates to the way in which these are achieved on a day-to-day basis (i.e. the constraints of time and resources) and how each professional contributes to a pattern of care. This aspect also includes an understanding of the boundaries of each professional's contribution, where these meet and where they overlap. Finally, it includes an understanding of the rationale behind a professional's contribution to a patient's care – that is, knowing why a professional is making particular decisions and taking certain actions.

In the next three chapters we shall explore in some detail three levels of analysis – *organisational, individual* and *group levels* – in order to understand more clearly how these influence the ability of professionals to work collaboratively by communicating effectively and understanding how each member contributes to patient care. The organisational level will be dealt with first, as the context within which teams work will influence the very structure of the team, and will constrain or enhance the possibilities for interaction. The influence on the individual will then be addressed, as the professional background, status, experience and personality of team members will obviously shape the potential of the team to develop collaborative working. Finally, group processes will be examined, since these may be influenced by both the external environment and the internal contribution of the team members. We shall use scenarios and quotes from the case studies to illustrate how different organisational structures and processes, individual philosophies of team-working, and group issues can inhibit or promote professionals in providing team care for patients, and the benefits or otherwise which result.

Although it will become clear that, in our study, *integrated working* seemed to provide evidence of benefits to patients which other types of working did not in any consistent pattern, it is not suggested that this way of working is the *only* way to achieve such outcomes. Nor is it suggested that the level of collaboration that was seen in the 'integrated' team is the only way to operate – some teams simply would not have the time or accessibility to work in this way.

Although part of our argument is that, in our study, *integrated working* seemed to be an effective way of consistently providing benefits for patients or clients, setting this up as a 'yardstick' of multiprofessional working for students to aspire to in their clinical experience may be limiting and ultimately demoralising. It may be more useful for students to reflect on the nature of the context in which they are working, and how this might impact on multiprofessional teamwork.

We do suggest that if collaborative working in multiprofessional teams is to be at the forefront of trust practices, then teams would need to develop the means for ongoing discussion and agreement about a system that is appropriate for them. Furthermore, teams would need to develop a shared understanding of what they want to achieve and how to achieve it. Certain demands would need to be met in order to achieve this. As will be seen in the next chapter, these relate partly to the level of support that is given to collaborative working by the organisation. In Chapter 4 we shall see that they also relate to the degree to which professionals can learn strategies for overcoming problems of professional culture and develop awareness of the need for reflection on individual beliefs about working with others. Finally, in Chapter 5 we shall see that they also relate to how team members understand and cope with issues of group process in the context of issues related to power, authority and professional culture.

The impact of the organisation on teamworking

3

INTRODUCTION

In Chapter 1 we identified the direction for multiprofessional teamworking as proposed by government policy. We also examined current thinking in local trusts, both acute and community sectors, in terms of teamwork, the agendas which drive their policies and what that has meant for staff. However, this perspective came from senior management. Organisational theory identifies both the interconnectedness of different levels of organisation and how each impacts on the other, and the often conflicting agendas to which these levels may ascribe. These different agendas will subsequently shape the meanings that are given to particular concepts (Van den Ven, 1976; Katz and Kahn, 1978; Randolph and Dess, 1984; Spurgeon 1999). That being the case, we would need to ask how people who are actually working at the 'coal-face' feel the impact of policy decisions and the subsequent changes to organisational structures and processes. How do they understand 'teamworking' within that framework? Furthermore, for those who are required to work across organisations, how do changes relating to teamwork in their trust match those of other trusts or other agencies?

From our study it was evident that the way in which an organisation functions has a profound effect on whether teams can perform to the best of their abilities. The issue of organisational context should not be underestimated. Research into organisational change within the NHS as far back as the 1970s attested to the problems of educating or training people to operate in a particular way, only to find that acquired skills and knowledge were extinguished rapidly when they were back in an unsupportive workplace (e.g. Quilitch, 1978).

This chapter will identify several issues relating to organisational structure and process which were seen to have a negative impact on teamworking, and will present evidence of how some organisational structures and processes can support teamworking more than others. We shall raise issues which organisational senior management needs to consider if collaborative multiprofessional working is to be effective, and we shall flag up implications for professional education which would support a student's future teamwork.

Our study indicates that there are four main organisational issues which influence teamworking. These are: recent governmental policies, the diversity of the patient populations with which teams have to work, the degree of team-oriented structures and processes, and opportunities for working closely. None of these are distinct; recent policies impinge on patient populations, and patient populations are associated with the way in which teams have been constructed within the organisation. However, their separation stems from professionals' own identification, and as such gives us a useful means of describing and discussing the organisational context.

Recent government policies include bed management and the Care Programme Approach (CPA). The introduction of the former has implications for the levels of stability and predictability in the environment through which professionals have to negotiate a pathway of care. In our study, both communication and understanding of others' roles were compromised, giving rise to frustration among professionals. Allegiance to professional rather than team groups was reinforced, and the outcomes for patients were detrimental. Introduction of the CPA involves the development of a new key-worker role within community mental health teams (CMHT). In our study this created problems. The role was contested between various professionals within the CMHT, in terms of both its meaning and its allocation. Again this raised difficulties of communication and role understanding, and it exacerbated professional defensive behaviours. As a result, team allegiance was diminished.

The *diversity of the patient population* with which teams had to work related to two issues. The first of these was the extent to which professionals were expected to work with patients outside the designated population defined by the team. This meant that professionals needed to prioritise their work, sometimes to the detriment of work with patients within the team. This competition for professionals' time was frustrating both for themselves and for other team members, and it put team allegiances under strain.

The second issue concerned the situation in which teams of professionals were brought together where there were very different patient foci. Not being able to work to a shared focus created problems with regard to communication and knowing who was contributing in what way to a particular patient's care. Allegiances were formed around diagnoses, therapeutic intervention or professional groups.

Team-oriented structures and processes related to two aspects, namely the degree of collaboration across professional management and the extent of collaborative communication structures. In the former, this applied both within an organisation and across organisational boundaries. Lack of collaboration across management structures was seen to inhibit the development of team practices and, through arbitrary decision-making, to create unpredictable situations for team members, often at odds with team function. Frustration and professional defensiveness resulted.

In terms of communication structures, where these remained within a professional group there were opportunities for reducing the effectiveness of interprofessional communication by professionals being unaware of or misjudging others' contributions. These reinforced professional rather than team allegiance.

Opportunities for working closely were important in two ways. Where people were located together in order to practise, there were opportunities for learning about each other's contributions. Working separately made this more difficult, but the situation was compromised further if professionals had no central location where they could meet to discuss team practice and patient issues. In addition, professionals who did not work closely were denied the opportunity to engage in ongoing, *ad hoc* communication about particular issues, and to form social and thus team bonds.

All of these structural issues and their associated processes therefore had implications for the way in which teams were able to function, and consequently they had implications for patient care. Where professionals were shielded from the fall-out from current policies, where the team shared a patient focus without competing priorities, where management and communication structures were shared, and where opportunities to work closely were possible *and were grasped*, patients were seen to benefit. Where these criteria were not fulfilled, the continuity and consistency of care were compromised, referrals were seen to be inappropriate, ambiguous messages were given, and there was a lack of comprehensiveness to the decision-making and actions taken in relation to patient care.

Using scenarios and quotes from the case studies, the next four sections will explore in more detail the way in which these organisational structures influenced teamwork.

THE EFFECTS OF RECENT GOVERNMENT POLICY ON TEAMWORKING

Bed management policy was brought in by the previous (Conservative) Government to maximise the number of patients being cared for in the hospital setting at any one time. This was done in order to reduce waiting-lists by streamlining the management of patient throughput. Chapter 1 identified how senior management has attempted to overcome some of the fall-out from such policy implementation, but it is clear that those working in the acute sector are still facing extreme difficulties. This was epitomised in the medical ward, where professionals demonstrated the most 'fragmented' working seen in the study. As a general rule, within the trust it was often the case that patients were placed as outliers to specialist areas of care in order to fill available beds. This resulted in professionals (other than nurses) having to visit a large number of wards in order to see their patients – in some cases eight or ten wards instead of one or two as had traditionally been the case. By the same token, the outcome for an individual ward, (e.g. the medical ward) was that a large number of doctors and other professionals, such as PTs, OTs and specialist nurses, would need to visit their own patients in a constantly changing pattern. This was compounded by the fact that medical staff had become more specialised, thus necessitating the input of a greater number to any one ward. Furthermore, it was now expected that patients would spend only as much time as was necessary within the acute sector. Thus the rate of turnover of patients in the ward was high, with some only staying two or three days.

The combination of these factors changed the nature of professionals' interaction with others within a central practice base. Despite the fact that it had been designated as a 'respiratory ward', the large group of visiting professionals should arguably not have been called a 'team' at all. Professionals from the different specialisms did not necessarily need to have contact with each other, their chief point of reference being the nurses.

This fragmented picture was reinforced by the fact that there was also a turnover of professionals – some expected, because of the nature of their role, and some unexpected. The junior doctors, PTs and OTs were on periodic rotation as part of their post-graduate education. The nurses suffered a shortage of staff, requiring 'bank' staff input on a regular basis. Therefore not only was there a rapid throughput and changing nature of the patient population, but this applied to the 'team' as well. The environment for collaboration with others was therefore very unstable. It was also extremely unpredictable. In terms of the dispersal of patients, professionals who had to visit a large number of wards would experience ramifications for the amount of time spent in any one ward, as was identified by one house officer (HO):

> Most of the time I have been walking on my feet not seeing the patients, just walking from ward to ward. My actual working time is four or five hours and walking time is three hours.
>
> (HO)

It was felt that previously a particular consultant's ward round and the pre-ward-round visit by house officers and registrars would have taken up an appreciable part of the day, as they would have been seeing a large number of patients. Now a consultant and his or her 'firm' were seeing fewer patients in the ward in a shorter time. Because of the large number of wards being attended by professionals, the possibility of being able to predict arrival at any one ward was limited, thereby causing further problems for the ward staff. The nurses would also need to manage several similar events throughout the day. In this situation, interactions between various professionals were necessarily brief, if indeed there was any interaction at all. Ensuring that, amidst the flurry of activities, the appropriate nurse was available to talk to the relevant visiting professional was extremely difficult.

Not surprisingly, this situation greatly compromised communication, and it became difficult to establish what other 'team' members were doing, or why. For example, nurses on the ward did not know when other professionals would arrive on the ward, nor who they would be. By the same token, despite the named-nurse system, because of the shift rotation of nurses and the use of 'bank' staff, visiting professionals did not know who to go to for advice and information about patients. The problem of not knowing when various professionals would be coming to the ward was compounded by the fact that visiting professionals did not exhibit consistent patterns of communication with the nurses. Some professionals would wait until a nurse was available to inform them of what had occurred and any decisions that had been made, while others did not. The nurses, because they were frequently engaged in caring for patients behind pulled bed curtains, often did not realise that other professionals were in the ward. For many visiting professionals it was simpler to write in the medical notes and assume that the nurses and other relevant professionals would read them. As attested by several of the nursing staff, this was by no means always the case, and often either information was not communicated at all, or it was miscommunicated. For example, one detrimental situation resulted in which a patient was 'fasted' for several hours unnecessarily, and another patient missed a long-awaited appointment because the timing was misunderstood.

The missed opportunities for communication resulted in inconsistencies in patterns of care, some of which were vital for the patients' well-being. For example, one of the respiratory PTs expressed concern that lack of communication had led to disjunction in the care process. She spoke about the difficulties in linking her intervention with that of the nurses in order to maximise the beneficial effects for the patient. She came to the ward to perform chest exercises with particular patients that required the prior administration of drugs through a nebuliser, which was to have been organised by the nurses. The PT had indicated that the drugs needed to be given about 1 hour prior to treatment in order to maximise the effect of her therapy. She believed that the nurses were often late in doing their drug rounds, so that when she arrived not enough time had elapsed, or the patients had not received the drug at all. In either case, it was possible that she would be unable to perform the treatment on that day. However, the PT was also observed to attend the ward in a random fashion, sometimes early in the morning, and at other times not until the afternoon. When the nurses were asked at what time they would expect the PT to visit, they expressed no awareness of a particular pattern.

A direct result of nurses not knowing the pattern of professional input, and thereby missing the opportunity to communicate with other visiting professionals, was that the nurses would contact them at times when they might be busy on other wards. For example, they regularly contacted doctors using their 'bleep' system. This was a source of frustration among the nurses and resentment among the doctors. Some of these professionals were clearly stretched to the limit with work in other areas, and felt that the nurses did not understand how hard they *were* working, and had contacted them unnecessarily.

Operating in an unstable and unpredictable environment severely limits the knowledge which individuals within a 'team' could develop about the practice of other professionals (i.e. their roles in action). For the greater part of the working day, these roles may be hidden from each other. The brief and unexpected visits that were made by other professionals compromised nurses' availability to attend the patient and so witness what the professional was doing, and how. This problem was seen even where roles were well established. How much more difficult, therefore, was the situation when new roles were introduced. This problem was highlighted by the introduction of a discharge planning role to help support the bed management policy. A specialist nurse had been employed to co-ordinate the discharge of elderly patients in particular. She was aware that, despite the fact that she reiterated her role to her colleagues on a regular basis, lack of ongoing visibility made it difficult for her to build up the credibility of her contribution to the process of care. A successful discharge might or might not be attributed to her – others would simply observe that a discharge process had or had not been achieved smoothly.

Where teams are shielded from the effects of the bed management policy, they operate in a more stable and predictable environment. This type of environment helped to underpin the 'integrated' working that was seen in the rehabilitation unit. As with most rehabilitation care, patients remained in this unit for long periods of time, 6 months being considered a minimum for effective therapeutic outcomes to be achieved. In addition, many of the team members were also long-standing, with some staff having worked in the unit since its inception. This team stability provides the opportunity for two main developments – first, the building of relationships between team members, and between professionals and patients, and secondly, the growth of expertise about the patient group.

With regard to relationships between professionals, stability enables team members to develop an understanding of each other's strengths and weaknesses in relation to their role, and also at a personal level. The ongoing nature of this exposure enables professionals to learn how to manage these aspects within the team context. In this team, many members clearly understood one another's role – a many-layered concept that will be explored further in a later chapter. However, the stable environment in which various aspects of other team members' practice were exposed also enabled them to understand how their colleagues actually *coped* with their role within the team. Where there is stability, a team member can gauge another's ability to contribute effectively. Where detrimental patient care is seen, it would enable other team members to develop ways of managing that deficit.

Stability can also enable individual professionals and the whole team to develop a relationship with patients. In many situations, individual practitioners have ongoing relationships with individual clients or patients. However, other professionals caring for the patient will change. Both the long-term employment of staff and long-term residence of the patients enabled a 'team' relationship to develop with the patients in a setting such as rehabilitation.

The 'integrated' rehabilitation team's use of collaborative practices enabled patients to see professionals interacting, and to determine how those interactions provided a congruent pattern of care. For example, a physiotherapist and an OT were seen working together with a patient on one aspect of his standing position relating to the muscles in his trunk. The physiotherapist and OT had been trying to massage the muscles on one side of the patient's back in order to enable him to sit straighter, before asking him to stand in the same position. The physiotherapist left half-way through the session. The patient then asked some questions about what the professionals were doing, and the OT explained the principles of movement espoused by many of the professionals within that team, and how the techniques of the session related to those principles. The patient later said that this interchange had helped him to feel very secure, because both professionals had told him the same things. As a result, he had become more confident that they were 'aiming in the same direction'. In this way, patients could develop trust in the team, rather than an individual, giving them the confidence to express their own feelings about their rehabilitation.

The stable environment would also provide opportunities for team members to deepen and broaden their skills and knowledge in their particular field. This team was highly motivated in terms of rehabilitation processes, and had a predilection for reflection and evaluation. Stability enabled them to use these skills to develop processes of care and therapy, either from attending relevant programmes of education and conferences, or from observation of other rehabilitation teams. Where members of the team attended such programmes, conferences or other rehabilitation establishments, then part of the team process was for them to provide feedback to the rest of the team.

The work of this team was also highly predictable. There were no emergency admissions to the unit, patients being admitted by means of a negotiated process over several weeks. On admission, the team was able to timetable their work to a large extent. This process enabled professionals to predict one another's movements on a day-to-day basis, reinforcing their ability to determine when they would be most likely to make contact with another member to pass on information or discuss relevant incidents. It also enabled team members to prepare patients for the next aspect of therapy or care. With a predictable context, continuity of care can be maintained to a high degree, as it is easier to piece together various team members' contributions. In this setting it was also easier to maintain the 'carry-over' process, as both nurses and other therapists could be with their own patients while certain therapeutic interventions were being performed. By showing other team members how best to continue in the absence of the therapist responsible for leading a particular intervention, it was also ensured that patients received consistency of care.

We have cited these two extremes not to show that the 'integrated' team had all the answers to collaborative working – they did not. Furthermore, to some extent they existed in a privileged environment within the current NHS, and that has to be acknowledged (although other research conducted on a less isolated rehabilitation team within the acute sector has shown similar patterns of collaborative working; Miller *et al.*, 1997). However, the degree to which this team was able to provide effective patient care, given the level of stability and predictability that they enjoyed, should give us food for thought with regard to changes to organisational structures. Policies such as bed management have had far-reaching effects on the ability of professionals to form collaborative teams. Amelioration of some of the fall-out of the policy is a task that could be tackled by senior trust management, and indeed there was evidence of such developments within our study. For example, the introduction in some trusts of medical admission wards, where professionals are attached to the ward rather than to a particular specialism, have provided better opportunities for the development of collaborative working.

What should these changes mean for students?

> First, it is important that students begin to understand the context within which they are operating in teams – the organisation, its policies, structures and processes, and how these might impact on the team.

Secondly, students need to realise that best practice in terms of teamwork may not be possible in all environments.

Furthermore, fragmentation due to policies such as bed management can disrupt the ability of professionals to communicate with each other and to understand what others are contributing to patient care.

It is important that students learn how and why communication difficulties develop in contexts such as acute care, and the types of structures that can help to enable greater consistency of communication.

Students also need to learn the barriers to understanding the contribution of others as a team member – for example, where professionals are peripatetic and much of their role is hidden.

The *Care Programme Approach* (CPA) (Department of Health, 1990b) was the second policy change that created problems for a specific specialism, namely community mental health. These difficulties related *to cross-organisational process differences and to differences in interpretation of a fundamental aspect of the approach, namely the key-worker role*. The way in which two different organisations approached the CPA highlighted the problems faced by teams that needed to work across organisations and reinforced, in our study, the fragmentation of the CMHT.

This system was introduced as part of the work of the CMHT following an acknowledgement by the Government that the Community Care Programme was not offering sufficiently effective care for clients once they had been discharged into the community (Department of Health, 1990b). However, the approach was designed to cover *all* clients who were eligible for CMHT care, whether they received in-patient care or not.

Part of the approach involved the development of a care plan based on the level of mental ill health suffered by the client. It was the intention that those clients with the greatest needs, or who were the most severely ill, should receive the fullest range of services and the most stringently monitored plan. The levels were identified as follows:

- *level* 1: individuals with low support needs (e.g. the person experienced a period of emotional or psychological distress, but was likely to remain stable);
- *level* 2: individuals with serious mental illness, requiring 'sectioning' after-care, or with complex health and social care needs;
- *level* 3: individuals with severe mental illness, or with complex health and social needs, at significant risk, volatile, and possibly needing supervision on the Supervision Register.

This categorisation of individuals according to the three different levels created the first problem for the CMHT in our study. Initially, at senior management level, the local trust had developed joint documentation for the CPA in consultation with Social Services. This included a client registration form, and an 8-page multi-assessment form that included both psychological and social assessment. It was the intention that these forms should be used for all individuals being seen by members of the CMHT. However, the CPA forms were only used by health professionals. Supported by their own management, the social workers continued to use their own specific Social Services forms for their own social assessments. These forms were also designed to describe severity of mental illness, but related to 'funding bands' which the social workers then used to develop care packages for clients. Both social workers and CPNs considered that these forms provided a much fuller social needs assessment than the CPA form, but they were a source of frustration for two reasons. First, and most unfortunately, they ran in the opposite direction to the three levels of the CPA – that is, level 1 represented the most severe mental illness. Not surprisingly, this caused confusion when clients were being discussed, with the potential for mistakes to be made with regard to documentation of the severity of a client's illness. Secondly, because the Social Services form was much more complex, it gave the CPNs reason to insist that this form should be completed by the social workers, despite the duplication of information that this entailed. In the process, this reinforced the existing dissent between the professional groups with regard to a fundamental aspect of the CPA, namely the key-worker role.

In the CPA, it is stipulated that one person from within a CMHT should be identified as a key-worker for each client. This professional would be responsible for co-ordinating the 'registration, assessment, planning and review' of their client's care. Ideally, the key-worker should be a professional who already has knowledge of the client and has built up a relationship with them. However, the choice of professional depends on the level of mental ill health to which a client has been allocated.

The most seriously ill people would need full risk assessment both in terms of self harm and harm to others in the community, and in terms of regular and frequent monitoring. For this reason they may be deemed to require either CPNs or social workers as key-workers, as these professionals work most regularly and closely with clients. Other professionals who are not in such regular contact with clients in the community, such as the psychiatrist or OT, could be key-workers in cases where there are low-level mental health problems.

If a client has been seriously ill, and has required in-patient care under certain sections of the Mental Health Act, it is necessary for a meeting to be arranged before their discharge. This meeting should include the client and relevant members of the in-patient staff and CMHT, and requires the development of a care plan. As part of the meeting it should be discussed, written up and signed by the professionals and the client. Another intention of the approach is that those clients who are in hospital on a voluntary basis should have a meeting to plan for their discharge. However, in our study it was acknowledged that this did not always happen in the same formal way. In either case, decisions with regard to the discharge care plan need to be negotiated with an appropriate key-worker. As suggested above, the allocation of this role was a cause of much dissent and frustration for the CMHT in our study. This was partly due to the nature of the role contested between the health and social services.

For both the trust and many of the CPNs in the team, understanding of this role was that the key-worker would need to be aware of all psychological, medical and social interventions in order to *co-ordinate* a client's care. However, they would not necessarily be responsible for *actioning* the interventions. In *this* sense, as key-workers, the CPNs would still make their own assessments but would leave social assessment to the social workers (using their own more complex forms). They argued that this was important because of social workers' more detailed understanding of social assessment. However, the social workers had a different understanding of the key-worker role that related to their service's previous practice. Social workers had been involved in case management for some time. This meant that an identified case manager would be responsible not only for co-ordinating aspects of a client's care plan, but also for *executing* all aspects of that care plan. It was this interpretation of key-working to which the social workers subscribed. With the introduction of the CPA, the key-worker role was now one that any member of the CMHT could be required to take on. As far as the social workers were concerned, this meant that the CPNs would not only include more social awareness in their thinking, but would also add a social aspect to their work. However, this did not readily occur.

The CPNs argued that not only was this not their trust's interpretation of key-working, but that in any case they had neither the time nor the skills, as key-workers, to manage all aspects of client care. They protested that the social workers had smaller case-loads that allowed them to pursue housing or financial problems thoroughly. This was true, but the social workers felt that the depth of work they were expected to undertake with each client made their case-loads comparable to the larger ones of the CPNs. They were unhappy that they should still be required to take on the main burden of housing or employment problems, and they felt that the CPN role should include wider activities such as social assessment of their clients.

This situation was further heightened by the fact that social worker numbers were reduced within the teams. As a result, social workers started to refuse to take on further work, not only the key-worker role, but also housing and financial problems, where CPNs were key-working. Both professional groups felt overburdened with the work of the CMHT, but the CPNs felt that they were unprepared and therefore unwilling to carry out the complex assessment and intervention required for the clients. Key-working became 'the ball that nobody wants to catch' (CP).

This problem was compounded by current health service expectations of the CPN role and a shift towards greater involvement in statutory processes for the social workers. The CPNs' earlier role in the CMHTs had mainly been to deal with GP referrals of people with relatively mild mental health problems. This had allowed them to engage in both therapeutic and health prevention work. Now they were being required to manage clients with chronic and severe mental illness. This shift in emphasis demanded that CPNs look more broadly at the influence of social aspects of their clients' lives in order to offer the most appropriate care. Indeed, they might need to be involved in managing some of these aspects of care. Many CPNs in this setting felt unprepared for this altered role and responded in one of two ways – by seeking training to enhance their skills and knowledge, or by standing firm and saying that this was not the role they wanted to take on. This latter group felt that it would mean the loss of skills they had spent years acquiring; they felt that they had a monitoring and therapeutic role and did not want this encroached upon.

The traditional social worker role had included managing all the social aspects of client care, such as housing, unemployment and therapeutic intervention with regard to family therapy. Because of their statutory duties and their social focus, they had tended to deal with the more severely mentally ill, or those with chronic problems. The increase in statutory work and the reduction in their manpower now meant that certain aspects of their work, such as therapeutic intervention, were no longer possible. As with the CPNs, some of them felt deskilled as a result.

The change in emphasis for the CMHTs towards the more severely mentally ill meant that the roles of social worker and CPN now overlapped to a larger extent; the boundaries between 'social' and 'health' input had blurred. Because of the severity of their clients' mental illness, and the subsequent chaos that it often caused in housing and employment, clear divisions in client care were now inappropriate. It was difficult to untangle what was 'social' from what was 'health'. Did a lack of housing and employment lead to the mental illness, or was it the other way around? Some CPNs acknowledged that their clients' main problem was maintaining housing, so that to define the nursing contribution to their care as only therapeutic or medical monitoring would have been inadequate. If a person did not have their basic needs met, what would be the impact of therapy?

As a result of this role confusion, many CPNs felt that, as social workers were not doing what the CPNs regarded as their role, they did not now understand what they *were* offering to the team. By the same token, several social workers felt that the CPNs were being professionally 'precious' by adhering to their 'old role'. They understood that CPNs might require guidance and assistance in the more complex cases, but still they felt that this was appropriate for *members of a CMHT*. With regard to resolving who did what in the team in relation to the key-working role, there was little active support from either professional group's management. As a result, these professionals became entrenched in unhelpful positions. Far from being a mechanism for including and co-ordinating team members' activities with a client as a 'team' process, the key-worker role was used to reinforce further the professional role boundaries (this problem is corroborated by Simpson, 1998).

The introduction of the key-working role as part of the CPA focused the already contentious professional role issues within the CMHT. However, it was evident that the CPA could have been introduced as a more cohesive cross-organisational policy. The fact that there had been joint development of documentation showed that cross-organisational collaboration was possible. However, the lack of joint understanding of what different aspects of the CPA involved when it was put into operation fundamentally undermined its introduction. Despite entreaties from both CPNs and social workers to their respective managers, at no point prior to or during the study had both managers met together with the teams to talk about the problems of role change and how the current issues could be dealt with. Instead, each professional group had met with its own manager for a session on the rationale and working of the CPA. This was a missed opportunity for team practice development of major proportions.

Unlike the introduction of the bed management policy, the CPA had the potential to create effective collaboration among the various members of the CMHT. However, the way in which it was introduced, with the implications for practice apparently not thought through sufficiently, only served to divide some professional groups further. Cross-organisational working is fraught with problems of mismatching policies and mismatching cultures. Here one policy was introduced for both, but each interpreted the working of the policy differently. This highlights the need for ongoing discussion at all levels in order to identify and work through these differences in understanding, and a later section in this chapter will deal with this issue in more detail.

For students who need to understand how best to achieve collaborative practices, this has illuminated the problems of differences in meaning, and thus the implementation of policy across organisations (it is acknowledged that differences in meaning have implications for professionals within one organisation, and this issue will be dealt with in a later chapter).

> Students should be made aware of the specific barriers to collaboration that are involved in cross-organisational working.

DIVERSITY OF PATIENT POPULATIONS

A second major influence on teamwork is the degree of similarity of the patient/client population *within* teams, and the degree of competition for people's time *outside* the team. We would argue that only where professionals are required to focus on one group of patients does the *need* to develop the means of caring for those patients as a team become vital.

Having a single patient group on which the whole team could focus all of its time was the good fortune of the 'integrated team.' All of the staff (except junior PTs who were on 6-monthly rotations) were permanently and solely assigned to the rehabilitation unit. This meant that none of the team members had to deal with the problems of competing prioritisation of other patients outside the team. As a result, not only did the team have one focus for their work, but they were able to offer 100% of their working time to these patients. It has been argued that having a single purpose for action – a shared focus for whatever work the team would decide was appropriate – would be fundamental to the success of multiprofessional teamworking (e.g. Schein, 1985; Poulton and West, 1993).

The sharpness of this focus enabled the development of specific ways of addressing patient care and therapy, as all patients were initially dealt with by all professional groups and, to a large extent, during the course of their programmes. Because all of the professionals *needed* to be in involved in detailed communication and to understand what their colleagues were doing, how and why, this helped to provide the impetus for the team to develop a tight system of structures and processes. These were designed to optimise the amount and quality of communication, the degree to which members understood the nature of others' contributions, and the rationale behind that contribution. This also meant that there was no diffusion of their skills and knowledge through the need to perform a wide range of different aspects of their professional role for a diverse patient group. For example, the OTs were able to concentrate on particular aspects of occupational therapy, developing specialised knowledge and skills related to the identification and management of cognitive deficits in their patients.

To a large extent the two *core groups*, in the diabetes team and the child development assessment team, also shared a similar situation. However, whilst none of the core group members in the diabetes team had any other calls on their time, being a member of the core group in the child development assessment represented only part of these professionals' roles. As such, outside competition for their time *could* have been possible. The SLT, HV and consultant all had other roles either in the community or, in the case of the HV, as a liaison service for a child sitting-service within the hospital. However, unlike the peripheral members of the team, most of their external work was sessional, made by appointment and predictable (although sometimes heavy in terms of volume). This meant that they could not be called away during the time when they worked together in the Centre, thus compromising this aspect of their work.

One outcome associated with being assigned to a specific group with a specific focus (e.g. the same population of patients) is a sense of group belonging (Brown, 1988). This feeling of allegiance to a group is partly bound up with members identifying with its particular focus – a sense of all people moving in the same direction with the same purpose. With few exceptions, the 'integrated' team and the core groups all felt that they shared a strong 'team' allegiance. This was demonstrated in many of their behaviours (the way in which this was manifested and the problems associated with the few who did not share this sense of belonging will be discussed in a later chapter).

What of the peripheral members in the 'core and periphery teams', and those operating in 'fragmented' teams? As might be expected, team allegiance was compromised or non-existent. We commented earlier that there were two different problems with regard to the patient population – first, where there were competing patient demands *outside* the team, and secondly, where there was a lack of single patient focus *within* the team. The first problem applied to one core group and the second applied to the other. For some of the 'fragmented' teams there was a combination of these two problems. In all of these cases this was the cause of conflict with regard to team practice and the relationship with other team members.

Competing demands outside the team were a problem for the peripheral members of the diabetes team. Although all professionals *did* have a shared population of patients as the focus for their work, and had been able to develop a shared approach to patient care, their responsibilities outside the team compromised the time that peripheral members were able to give to the team. The diabetes team exemplified the situation where a specialist group was struggling to work in an organisational environment that demanded the attention of some members for wider tasks within the hospital. Like many professionals, although members were assigned to the diabetes team, not all of them were *solely* assigned. For the hospital chiropodists and dietitians, their role in the team was simply one of many in their daily work. As other calls on their time included responsibility for more acute work, their priorities of working were sometimes in conflict with their work in the Diabetes Centre.

This lack of sole assignment of some members of the team created difficulties for the core members, for whom the work of the team was paramount. For example, when assessment sessions were running for new groups of patients, they expected dietitians to stay until the end for a short debriefing. However, the dietitians often withdrew to their office to 'complete their paperwork'. When they were holding monitoring clinics in the out-patient department, the core group expected all patients who were being seen by the dietitians to be diabetic, but in fact the dietitians booked in other patients during the session. If members of the core group wanted a patient to be seen urgently, they expected the dietitians to make space in their day rather than the patient having to wait. Core group members felt that because of the dieticians' reduced attendance, communication was adversely affected in terms of 'missed opportunities'. These related to clinical discussion and informal conversation, and patients having to wait for information as well as treatment.

This lack of consistent attention to the work of the team angered the consultant and the specialist nurse in particular, and their feelings were made known to the dietitians. Both core group professionals had a strong commitment to the concept of a specialist diabetes team, and felt that all of its members should be specifically assigned, and that their prioritisation should be *primarily* to the diabetes team. Only by having such a focus did they feel that team members would provide the consistency and continuity required for their patients. The consultant, in particular, commented that specialism went hand in hand with greater motivation, since presumably the professional who joined such a team would be making a positive career choice.

The situation fuelled a lack of understanding about the dietitians' role among core members. Much of the dietitians' work elsewhere was invisible to them, and they interpreted their lack of response as obstructive rather than inevitable, given the acute nature of the dietitians' other work. For some teams, lack of role understanding may be overwhelmed by the organisational situation, with professionals' desire to know more about the contribution of others able to make little impact. However, in this team, the core group seemed to be *unwilling* to accept the limitations for the dietitians – they did not want to know about the wider role that was causing the problems. Not surprisingly, peripheral team members felt that they were being unjustly treated. Because there had been a reduction in dietetics manpower, the manager of this group believed that there was no room for manoeuvre of the dietitians' position, and was angry about the apparent lack of understanding shown by members of the core team. She and the other dietitians refused to be 'bullied' into meeting criteria set by the diabetes team over and above their own professional criteria. Prior to the study, the dietitians had withdrawn from the team meetings as a form of protest. Instead of allying themselves with the diabetes team, monoprofessional allegiance became more evident.

This aspect of organisational influence on teamworking needs to be understood by students.

> Students need to learn that competing prioritisation of patient care outside the team challenges team allegiance, and can reinforce professional allegiances.

Lack of single patient focus within the team was the problem for the child development assessment team. Many different patient groups were seen by this team, none of which overlapped for the whole team, but some of them overlapped for groups within the team. In this situation, the purpose of collaboration itself becomes redundant to some extent. The pattern of patient groupings was as follows. The SLT in the core group had a focus involving the early-years provision of speech therapy to children with more complex special needs. She did not see children once they had entered educational provision (often at 3 years of age). This heavily overlapped with the focus of the playroom teacher and one of the nursery nurses. However, these professionals also worked with young children with physical and sensory problems such as cerebral palsy and blindness (some of this work overlapped with that of the PTs and OTs). The consultant in the core group had a wider but partially shared focus with the SLT, and a matched focus with the playroom teacher. The HV's work was shaped by those seen in the centre, therefore matching that of all these professionals.

In contrast, the PTs saw all children from the hospital population up to the age of 16 years who required physiotherapy, and children with special needs in schools, as well as younger children who required the service. Similarly, the clinical psychologists were members of the Child and Adolescent Mental Health Service (CAMHS), which was responsible for all children up to the age of 16 referred by the hospital, community and Centre consultants with behavioural problems. This meant that only a small proportion of PT and CAMHS time could be spent dealing with children with special needs who also had behavioural problems. However, the needs of some of these children would have overlapped with the work of the SLT and playroom teacher.

This lack of a single population group, and thus a single focus for work, can restrict the ability of a group of professionals to develop a shared approach to care, and consequently an overall team direction. The need for in-depth discussion and the sharing of specific professional knowledge across the 'whole team' would, arguably, not be required in the same fashion. Furthermore, the development of in-depth role understanding across the 'whole team' would not be as relevant, as ongoing professional interaction would not necessarily occur.

The core group did share a focus for care. Over a period of several years, the emphasis of the *therapeutic* work in the centre had shifted from those children with physical problems such as cerebral palsy and blindness to those with language and social interaction disorders. There may have been demographic reasons for this, but the change may also have been partly related to the strength of the core group and their interests. It was evident that language and social development groups, in addition to individual speech therapy sessions, dominated the Centre programme for the week. In relation to the assessment and language disorder aspects of the work, there was a 'team' that shared a focus, had developed a philosophy of care, and had a sense of direction *for itself*.

The more peripheral members of the team, such as the PTs, were to a large extent isolated by the nature of this dominant therapeutic intervention. Even when they could have attended meetings such as a general case-review session that would have required their input, they seldom made an appearance. However, this legitimate reason for the PTs' dislocation did not apply to professionals such as the clinical psychologists, and the reasons for this will be discussed in the next chapter.

We have described two problems concerning patient population that partly contributed to the development of the 'core and periphery' type of working. Both of these problems afflicted the teams who displayed *fragmented* working, albeit the difficulties caused by lack of a single patient focus were the major source of concern. For example, on the medical ward, because various types of patients were admitted to the ward, they required a variety of professionals to care for them. The number of visits that were made to a ward by a particular PT, OT, house officer or consultant would be determined by the number of patients belonging to a particular category in the ward. Thus it can be seen that the shared patient population of the medical ward team would shift and alter as the patients changed. Because the professionals come from different specialisms, it would not be necessary for them to communicate with or understand the contribution of professionals from other specialisms. The only group with which they would consistently need to communicate would be the nursing group, as *they* would share their focus of care with whichever visiting professional was relevant to the particular group of patients.

Similarly, within the CMHT, the team members' shared administrative base gave them an opportunity to discuss clients during their working day. However, there would be little *reason* for communication, other than social interaction. As suggested earlier in the description of the teams, the focus of the CPNs and social workers was either different or, where there was an overlap, clients tended to be taken on by one or the other. Despite the fact that the CPNs are currently expected to be moving their focus from clients with relatively minor mental illness referred by their GPs, to more severely and long-term mentally ill clients who may well be referred via the consultant, there is ambiguity about the extent to which this was achieved in our study. The adherence to the guideline of a 20%/80% split was contested by other professionals in the team, who felt that the split was more in favour of the less severely mentally ill, which meant that the potential for others to share a focus for teamworking with the CPNs was therefore uncertain. By contrast, the social workers dealt mainly with the severely or chronically mentally ill. Both the consultants and the OT shared the clients of the other professional groups, so their case-loads spanned both. In effect, their communication was usually with either one of the professions, but seldom with both.

In the PHCT, each professional group would be responsible for a percentage of the doctors' patients. The very nature of combined practices means that while some patients will be seen by various GPs in a group, in general terms these doctors work as autonomous practitioners with their own lists of patients, to whom the other professionals offer a variety of services. These will therefore be different populations of patients. In some ways this reflects the situation in the ward setting where the *nurses* were the profession with whom every professional had contact, although they did not necessarily need to be in contact with each other.

How does the situation where different professionals have different patient populations affect these types of team? Using the CMHTs as an example, the most problematic outcome is the lack of identification of exactly where the various professionals share clients, and where they do not. It is possible that patients could be receiving either multiple input where less is necessary, or inadequate input. With some professional groups working 'in the dark', this could give rise to ambiguous messages from the various professions, duplication of effort due to unacknowledged role overlap, and thus reduced time for other client input. It is also possible that professionals may wrongly assume that someone else is seeing a particular client.

As was described in the last chapter, the lack of structures such as systematic case review meant that, even if the two CMHTs had had a tight patient focus for their input, a helpful process for identifying progress (or otherwise) was lacking. In a situation involving different foci for care, this would seem to be a major omission. The outcome for these two teams was an acknowledgement that some people 'slipped through the net'.

The lack of shared focus makes it difficult for all members of fragmented teams to understand and therefore predict the work of other team members. One outcome of only some professionals in a team sharing a patient or client group is that 'teams within teams' may develop. Only these people would need to communicate in-depth and understand what each professional is bringing to the care of *their particular patients/clients*. If the focus of team members varies and changes, and those professionals within the team do not *need* to communicate with each other, then the entity that is known as 'a team' does not actually exist. This was reflected by the nurses in the medical ward who described 'the team' as all those who came into contact with all of their patients – almost the entire hospital staff excluding nurses!

Although the 'fragmented' teams ranged from a small designated group of professionals to a larger semi-permanent group in the PHCT, to an amorphous and shifting number of professionals in the medical ward, in none of these was there a sense of *belonging* to a multiprofessional team. Although other issues impacted on the difficulties of these groups in developing a feeling of being 'in a team', the lack of a shared patient population would seem to be an important missing aspect of the substructure.

Professionals in all of these settings also had to cope with competing priorities for their time in a specific team. As stated earlier, this seems to be highly detrimental to the development of a sense of team allegiance. In the medical ward, for example, those who were left to manage problematic situations (i.e. the nurses) felt that visiting staff did not always give the patients in the ward sufficient priority. Although the nurses may have understood the diverse nature of the doctor's role, accepting it when they needed a doctor's input as a 'team' member was far more difficult, and helped to reinforce monoprofessional allegiance. It was common for nurses to complain that they could never access house officers easily once they had left the ward. Although the doctors had pagers, because of other calls on their time (some of which may have been of a more serious nature than they would deal with on the respiratory ward), nurses might have to wait for some time before the doctors came to see their patients. In situations where the nurses felt they had to 'badger' the doctors, and where those doctors did not attend for several hours, the nurses had developed the system of writing every attempt at communication in the nursing Kardex. This was commented on adversely by the doctors, and one perceived this as defensive behaviour (i.e. in a bid to protect their professional reputations – this had become a stick with which to beat the doctors).

A similar situation can be seen in the CMHTs. Some social workers (approved social workers, AWSs) have extra qualifications that give them powers to 'section' patients with severe mental illness who require in-patient care. This system operates separately from the work of the CMHTs, as part of the Social Services mental health resources. Social workers are regularly 'on call', during which time they are expected to prioritise their ASW work over that of the CMHT. This could mean that they are absent from team meetings or ward rounds. In our study, this situation appeared to be accepted, or at least not commented upon adversely by the CPNs. However, one consultant was extremely frustrated by the way in which this (and other priorities, such as training) took the social workers away from what he perceived to be important times for discussion, such as discharge planning meetings. He felt that their absence severely hampered the ability of others to make comprehensive decisions. Since the client always attended these meetings, this would also enable professionals, such as the social worker, to gauge their condition and to assess whether discharge was appropriate. The fact that these meetings were not consistently attended by social workers compromised their crucial input in determining factors such as the accommodation obtained, follow-up resources available and financial arrangements made.

The following situation illustrates how social work input could have shaped the decision-making process differently. One of the consultants and a social worker had each separately seen the same client who had attempted suicide. The consultant's diagnosis was that the man had a personality disorder, which led him to believe that the suicide bid was attention-seeking rather than a serious attempt to kill himself. At the ward round the consultant wanted to arrange for the patient's discharge, but was unsure how to proceed, as the social worker was unavailable. Without specific information from this professional the consultant could not know that the man had been in alcohol rehabilitation, where he had been extremely depressed and had made previous suicide attempts. Vital information of this nature would have allowed the consultant to make a more accurate assessment of how best to manage this patient.

In fairness, the social workers also found that their ASW work competed inappropriately with their time in the team, as it frequently interfered with appointments with clients. It also meant that information that should have been given at the meetings had to be relayed by written report or telephone, taking yet more time from the already limited amount they had available for the team's work.

How does a team develop a sense of integration if its members either need to focus regularly on events outside the team, or have no one focus within the team? Within the rehabilitation team, prioritisation was not only firmly located within the rehabilitation specialism, but it also related to one specific group of patients within that specialism. This gave the team a sharp focus that helped to foster attention to patient needs as a primary goal for *the team*, rather than as individual professionals.

> It is important that students understand that organisational structures which group professionals together without a single focus for their work, in terms of a patient population, are unlikely to foster collaborative teamwork.

Given that many 'multiprofessional teams' seem to be defined by broad function, rather than specifically by what they do, developing a sense of belonging to a venture known as 'teamwork' under these circumstances may be impossible. Perhaps multiprofessional groups working under such adverse conditions need to identify where natural partnerships occur and then foster better working between the individuals concerned. This should then be acknowledged by the organisation, rather than the prescription of professional groups as teams in what seems to be a rather indiscriminate fashion. The creation of smaller teams of professionals that focus their activities on an appropriate number of patients may not only help to sustain a high level of cohesion among professionals, but also ensure that patients have a sense of *their* nurse, or *their* OT, for example, within the wider framework of *their team*.

THE TEAM ORIENTATION OF ORGANISATIONAL STRUCTURES AND PROCESSES

In this section we shall argue that, if teamworking is an organisational priority, then *the way in which an organisation develops its structures and processes would need to reflect an emphasis on teams, rather than on individual professional groups*. By this we mean that management structures and communication structures need to be developed in a framework which recognises responsibility both to the professional and to the team grouping. To some extent, as was seen in Chapter 1, it is clear that some senior trust management is starting to take this on board. However, among the different types of working that were observed in our study, separation of these structures and processes into professional divisions was more apparent.

The degree of collaboration across management structures has the potential to impact on teams, and in our study this had both a practical and a cultural component. First, it influenced the way in which teams were able to *develop 'team practices'*. Where 'integrated working' was observed, managers were in communication on a consistent basis. This resulted in the development of ideas from 'the coal-face' that could change the way in which professionals worked together. These were then transformed into concrete practice development. Furthermore, enabling team practice development can encourage a *team culture*. Where 'core and periphery' and 'fragmented' working were observed, separate management structures were evident. The development of team working under these circumstances may well only relate to individual professional groups and, through this pattern of support, help to foster professional rather than team allegiance, and reinforce monoprofessional rather than team cultures.

The size and degree of separation from its trust had enabled the 'integrated' rehabilitation team to have middle management representation within the team – a factor which did not apply across all teams' professions in the other forms of working. These managers, in turn, were part of a collaborative management structure that was led by a non-clinical director. In effect there was parity of status at this level, encouraging equality of professional input. Although the director had the final say in decisions, his non-clinical position allowed appropriate weight to be given to other management team members' input. This multiprofessional structure in which each manager also has a clinical aspect to their role makes it possible to promote team members' *primary allegiance to the team*, rather than mainly to their own professional group.

Regular meetings of this managerial layer enabled ideas from the professional groups to be raised and discussed. It was also possible for decisions relating to team practice to be negotiated and fed back to other team members. As the unit was largely autonomous, the director was then able to action any agreements. This pattern of joint discussion and communication with other team members enables a team to develop – in a multiprofessional manner – both clinical and administrative strategies for patient care and team function.

One issue that was discussed in this team was inconsistent communication between some nurses and therapists. This was seen to be a particular problem where some nurses and nursing assistants who potentially did not have the same understanding of rehabilitation processes were required to 'carry over' therapeutic procedures. In several of the weekly managers' meetings, ways of overcoming this problem were explored. One of these had been to introduce, in addition to the daily nurses' handovers, a weekly multiprofessional handover. Since many nurses and nursing assistants attended these meetings, this provided an opportunity for other professionals to explain in detail the procedures relevant to particular patients, and the underlying rationales for the actions to be taken. The ongoing interaction between the managers of the different professional groups therefore provided the opportunity to develop better 'team practice'. It also helped to encourage and reinforce team allegiance that was equal to professional allegiance.

Within the other 'core and periphery' and 'fragmented' teams there was no such unifying structure. Separate line management has the potential to create two problems for collaborative teamworking, namely the *practical problem of inhibiting change*, and *reinforcing monoprofessional rather than team cultures*. In the former case, even if a team sits down and devises an approach which requires changing multiprofessional structure and process, how can that be achieved if management does not communicate to discuss and agree the changes? In the latter case, how can a team culture develop where unilateral decision-making is common? This has the potential to create interprofessional conflict by sustaining the attitude that team allegiance is less important than monoprofessional allegiance. In turn this governs the level of effort and commitment to a particular team (McGrath, 1991; Delaney, 1994; Pritchard and Pritchard, 1994). Although in our study separate management was generally perceived to be divisive in nature, only where there was fragmented working did this extend to conflict within the teams.

It should be emphasised that we do not intend to undermine the support given by managers to individual professional groups. Our study showed that some of the actions that were being taken seemed to be positively promoting the development of particular professions. However, in terms of the development of collaborative teamwork, the lack of discussion of issues relating to team practice, and unilateral managerial decision-making (no matter how positive) seems to be inappropriate. The following examples from both 'fragmented' and 'core and periphery' working illustrate this point.

One of the CMHTs had spent time the previous year developing joint approaches to client care in response to the introduction of the CPA. One of the main proposals which resulted from the discussions was the need to put a 'team co-ordinator' into post, and the subsequent development of multiprofessional structures such as joint referral and allocation of clients. The resulting document was given to the CPN, OT and social work management, but as far as the team was concerned this was not discussed as a joint managerial venture, little information was fed back to the team, and the ideas were not implemented. This had a demoralising effect on the team, several members of which had left before our study took place.

In the diabetes team, the lack of specific and sole allocation of dietitians had long been a source of irritation to the consultant and the diabetes specialist nurse. Despite the case being made by both of these individuals to their own senior trust management, it was not possible to alter the way in which the dietitians organised their work, nor to obtain the resources for an additional dietitian. While this was understandable given the shortage of resources in the trust, it was perceived that the lack of negotiation across professional management did little to help to find alternative solutions to the problem.

Finally, in the child development assessment team, several professionals wanted change in order to facilitate better management of such a disparate group of individuals. It had occurred to the SLT, playroom teacher and HV that creating smaller teams structured around the different foci would recognise the different working emphases, and enable professionals to collaborate when this was relevant. These ideas were discussed at the team's 'away-days'. However, this system seemed to frustrate team members more than it helped them, since nothing meaningful was seen to develop from the discussions. Core group members recognised that the 'away-days' were in fact 'toothless' because of the subsequent lack of communication between management personnel. The lack of a cross-professional management structure meant that there was no route by which the regular promotion, discussion and development of ideas could occur. This was also recognised as helping to perpetuate the peripheral position of individuals such as the clinical psychologists and PTs.

Over time, the lack of team progress demotivated several professionals. Given that many members were aware of the need for time together to discuss practice, it was disappointing that these discussions were largely fruitless. If multiprofessional teamworking is to be a fundamental fact of organisational life, it would seem that further thought should be given to developing ways in which management structures could include cross-professional discussion to help to facilitate team practice. As was suggested in Chapter 1, the concept of multiprofessional structures such as executive boards at senior trust level has been made concrete, but it still leaves a large gap between the top echelons of the organisations and those working in clinical settings. In order to develop and maintain team practices rather than merely professional practices, it would appear to be necessary to consider how this could be achieved for middle management.

A second outcome of separate management is the likelihood of unilateral and divisive decisions being made on behalf of individual professional groups within teams. This creates unpredictable situations in which professionals can be taken unawares and are subsequently ill-prepared to handle a new context. Evidence of this was seen mainly in the 'fragmented' teams. For example, changes in patterns of attachment to the PHCT and the shifting nature of the professional input to the 'team' had been difficult for all team members. The doctors in particular had become concerned about these changes, to which they had made no contribution in terms of the decisions that were made. They remembered a time when they had seen one or two designated midwives in the practice with whom they felt that they had developed an effective collaboration. Now they felt 'left in the dark' about what these changes meant for their practice, but above all they were aggrieved at the lack of information from midwifery management. This was demonstrated by the following incident.

One midwife attending the practice at the beginning of the study was requested to withdraw her services in order to rationalise the delivery of care in the area. She left without saying good-bye to anyone, and no one seemed to know who was coming in to replace her, nor when they would be arriving. Only the HV had been informed of the situation, and this reflected her rather closer relationship with the midwife. When the new midwife arrived she presented the GPs with a new protocol for shared care, developed by the local trust, and requested that they all meet with her to discuss it further. This protocol was developed without input from the GPs, despite being called 'shared care'. One GP was particularly angry since on first reading it appeared that the changes would restrict medical input until late in pregnancy. For this GP, who had a strong interest in antenatal care, this was unacceptable. Fortunately, the midwife had anticipated the GP's reaction, and in fact felt similarly aggrieved that this had not been a joint venture. An agreement was reached between the GPs and the midwife, but in the interest of teamwork it did not seem appropriate that the situation had developed in the first place.

In the CMHT, too, the separate processes of decision-making at management level also seemed to be more intent on strengthening the divisions between professionals than on supporting joint working. There was no discernible feedback of information between health and social services' upper-middle management during the study. This cross-organisational problem was further exacerbated by the managers having to abide by different organisational policies. Where teams consist of members from other trusts and/or agencies, the opportunities for areas of conflict to arise are often multiplied, and the working of the CMHT was no exception to this. As a result of this lack of communication, and the differences in agendas, what should have been a series of team discussions at which representative managers were present to field questions in fact became a source of acute distress for many team members.

Within the CMHT the trust had opted to redraw the consultants' geographical boundaries of care, which then differed from the Social Services boundaries. This meant not only that the CPNs within the two teams had to change around, but also Social Services then required the removal of several social workers. The subsequent strain which this might put on the team resources was not discussed with the teams. In fact, it was not even discussed as a social work concern. This apparently arbitrary approach to decision-making, and the abrupt withdrawal of social work support, affected all members of the CMHTs. All of the professionals felt extremely frustrated, and this fed into a situation which was already contentious with regard to team roles (as was discussed earlier). Although it was understood that the social workers were affected by the reduction in *their* manpower, and were finding it difficult to meet the demands of their new workloads, this still generated anger among other team members about perceived support. For example, the CPNs felt that they were being asked to tackle issues such as housing and finance for which they were ill-prepared. However, as 'grass-roots' workers, they felt largely powerless to make fundamental changes to team practice which could help to overcome the problems.

The extent of professional separation was also reinforced at lower-middle management level, and this was highlighted by a further incident. The teams were relocating to a base in a new mental health complex, and had been invited to look at their new offices. This was promoted as a 'whole team' day out (i.e. the combined staff of the two mini-CMHTs), yet when team members arrived at the hospital, the social work manager and the CPN manager each took their professional group aside to discuss practical issues relating to 'teamworking'. When they were asked why this had happened, the CPN manager said he felt it was 'not my place' to ask the social workers to join the CPN group, and the social work manager concurred with this view. Such actions do little to foster a sense of belonging to a unified multiprofessional group.

Since many teams, particularly those which operate in the community, are required to pursue team actions with professionals from different organisations, this raises important issues for communication and the development of team practices. It demands that organisations should pay greater attention to developing joint management structures, in order to help to bridge the divide in cross-organisational working. This needs to be done in order to encompass differing agendas and policies and the way in which they impact on multiprofessional teams. Unless closer working relationships evolve, and unless those individuals who are most intimately involved with the outcomes of those policies are included in the discussion process, mismatched policies will continue to develop (Øvretveit, 1990). These issues also need to be brought to the attention of students who are entering the working environment.

> Students should understand the impact of separate management structures, and how they can not only hamper aspects of team practice change, but also reinforce monoprofessional cultures.

Since it is likely that separate management structures may reflect the general structural nature of the organisation, and thus the processes which derive from these, it is important to understand how they also affect teamworking. One problematic area for many teams in our study was *the use of separate communication systems by the different professions within the teams*.

Within our study, the evolution of joint communication systems was generally regarded as a fundamental aspect of the 'integrated' team's good practice. It is important to remember that this team was able to pursue the development of its own structures and processes partly because of its separation from the main trust. This option may not be open to many teams, especially those operating within the acute sector where they would need to conform to a large extent to the general structure within their own trust.

As part of a joint communication system, the 'integrated' team had developed collaborative note-keeping. This consisted of all assessments, notes identifying patient problems, monitoring of goal achievement, and case-conference reports relevant to each patient. A separate section in the notes was allocated for each problem identified. The problem was stated, its actual or possible antecedents were noted, long-term goals were defined, and short-terms goals which would provide measurable steps towards those long-term goals were identified. Each professional's entries in the notes were made under the appropriate problem section and followed a prescribed formula known as SOAP (acronym for the patient's **S**ubjective responses, the professional's **O**bjective observations, the professional's **A**nalysis of the situation, and the **P**lan for future action). Where two professionals had worked together on a joint session, this was recorded as such. All professionals were expected to contribute to the notes on at least a weekly basis.

At the beginning of the notes, a list of specialist words and abbreviations had been compiled together with appropriate definitions. This not only helped professionals to learn each other's professional language, but it also ensured that all professionals understood each term to mean the same thing. Six-monthly sessions were held for all professionals within the unit in order to initiate new members into the process, and to enable staff to express their views on the note-keeping operation. Thus the system was still evolving, and because this was a joint process, most team members felt as if they 'owned' the product – a situation which helped to promote the unity of the team.

Collaborative note-keeping was deemed to have several positive outcomes. First, it was felt to be extremely useful in terms of monitoring patient care. For example, the therapists and some of the nurses felt that it had shaped their thinking about the pathway of patient care and how it encouraged better problem-solving: 'it keeps you on the ball, and it keeps you thinking "what's my next goal, is it patient centred, is it functional?"'(SLT).

It was also seen to develop professional trust, knowledge and team cohesiveness because of the 'openness' of the notes. In addition, these notes were readily accessible and contained most of the information relating to patient progress, so there were fewer opportunities for inaccurate or missed communication (although the level of nursing input could be inconsistent, a subject that will be discussed further in Chapters 4 and 5). The pattern of a patient's progress in relation to all professional input also enabled the team to develop a more comprehensive picture of that progress.

To a small extent, collaborative note-keeping had also developed in the core group of the child development assessment team. This was a less formal system in which each professional's ongoing assessments were brought together in regular discussion sessions, from which the findings were written up as a joint statement, and plans for future care were decided.

The use of multiple communication systems was considered to be a major source of problems in 'fragmented' working. For example, not only did each professional group in the medical ward team keep its own set of patient case-notes, but also some of these were unavailable to other members of the team. Only the medical and nursing notes were kept on the ward, while other professionals such as PTs and OTs kept their notes with them. Furthermore, because of the nature of rapid and frequent visits to the ward by different professionals, the notation in these different sets of notes varied across the professional groups (i.e. they did not have time to write notes other than their own). Typically, the medical staff and the specialist nurses *always* wrote in the medical notes (the latter professionals would also write in the nursing documentation if they felt that this was appropriate). The nurses *always* wrote in the nursing documentation but nowhere else. Apart from their own notes, the PTs, OTs and medical social workers would sometimes write in the medical or nursing notes if there was something they considered to be particularly relevant to include. However, none of these professionals *always* wrote in either or both sets of notes.

In addition, in general terms it was observed that the medical staff did not read the nursing documentation or look at the patient care plans, whereas the nursing staff realised that they would need to be fully aware of the information written in the medical notes, particularly on their own patients. In this type of situation, unless professionals consistently alert other professionals in the ward to the decisions and actions they have taken, there is enormous potential for lack of communication or even miscommunication to occur – both were observed during the time of the study.

For example, one nurse identified that it was not always part of their routine to document what they had been told, or to read the medical notes and then document them in the Kardex on a regular basis. This situation was felt to be responsible for a great deal of both monoprofessional and multiprofessional communication problems. The nurse cited an incident which had happened earlier in the day:

> There was a patient who had been waiting to see the consultant, and a nurse in the other team said to me 'what's happening with this patient?'. Now I knew four days ago that the patient was waiting to see the consultant. He's actually seen the patient and referred him to St Thomas's, but we only found that out through reading the (medical) notes. Although I knew that he was going to see the patient, no one had reported that in the handover.
>
> (Nurse)

Some teams, such as the CMHTs, *could* have developed joint communication systems. Professionals joining these teams from other nearby locations spoke of CMHTs which had developed joint referral, allocation and systematic review systems, and as described by Onyett *et al.* (1996), this is now common practice in the majority of CMHTs. One of the reasons for the continuation of monoprofessional communication structures (i.e. the separate patient groups which the professional served) has already been discussed in an earlier section. For the OT who took cases from most members of the team, the lack of joint communication structures was particularly problematic. This state of affairs meant that, *de facto*, the OT was a secondary referral service. Because she had to wait until each professional had made a decision about whether to refer to her, she felt that this limited her opportunities to contribute to the whole process of patient care. Furthermore, because of the separate referral, allocation and assessment processes, she lacked information about how the team worked. As a result she found it very difficult to prioritise her work, which she felt compromised OT input to patient care. Since she had previously belonged to a team in which all communication structures and processes were team based, this reinforced her feelings of alienation from these CMHTs.

The use of joint communication structures, such as more collaborative note-keeping, assessment and monitoring processes, and the allocation of professional input, are all vital for preventing problematic communication. The resultant effect for patient care was clearly demonstrated in the CMHTs, where it undermined continuity and consistency of care. Furthermore, the use of such structures is fundamental to providing opportunities for the development of team cohesion, and thus motivation with regard to the processes which the team undertakes.

> Students entering teams that have very diverse methods of managing their communication should reflect on the nature of the structures and processes with which they have to work. They need to understand the problems associated with separate systems of communication, and to identify strategies for overcoming the resulting inconsistencies.

OPPORTUNITIES FOR WORKING CLOSELY

The final section in this chapter will examine some very basic aspects of organisation which can provide the *opportunity* for team members to work collaboratively. These relate to the *centrality of location in which the team operates*, and the *purpose of being in that location*. By this we mean whether team members share a workplace and, if they do, whether this relates to the clinical or administrative aspect (or both) of their practice.

The centrality of location of team members was considered to be an important issue by many individuals in our study. Of course, being together on one site should intuitively make collaboration easier to achieve, primarily because it enables individuals to take up opportunities to engage in ongoing, *ad hoc* in-depth communication about specific issues, and to form social and thus team bonds. This is reinforced by the findings of earlier research (Abramson, 1990; Furnell *et al.*, 1997). Secondly, depending on the purpose of the professionals being together in one place (i.e. whether it is clinically or administratively related), centrality of location provides opportunities to develop in-depth role understanding. Together, these two factors can enable patient care to become more streamlined, as relevant professionals are available in one place to provide their services, rather than dispersing them across hospital or community practice settings. (Obviously it is appreciated that domiciliary services cannot be subsumed within this type of structure.) The development of specialist areas in hospitals, such as the medical ward being part of a 'respiratory village', and the Diabetes Centre, attest to the fact that this notion has been taken on board by trusts (although, as we have already mentioned, policies and thus structural and process change can undermine these developments).

We examined a number of teams in which ostensibly the majority of team members were able to work together in one place – for example, the rehabilitation unit, the Diabetes Centre, the Child Development Assessment Centre and the CMHT (in the general practice setting and the medical ward – both 'fragmented' teams – a high proportion of team members visited the location rather than being based in it). The fact that the teams exhibited the entire range of different types of teamwork described in the previous chapter illustrates that simply bringing people together to work in one place is not the answer to creating effective teamwork. Some of the reasons why this does not work have already been identified in this chapter; others will be dealt with in Chapters 4 and 5. However, the point to emphasise here is that centrality of location simply provides a basic ingredient for collaboration, namely *opportunity*.

In the case of the team that was working in the rehabilitation unit, this opportunity was grasped. We have shown how the work of this unit was underpinned by a lack of conflicting and competing factors external to the team, and we have described how the joint management supported teamwork. The fact that the team worked at a location which provided central, open spaces for working and communal rooms for team members to use for eating and discussions helped to reinforce those factors.

For example, team members would frequently congregate in the nurses' station or the large therapy area to discuss a particular issue. Working close to each other enabled professionals to allocate time for structured meetings without the need to travel, thus making maximum use of their available time. In addition, they used every opportunity to communicate as they came into contact. Although each profession had an office in which they held their own meetings, in general there was open access to all rooms. This encouraged individuals to stop and talk when they were passing other's offices.

A major advantage that working in the same place gave to this team was the opportunity to observe each other's practice, since much of the work with patients was conducted within a common area. Initially this was a double-edged sword for new professionals, as they were 'on display', which could have been interpreted as a negative aspect of the environment. However, as members became used to working in front of other professionals, this became the source of practice development, both individually and as a team.

Finally, because the unit had a communal space in which all professionals could take breaks, they could develop social relationships with each other. This communal area also gave individuals an opportunity to discuss aspects of interactions between themselves and patients, between team members, or between the team and the rest of the trust which might have been considered to be 'politically incorrect'. In short, they could 'let off steam', and this opportunity was regarding as helping to cement working relationships.

The geographical proximity of individuals in this unit did not guarantee development of a joint communication system, understanding of each other's roles, and close personal and professional relationships. It simply provided opportunities which team members could take advantage of or not, as they wished. The example of one new member who did not take those opportunities clearly demonstrated that being able to work together only represented part of the picture (see later chapters).

The opportunity to develop understanding of professional contributions to a team effort may be reduced if individuals do not actually practise in a central location, but simply use the base for their paperwork and for any team meetings. This situation was seen in one of the 'fragmented' teams, namely the CMHT. There had been a deliberate decision by the trust to bring professionals together under one roof in the hope of achieving greater co-ordination of service delivery. However, in this team clients were seen either at home or in an out-patient facility. Occasionally they were seen in rooms off the office area, but this was solely a one-to-one exercise between the professional and their client.

This type of practice would require that, at some point in their day or week, professionals would find time to discuss what they have individually been achieving with their clients. The central location of their administrative resources (i.e. their desk-space, case-note storage facilities and computers) could have given the CPNs, social workers and OT many opportunities for communication, and the opportunity to learn what other team members were doing, in what way, and why they were taking the decisions and actions that they deemed to be necessary. Because the teams were not in general offering an emergency service, it would have been possible to set aside regular time for a daily 'debriefing'. However, team members did not identify a time other than the weekly 'case-review' meeting as useful for discussion, and communication in the latter setting was varied. Although, as has been discussed, there were limited occasions on which a *team* discussion of a particular patient was relevant, this meeting could have identified exactly where patient care could be a team venture, and thus have promoted closer collaboration. Professionals could have become aware of where their contribution fitted in the pattern of care and where patients' needs were not being met. Since this meeting was described by several members as being fraught with problems (why this was so will be discussed in the following chapters), the few opportunities which did occur for discussion and debate about the management of particular patients were rarely used effectively.

Whilst discussing this topic, it is important to mention the alternative case in which professionals are situated away from a central location yet are still deemed to be fundamental members of a team. Here collaborative teamwork may not relate to geography, but to history. Where team members have been able at some point to *develop* effective collaboration, with its outcomes for both patients and team members, then it may be possible for changes to the patterns of team interaction to have little effect. For example, in the diabetes team, one of the core members – the podiatrist – visited only periodically (about once a month) for a special clinic session, and was present for a weekly clinic in the out-patient department. His involvement with the team in terms of face-to-face contact was small, yet his credibility as a core group member, and his allegiance to the diabetes team and its work were not questioned. The reasons for his position, despite his infrequent visits to the Centre, will be discussed in Chapter 5, but it is clear that an ongoing presence need not necessarily be a criterion for effective collaboration.

By the same token, ongoing presence in both a clinical and an administrative sense may still preclude collaboration. For example, the clinical psychologists in the child development and assessment team had an office in the Centre which they used daily, and held regular clinics in the Centre, yet were universally regarded as the most distant members of the team. Others in the team found communication with these professionals difficult to achieve, and understanding of the clinical psychology role was limited. This distancing was largely seen to be the choice of these professionals, and their lack of interaction with the team was identified as compromising patient care on a number of occasions.

What conclusions can we draw about the role of central location and the purpose of being in the same site? The study would seem to suggest that geographical proximity, as a basic requirement for collaboration, may be important in helping to foster initial team cohesiveness through the facilitation of social communication. However, it may not be necessary in order to maintain that relationship. It also suggests that being able to talk freely with others during the period of the working day may encourage the development of effective communication. Finally, it suggests that where people practise together, opportunities arise for developing an in-depth understanding of how individuals contribute to the work of the team. However, it *can* be used as as easy excuse for poor teamworking where other more fundamental problems should be addressed.

This chapter has sought to explore the way in which some organisational issues impact on the ability of teams to work collaboratively. We have examined those structures and processes which help to promote in-depth multiprofessional communication, role understanding, the development of a shared vision of teamworking, and a sense of belonging to the team. However, the presence of a consistent, supportive system of structures and processes to support teamwork was only observed in one situation. More commonly seen were systems that only partly supported – or indeed even seemed antithetical to – collaborative working.

The changes to structure and process that have been incurred by the introduction of recent policies cannot be ignored, as they have created chaotic, unpredictable working conditions and instigated new and contentious roles for unprepared professionals. Extant structures and processes have been seen to compromise patient care and the development of team allegiances. This has occurred as a result of requiring that professionals make difficult choices in having to attend to priorities outside the team. In addition, the lack of attention that has been paid to how teams focus in terms of the patients they serve has resulted in inappropriate 'team' formations. These structures and processes have also, through the persistence of a professional rather than team orientation, inhibited the development of team practice and given rise to professionally defensive behaviours. Finally, although working under one roof would seem to be a useful way to promote teamwork, without the presence of other supportive organisational elements it is unlikely to have the desired effect. Spurgeon (1999) has identified the 'indiscriminate advocacy' of teamwork by NHS trusts, irrespective of the tasks or the settings within which teams find themselves. In our study, the way in which teams were largely unsupported by their trusts in developing collaborative working highlights the gap between the rhetoric related to teamworking and the reality.

If the push towards multiprofessional teamworking is a real phenomenon, that is regarded as essential to enhance patient care, structures and processes are required which support the growth of this type of working. Where this is limited by the need to introduce policies which may conflict with the maintenance of collaborative working, then senior management needs to consider what strategies could be developed and introduced to help to ameliorate their impact.

> Students entering the health professions should be given a clear understanding of the organisation in which 'teams' function, and should be encouraged to learn strategies for managing fluid and unpredictable environments. This may mean being more open to more fluid role boundaries, and understanding the conflicts which may arise as a result of change.

Although the impact of external forces, such as organisational structures and processes, has been demonstrated to affect teamwork, the influence of individual team members will be equally great. The following chapter will examine the way in which each member of the team brings with them their own personal beliefs about working with others. These will be shaped by both personal and professional experience. As will be shown, some team members will have developed a cohesive set of beliefs about working with others, either in terms of collaboration or in terms of professional separation. Other team members will have rather vague notions of what working with others means, their assumptions being based on long-standing constructions of multiprofessional practice within a medical model. Where beliefs about teamworking did not match within the teams that we studied, difficulties and conflict emerged with regard to these different interpretations. Where beliefs were consistent with each other, depending on the nature of those beliefs, individuals either developed collaborative working or maintained the status quo without challenge.

4 The influence of individual beliefs on teamworking

INTRODUCTION

Important as the influences of the organisational context on teamworking are, it is also clear that the individuals within a multiprofessional team can make or break the ability of that team to work together effectively. In this chapter we shall explore how individuals may hold different perspectives on teamwork which then affect their approach to collaborative working. By this we mean the development of a set of beliefs which support or inhibit motivation towards teamwork, and that give different values and meanings to various aspects, which then shape the way in which individuals are prepared to operate in a team context.

Examining these different beliefs about and values related to teamwork is fundamental to understanding how education can contribute to the development of more effective collaboration between professionals. As will be seen in this chapter, the ways in which beliefs about teamwork shape understanding about what to do and how to do it as a team member seem to stem largely from those beliefs that are developed during the socialisation process of becoming a member of a particular profession. However, there are exceptions to the view that professional culture alone is responsible. Whilst not discounting the contribution of other aspects (e.g. personality) to the way that people feel about working collaboratively, in these cases previous experience of working in 'effective teams' seems to have influenced the way in which some individuals understand what is meant by teamwork. This then provides us with ideas about how education can be employed to help to overcome the difficulties which can be created by differences in beliefs.

Recalling the three types of working that were encountered in our study, it is evident that the same understanding may not be held by all members of a multiprofessional 'team', particularly where more 'fragmented' working is seen. Where professionals are encouraged by organisational structures and processes to remain within their own professional alliances then, as we suggest above, understandings of teamwork may be bound to a large extent by *professional cultures*. These cultures, and the power and status accorded to the professional groups, then impinge on the way in which individuals operate as a multiprofessional team. However, where beliefs about teamwork become incorporated as the *team culture*, then we would expect to find greater congruence between individual beliefs. This was only observed in one team. The implications for patient or client *team* care of whether individuals hold very different or similar views of teamworking were clearly identified in our study. We found that where there were different interpretations, this had the potential to compromise communication and the development of role understanding. As a result, the level of team learning was limited. Differences in views also exacerbated underlying resentments, undermined professional esteem, and created outright conflict. Where the focus of individuals' efforts was moved away from what should be their primary focus (i.e. the patient or client), to dealing continually with inter-professional problems, less effective care resulted.

Through in-depth observation and interviewing we were able to identify three different philosophies of multiprofessional working. By 'philosophies' in this context we mean a clearly articulated and coherent set of beliefs within which value and meaning are ascribed to specific aspects of working with other professionals. We have termed these philosophies *directive, integrative* and *elective,* and they will be described in the first part of this chapter. They represent two variants of understanding about *collaborative* teamwork (directive and integrative), and one which could be described as *anti-teamwork* (elective). There was another approach to working with other professionals that could not be identified as a philosophy. Particularly in the PHCT and the medical ward, individuals were unable to articulate their actions or intentions with others in such a developed way; multiprofessional teamwork was not really part of their agenda. As such they worked in *parallel* in response to a medical diagnosis with little consistent and structured interaction. However, there were identifiable assumptions being made which influenced how and why individuals worked with others.

We do not intend to imply here that there are no other philosophies of teamworking, but simply that this is what we found in the course of our study. Identification of these philosophies did provide us with a handle for explaining discrepancies in perceptions and actions between team members that did not appear to be accounted for by other factors. Moreover, the way in which people think about teamwork, and the power which may reside in those who hold perspectives which may not be as facilitative of effective collaboration as those of others, have important implications for the ease with which alternative thinking may be introduced.

After describing the philosophies we shall examine how they impacted on the three types of teamworking, namely *integrated, core and periphery* and *fragmented* working. Specifically, we shall examine where different philosophies came together within teams and how subsequent *mismatches in awareness of having a team focus, communication, understanding of role contribution and learning from others in the team* influenced patient or client care.

PHILOSOPHIES OF MULTIPROFESSIONAL WORKING

The different philosophies were initially identified by observing patterns of behaviour within the teams with regard to specific aspects, such as communication and awareness of role contribution. For example, with regard to communication, what was being said, how was it said and to whom? With regard to awareness of role contribution, what did team members do in certain situations, what were their expectations of others' roles, and what happened at the boundaries of those roles? These observations then prompted interview questions related to specific incidents. For example, how did team members perceive communication which had occurred, and what were their expectations of such communication within a team context? What did they see as their own and others' contributions at that point, and what was the rationale behind those perceptions? From these initial findings, more general understandings of teamworking were explored, such as interprofessional learning within the team.

It became evident that the understandings which individual professionals had of working with others lent different meanings to these elements. Although, as suggested earlier, there are other factors which impact on teamworking, having different understandings of teamwork was seen to inhibit professionals from working together effectively. Individual philosophies of teamworking appear to shape beliefs about the *need for a shared team focus, what constitutes effective communication and role understanding*, and *how role contribution is valued*. In relation to these, the different philosophies lead to different expectations of *learning from other team members*.

The directive philosophy

We found that the directive philosophy was most frequently held by members of the medical profession, and by some non-specialist nurses. First, it was based on an assumption of hierarchy where one person would take the lead by virtue of status and power, and might therefore be in a position to direct the actions of others. At this point, however, we need to differentiate between this set of beliefs and others where being a 'director' is not a primary objective. There were some professionals who assumed power in teams, but who did not feel the need to direct others' actions – they simply expected others to fall in with their wishes. For the 'director', team awareness was important, and being a team player was an acknowledged attribute. However, this was achieved from the position of 'team leader'. Secondly, this philosophy generated assumptions about what was appropriate in terms of communication, since the 'team leader' would determine *what, when, and how information was communicated, and to whom.* Although other professionals who held these beliefs often did not welcome these constraints, they colluded because they found it difficult to challenge the status quo. Thirdly, the philosophy made assumptions about understanding others' roles in terms of *task*s. Where roles were deemed to be lower in the hierarchy, they were valued for their service to the 'directive' role, rather than for having an intrinsic value in terms of insights into patient care. Finally, this philosophy had the potential to determine *the way in which professionals learned from each other,* since this was apparently defined by status. Those in *directive* positions believed that they could only learn from their peers or superiors, whilst they taught. Those who held this philosophy from a *directed* position did not seem to believe that other professionals could learn from them.

The integrative philosophy

We encountered this philosophy most frequently in the therapy and social work professions, in health visitors and among some nurses. The name is deliberately similar to that of the integrated form of teamworking, as there it was seen almost as an entire team belief system. In the *integrative* philosophy, professionals regarded the following criteria as fundamental to teamworking. First, there was a commitment to two aspects of being a team member, namely the *practice of collaborative care and therapy* and *attention to being a team player.* Secondly, there was an acknowledgement of the *complexity of communication*, which incorporated a belief that in-depth discussion and negotiation were important in order to develop a team understanding of the patient. Thirdly, there was recognition of the need to *understand different aspects of role contribution*, and their importance in the *development of negotiated role boundaries*. In this sense, whilst clarity of role was deemed to be important, this applied to core distinctions, with flexibility at the boundaries of roles being accepted as necessary for continuity of care. Fourthly, it was assumed that there would be *equal value assigned to each professional's contribution* to both the patient's progress and to other professionals' development. Finally, it was assumed that professionals would develop both as a team and individually by *learning skills and knowledge from each other*.

The elective philosophy

This philosophy essentially related to a system of liaison, and we encounted it most often in those working in the mental health services. The professionals who held this philosophy preferred to operate autonomously, and referred to other professionals as and when *they* perceived there was a need. Although autonomy of practice may not be at odds with collaboration, in this sense it was synonymous with *insularity of practice*. As such it would inhibit the development of a shared understanding of patient care. Secondly, there was an *attention to role clarity and distinctness* that precluded the negotiation of role boundaries. Thirdly, there was a belief that *brevity of communication*, in order only to inform others, was more appropriate than discursive interaction. This *may* be related to issues of confidentiality which are particularly relevant for many professionals who hold this philosophy. Finally, as with the directive philosophy there was an ascription to a hierarchical structure of professions in which *learning was only valued from those of equal or higher status*.

Parallel working

As suggested earlier, this was not a philosophy, but rather an approach to working in which professionals accepted that they needed to liaise with others and know what others' roles involved, but only to a limited extent. It was accepted that individuals worked within a hierarchy of professions and a hierarchy within each profession. Thus, responsibility was not primarily to the multiprofessional team, but to individual professional groups. Framed by the medical model, individuals understood that one group – the medical profession – would hold the power in the decision-making process, and other professionals would acquiesce and/or support those decisions by *working to* the medical profession. Although challenge was seen within this context, it was not a consistent part of decision-making in the multiprofessional arena. Each profession would have their own patient care/treatment/therapy plan, predicated on the medical diagnosis but developed on the basis of their own body of knowledge. Unlike the insular one-to-one practice of those who held an elective philosophy, care was a team process – but it involved a monoprofessional team.

Basically this was a 'do what I say' or *directive* approach to multiprofessional working, but *without* the concept of medical leadership. This is not to say that all other professionals would necessarily be satisfied with this state of affairs, but they would accept that the status quo would be difficult to change.

As with the elective philosophy, communication between professional groups was relatively brief. As might be expected, this largely involved information sharing rather than the sharing of professional perspectives. Similarly, understanding of others' roles was limited to knowing the tasks that would be done, and not the underlying rationales for why a particular action might or might not be taken. Sharing of knowledge and skills remained chiefly within professional boundaries, and although medical skills were taught to professions such as nursing, this was not generally a reciprocal venture. On the wards, nurses working with junior doctors showed them 'the way things were done' within the parameters of ward process and routine medical tasks, but not with regard to the nursing contribution to care.

THE MEANING OF TEAMWORK

The above descriptions now provide us with a framework in which to explore further some of the ways in which holding specific philosophies can shape the meanings that are ascribed to various aspects of teamwork, and how they affect behaviour where meanings either conflict or are consistent. Specifically, we shall examine *awareness of having a team focus, communication, understanding of role contribution* and *learning within the team*. Bearing student education in mind, this is particularly relevant when considering professionals' willingness or otherwise, to engage in interprofessional learning.

The examples that are cited in this section of the chapter are representative of the particular type of interaction being discussed. Many similar incidents and comments were identified during the course of our study with regard to the meeting points between individual philosophies.

Having a team focus

In terms of having a team focus, all of the professionals in our study would maintain that they had a goal towards which they were working – that is, providing the most comprehensive care possible for the patient, with accurate diagnosis, referral and continuity. However, only those who held *directive* or *integrative* philosophies would necessarily relate this to 'teamwork' (i.e. that people have shared goals, achieved by working alongside or with others). Those who held an *elective* philosophy tended to view teamwork as a threatening concept, with professionals unsure about or even hostile to the idea of working in a more collaborative fashion. For them, the *one-to-one relationship with the patient* seemed to be more important in their practice. This may sound rather presumptious on our part – that we might be critical of someone who prefers a one-to-one relationship with their patient or client. However, this relates more to emphasis. For professionals who held *directive* or *integrative* philosophies there was an attention to their relationship with other professionals in the pursuit of patient care that went hand in hand with the relationship they had with their patient or client. As suggested earlier, the emphasis in *parallel working* differed from the three philosophies in that responsibility for patients lay with the professional group rather than with individuals, thus encouraging a situation in which any 'teamwork' referred to was a monoprofessional venture. So how were the various beliefs about teamworking manifested in the teams?

In these first examples we shall examine *the difference between integrative and elective beliefs*. In the 'integrated' team, the majority of individuals believed that they should operate *together* to make decisions and define actions to be taken with a particular patient or client. They understood that unless decisions were made as a team, with the development of structures, processes and strategies that supported decision-making, patient care and therapy could suffer as a result. The development of and subsequent participation in joint working practices further reinforced and perpetuated these beliefs. This ensured that team newcomers would be in no doubt about how strongly this way of doing things was adhered to. The level of motivation to support an integrative approach to multiprofessional working was based on the fact that the team had identified the benefits that accrued to patients as a result. As stated in Chapter 2, where beliefs about teamworking were shared, and where these had been harnessed to provide a systematic approach to patient care, it was possible to see that patients benefited in the following ways. There was *continuity and consistency of care*, a *reduction in the number of ambiguous messages given to patients by different members of the team, appropriate and timely referrals*, and a *holistic perspective combined with a problem-solving approach, which ensured the most effective team decisions and actions*.

In addition to having a high level of motivation regarding the concept of collaborative working, many members recognised that attention should be given to individual and team concerns as well as to those directly related to patient care. This dual approach to the team's primary tasks *and* its internal needs has been identified as fundamental to the evolution of effective teamwork (e.g. Schein, 1985; Øvretveit 1995). Both aspects of teamwork demand an ongoing effort from individuals, and it is therefore essential that members believe that this is the best way to provide effective care.

Most of the members who were new to this team had no difficulties in adhering to a team-focused way of working. Indeed, individuals were deliberately recruited for their 'team' beliefs. However, the arrival of a new professional who held very different views created 'a tidal wave' in the team because of the almost diametrically opposed views to which he subscribed. Essentially, the new member felt that he should be able to choose how he operated with other professionals, rather than following a pattern of working in which there would be expectations of him as a fellow collaborator. He maintained an *elective* philosophy of working. He did not believe that collaborative teamwork was an important aspect of his day-to-day practice, but perceived it as a threat. Others noted his unwillingness and were concerned about his isolation from the rest of the team:

> It's kind of like you are pulling a dog that doesn't want to come. You are pulling at its lead and it's like it's digging its paws in and saying "I'm not coming". I get the feeling with him that he's stuck in the position he's in. You could try and try and try but I'm not sure the will would be there.
>
> (OT)

As far as this newcomer was concerned, collaboration at this level was not necessary. Because teamwork was not important him, he opted to devise his own rules with regard to how he operated. He avoided systems such as joint note-keeping and joint working, he did not negotiate patient appointments with others, and he eschewed attendance at team meetings. This behaviour made it difficult for others to predict when, how and why the new professional would be undertaking patient interventions. In effect, his different belief system culminated in methods of operating which were almost completely at odds with those of the other members of the team, and left them feeling angry and confused. More importantly, it left them unsure about the way in which he practised. The outcomes they *did* see in terms of his work with patients were unsettling (as will be described later).

The meeting of an *integrative* philosophy and an *elective* one, in terms of being aware of the need for a team focus, was echoed in other teams. There were many professionals who felt as strongly that collaboration was the most beneficial way of working, both for patient care and for the team itself. Members of the core groups in both 'core and periphery' teams shared a similar awareness of and motivation towards teamworking. For these groups, the development of systematic ways of communicating with and learning from each other elicited similar benefits for their patients. Other peripheral members, particularly in the child development assessment team, remained aloof from collaborating in such a close fashion.

We identified earlier that those who held *integrative* philosophies *generally* included members of the therapy professions and some nurses. It was not common to find members of the medical profession who shared these beliefs. However, both of the core groups did include consultants. Although the diabetes consultant had a reputation outside the core group which belied these beliefs (see Chapter 3), within the core group he undoubtedly saw the benefits of working in an 'integrated' fashion. The other consultant also actively promoted this type of working. Both of these individuals had previously worked in teams that they considered had been very effective in terms of both team function and patient care. Both of them had experienced working collaboratively with specialist nurses, HVs and therapists, and currently spoke about how much they valued the professional skills and knowledge of these other professionals: 'We all work together as equals here, I don't like this idea of the traditional doctor and nurse divide, or any of the other professionals as well' (Consultant).

Because they had seen the outcomes of such working, they were both motivated to encourage the same approach to teamworking in their new environment. Unlike some other members of the medical profession in our study, they seemed to be able to step outside their professional culture and the long-standing hierarchical approach to multiprofessional working. One can only speculate as to what enabled them to do this, but on the basis of their current experience they were both working with professionals who, through organisational opportunities and professional attributes, had been able to demonstrate the importance of their own contribution to the work of the team. Time, ongoing exposure and challenge had reinforced the consultants' beliefs within these groups, and may also have been the factors that enabled them to take these beliefs on board in the previous settings.

However, outside the core groups individuals' beliefs varied. In the child development assessment team, the core group found it difficult to engage with some peripheral members, particularly the clinical psychologists. This group operated in what was termed a 'secretive' fashion, so that few people understood the exact nature of their role and what should or could be communicated between themselves and others in the team. As a group they were almost 'demonised' by others. Conversations between professionals often included adverse comments about the unwillingness of members of this team to interact with others. In addition, there was a strong feeling that these professionals acted as if they could assume rights over others by making demands for space and resources to which others were expected to agree. None of the members of this group joined the joint assessment, monitoring or evaluating processes that other members of the peripheral group attended on occasion. When asked for their ideas about teamworking, it was clear that what this group valued most was their professional autonomy. This was compounded by the nature of their work, in which confidentiality and the one-to-one relationship they had built up with their patients were paramount. Their unwillingness to develop a shared approach to working frustrated the members of the core group, but more importantly it compromised care for patients with whom they and other professionals were working (see in section below on communication).

Some individuals in the 'fragmented' teams also shared an awareness of the importance of developing a shared team approach, as is evident in this quote from a social worker in the CMHT:

> You need to know that as a team you can break their [the patients'] fall so that they don't smash themselves to bits when they fall off the tightrope of their precarious life. That's what you can do as a team, and you can't do that on your own. I don't think one person is big enough to have that many hands at the ready.
>
> (SW)

The OT in the CMHT also shared these views. She had come from what she perceived to be an integrated team, in which it was clear to her how the patients were benefiting from such a collaborative approach. However, together with the social workers and one of the psychiatrists, she found the practice in this new setting difficult to understand because it contrasted so negatively with her previous experience. Partly due to factors that have been described in Chapter 3, they were *unable* to develop the means for providing a systematic team approach. However, the members of this 'team-minded' group were all prepared to set aside time to discuss clinical issues, including those not directly related to their own practice. The psychiatrist held a 'directive' approach to teamworking and, as will be seen later, although this had ramifications for other aspects of teamworking, he did understand what collaborative working could achieve.

Like the clinical psychologists in the core and periphery team described above, other professionals in this team, including several of the CPNs and one other psychiatrist, maintained an 'elective' philosophy. Their lack of understanding of the need to operate closely with others was frustrating for the team-minded group. For example, the OT was disappointed that others were not coming to her with their opinions about clients and asking how, as a team, these people could be helped. She found that nothing was 'open and agreed and discussed'. When referring to her understanding of others' roles in the team, she felt 'in the dark', saying:

> In terms of what they actually do with people, I have my thoughts on it, but because we don't actually talk about it, it is very hard to know if that is true or not. I don't know what they do; do they go and see people, do they support them, do they talk to carers? I'm not sure.
>
> (OT)

Without this basic knowledge of how the team worked she found it very difficult to prioritise her work, yet she felt that her input could be provided much earlier on in the process of patient care. Because of the mismatch between her point of view and that of many others in the team, she felt alienated both from other members and from the decision-making processes that were occurring.

As suggested earlier many of the CPNs displayed less willingness to develop 'teamness', and some CPNs and one of the consultants showed *no* motivation to become part of the wider multiprofessional team – they did not seem to be prepared to make the effort to develop closer working practices. Like the clinical psychologists, one of the reasons for this was that they set great store by their professional autonomy. They spoke about their *own* interventions with patients as being of greater importance than team interventions.

The following comment made by a staff nurse (SN) from a local in-patient facility demonstrates how several 'outsiders' saw the team:

> this team is not patient-led . . . it is not a needs-led team at all; it is a professional-led team. It's about 'this is my work, and this is your work'; it is not about how we can help this patient.
>
> (SN)

The belief in self-governing, rather than being steered by team influence, supported their lack of willingness to be multiprofessional team members, and, as will be shown later, affected the way in which they communicated and protected their role in the team.

In the next example we shall look at the *differences between integrative beliefs and assumptions about parallel working*. For 'team-minded' members of the PHCT, such as the HV, the midwife and one of the GPs, their interviews and general conversations were rich in 'team' allusions. These included sharing knowledge, sharing similar approaches to care, and an awareness of the necessity of 'building' a team, rather than assuming it would simply happen. They had all endeavoured to promote the development of regular discussion and debate. Between them (although not all together), meetings were suggested and arranged which had helped to promote closer working relationships. For example, the midwife and the HV had noted the need for better co-ordination to improve antenatal and postnatal services. Previously they had not seen each other regularly, and the HVs had not always received information about aspects of the antenatal process such as the booking-in forms. They established a fortnightly forum at which they could discuss clients and any problems they were having with communication. As a development of these discussions they established new protocols for breastfeeding and for identifying clients at risk, and they improved the notification system. Both of them felt that these meetings had helped them to establish the nature of each other's contribution to the antenatal process, and the hand-over of information. Furthermore, the meetings had generated an alliance between the practice of two trusts, the mismatch of which had been of concern to them both.

Other individuals in the PHCT did not share these professionals' enthusiasm for such collaboration, but subscribed mainly to a *parallel* way of working. This greatly hampered the fostering of their 'team-minded' point of view. Although all of the GPs were perceived to be friendly and approachable, they did not use the same language to describe their interprofessional interaction as was heard from these other professionals, nor was their behaviour as facilitative of what others saw as 'teamwork.' In fact, some of them were perceived to act in ways which precluded an awareness of other professionals' reactions. For example, one GP would cancel his clinics at short notice, leaving reception staff to contact patients, and individuals such as HVs and the practice nurse to attempt to rearrange their own appointments with patients who would have been seen by the doctor. Unlike those in a position of power who hold a 'directive' approach to multiprofessional working, there was no sense in which most of the doctors in this setting wanted to lead the PHCT. Instead, they simply seemed to be making assumptions that they would perform their function, and that others would do what they were expected to do.

From this description of how subscribing to the different philosophies can cue people differently into thinking about the importance of teamworking, it is clearly a vital starting point when considering the way in which students are educated. Knowing that working together in a consistently collaborative fashion has identifiable benefits both for patients and team members is imperative for helping to motivate people towards operating in such a fashion with other professionals.

It is important to raise students' awareness of the importance of collaborative working by ensuring that they reflect on the benefits that accrue from following such a pattern of working.

One might imagine that the views of those who hold an 'integrative' or 'directive' philosophy would consequently enable them to develop collaborative 'ways of being' together. However, in terms of their day-to-day interaction, the meanings that they ascribed to communication and role understanding were in fact very different, and actually worked against achieving their identified goals. Not surprisingly, where the 'integrative' and 'directive' philosophies met the 'elective' philosophy, those aspects of teamwork were also compromised. In this section we shall consider how holding different philosophies can shape people's understanding of the term 'communication'.

Communication

Where professionals held an integrative philosophy, it was viewed as important that time would be given to discussion and debate, both informally and within regular forums. All of the professionals in the team would be expected to contribute, and all domains of patient care would be valued for their provision of a full picture of the patient's progress. In our study, professionals in the 'integrated' team and in the core groups of the 'core and periphery' teams spoke about how beneficial it was to gain these multiple insights, as they had the potential to persuade others to make changes to the path of action they were considering taking. They also understood the different components of communication. These included the need to engage in a rich, detailed forum of communication related to the focus of care (the patient), to discuss the concerns of individuals within the team, to ensure the development of team knowledge and skills, and to give time to the development of team strategies.

For example, in the 'integrated' team there were a number of regular meetings at which patient progress was discussed in depth, based on the use of a joint scoring system. At one meeting, two therapists each gave a different score for a patient's problem-solving abilities. Because of the magnitude of the discrepancy, the head of the unit asked one of the therapists why she thought her score was so low. She described how the patient had not been able to manoeuvre between his wheelchair and a plinth to do a 'low transfer' in a logical manner. She felt that he had a poor ability to think the manoeuvre through. The other therapist was surprised, as the man had performed very well in a formal paper assessment. The first therapist then reflected that it might only be in physical situations that the man experienced difficulty in conceptualising appropriately. As a result of this discussion, the two therapists decided to book a joint session to examine more closely how different settings might affect the man's cognitive skills. The outcome was the identification of problems of generalisability with regard to the man's cognitive skills that encouraged a different therapeutic approach.

Individuals also felt able to discuss their feelings of inadequacy, dislike and despair in the knowledge that their audience would be receptive and supportive. The nature of this communication could be identified as far more risky than that related specifically to patient progress. It would require a high level of personal and professional trust that others in the team would not only listen and provide support, but would also reciprocate. In terms of group process theory (Brown, 1988), it would indicate high levels of cohesiveness, which have in turn been linked to effectiveness.

As part of the need to understand and learn about others' roles, communication was seen to encompass learning from and teaching one another, both in terms of formal teaching, and in *ad hoc* exploration of issues as situations arose. For example, over the years the members of the diabetes core group had developed specialist courses for diabetes management on which all of them taught. This course development work gave the group another arena in which to reinforce their 'teamness' through displaying their own – and an understanding of each others' – knowledge and expertise, and it enhanced the trust which had developed between them. In addition, they attended conferences together, discussed the most recent research evidence together, and critiqued each other's work in terms of research papers, etc. This shared professional development was again perceived as increasing confidence in the expertise of others and reinforcing 'teamness' by taking their professional activities into other arenas.

Finally, as part of the 'integrative' philosophy it was felt to be important to set aside time to discuss strategies for team practice. This should include what the team was doing now, where it wanted to go, and how that should be achieved. This was recognised as being rarely pursued because it was not clinically related and others might regard it as 'wasting precious time'. However, it was felt that without such communication a team could 'drift' with no clear understanding of its purpose and direction. It was also recognised that because 'why?' questions could be asked at this forum, professionals would be able to develop a better understanding of each other's contributions, how the various roles fitted together or overlapped, and whether there were better ways of 'using' various forms of professional input.

In view of what we have said about some of the similarities between them, we shall now examine *how directive and integrative philosophies interpreted communication*. Furthermore, we shall examine the impact of the 'directive' philosophy for individuals who hold 'elective beliefs'. At first glance it would appear that the 'directive' and 'integrative' philosophies might have a shared set of beliefs about communication. However, in the 'directive' approach it was understood that one person directed the decision-making process and had the power to control communication made by others in the group. Furthermore, a challenge to the status quo was not expected. This could be extremely limiting for others who wished to share knowledge and information about a patient that was outside the parameters set by the person directing.

For example, one consultant in the CMHT spoke at great length about the systems that should be in place to ensure effective working. This included regular times for in-depth case discussion, to which all of the relevant professionals should be able to contribute. He was always present at these meetings and had actively striven to promote the importance of others' attendance. However, during meetings it was observed that *he* set the pace of the discussion, despite the fact that there was a 'rotating chair'. He would always start by telling people about clients he had seen, and would then ask for other people's input about those clients. Other individuals would supply any relevant information and then offer opinions about potential ways to manage the client. At this point problems would arise, as the consultant had difficulty in accepting challenges to his opinions and decisions.

This led to different responses from the other team members. Most of the CPNs tended to back down very quickly when the consultant disagreed with their ideas. However, one situation in particular had made two of the CPNs very angry, and although they did finally speak out about it, this was only after much agonising in their office. The consultant was renowned for making decisions on behalf of others without prior discussion with either the professional or their clients. On several occasions he had informed clients that their CPN would no longer be visiting them, without discussing with the CPN either what was being done or why. This obviously created difficult situations when the CPNs arrived to see their clients for prearranged appointments. For the CPNs, who were long used to operating independently as a referral point for the GPs, this was extremely frustrating and was perceived as threatening their professional autonomy. Not only did they believe that they were made to feel 'stupid' in the eyes of their clients, but they were angry that their own programmes of care could so easily be overridden. When the psychiatrist was finally challenged, his response was that his approach was in the interests of team resources. There was no negotiation on this point, and he could see no conflict in his actions. He appeared to be unable to understand that his behaviour had caused others to feel undermined.

The reasons why the CPNs finally challenged the consultant may well have included their feelings about the outcomes for patients that resulted from the curtailing of CPN care for particular patients. However, the threat to the CPNs' professional autonomy appeared to be uppermost in their minds. The consultant would argue that he had acted on the team's behalf (although how he would understand the nature of the progress that CPNs were making with individual clients may be doubtful). The CPNs, because of their emphasis on the one-to-one relationship, did not regard this as a valid argument (and this would also have been the response of those who held 'integrative' views, but for a different reason).

Those in the CMHT who held an 'integrative' philosophy did challenge on a regular basis. They were prepared to discuss client care by proposing ideas and opinions based on their professional knowledge, and in recognition of the fact that this should be able to sway decisions about programmes of treatment. Inherent in this was the concept that *challenge was appropriate in a multi-professional team*. Each individual acknowledged and respected others' input as having equal importance to their own, but expected to contest others' decisions if necessary, and for any such challenge to be given weight. They saw this process as fundamental to both client care and team development, in that a team needed to be dynamic.

However, despite the fact that the 'integrative' professionals expressed knowledge and opinions in meetings, the 'directive' psychiatrist used dismissive and indeed sexist techniques to enable his own views to lead to his decisions. While appearing to encourage challenge, he manoeuvred the situation so as to deflate it. For example, he would decide that the meeting would have to close because he was late for another appointment, or he would make comments which attempted to reduce the conversation to gender differences in opinion, thus undermining the importance of comments made by others (the relevant social workers and the OT were all female). Thus despite apparently offering opportunities for debate, the outcome was that he gathered the information and, then made the decision himself for the team.

Similar circumstances were observed in other contexts. For example, in the medical ward, a senior house officer (SHO) and a registrar apparently had an understanding that they should listen to others, but direct their actions. Thus the differences between those who subscribe to 'integrative' and 'directive' philosophies with regard to communication seem largely to be concerned with differences in understanding of notions of democratic process. For those who hold integrative philosophies, equal representation from members of the team is a 'given'. Underpinning that notion is the belief that, on the basis of their own professional knowledge and experience, a team member should be able to challenge what they feel are inappropriate decisions or actions, *for the benefit of the patient or client*. Whilst supporting what appears to be a democratic process, such as multi-professional debate, those who hold a 'directive' philosophy do not seem to accept challenge as part of that process, thus potentially decreasing the likelihood of optimum care being provided.

With regard to the 'elective' philosophy, those who chose not to communicate comprehensively with others not only failed to see the wider picture of the patient, but also prevented others from having full access to *their* assessments, decisions and actions. The newcomer in the 'integrated' team believed that brevity of communication was important, and as a result of his unwillingness to discuss anything at length, he did not attend any team meetings on a regular basis. When he did attend it was perceived that his contribution was unhelpful, providing little or no advice on particular patients, and remaining uninvolved in planning processes. Furthermore, although all the other members of the team wrote in joint notes, this professional declined to participate in the system, instead keeping his own notes locked in his office. The director commented:

> There is this whole thing about secrecy, about keeping things confidential. And that's anathema to us. Here's somebody who is keeping their stuff under lock and key; what does that say about us, in that he has access to everything we write, but we don't have access to the things he writes.
>
> (Director)

As a result of the newcomer's reluctance to reveal the reasons for his clinical decisions, and how he intended to proceed with a programme of care, resentment grew among other team members, and doubts were fostered about the extent of his knowledge and skills. Furthermore, patients in the unit were left confused and, in some cases, distressed about their future care, often receiving different messages from the newcomer and the remainder of the team.

The way in which this professional communicated was echoed in the 'fragmented' CMHTs. Some CPNs in these two small teams were more discursive than others, but in general they were a group who worked alone and *liaised* with others. They seemed to do this efficiently, ensuring that they left notes for relevant professionals if necessary. Although many of them attended meetings regularly, they often agitated for discussion to end and the meeting to 'move on'. Discussion of team practice was not generally popular with them. They considered their own practice to be more important. Indeed, their overriding concern seemed to be their clients. (This is not a negative value judgement; all professionals could be expected to be more concerned about their patients or clients than about team membership. However, this group attached *little* importance to team membership.) As suggested above, these CPNs were working with one psychiatrist who was very team aware, but who wanted to direct their actions. This behaviour on his part persuaded some of them to curtail their communication with him even further. They were not present at any observed discharge meetings at the in-patient facility, nor did they consistently attend team meetings.

The nature of communication for those who held 'elective' beliefs about teamwork appeared to be constrained by the issue of confidentiality in a way that was not problematic for other professionals. All professionals within health and social care expect to enter into a confidential relationship with their clients. Where services need to be co-ordinated across professions within health care there is an understanding that information about physical, social and psychological issues will be passed between professionals with regard to a particular case. Where other agencies are concerned, as for example when Social Services needs to exchange information with health care professionals, the client's permission would then be sought in order to disclose aspects of the client's family life, for example. However, in our study many members of the psychology and psychiatric services, would maintain that the whole basis for in-depth disclosure – in order for the professional to help the client – is predicated on the confidential nature of the interaction. This raises difficulties for teamworking, particularly if confidentiality is seen to be 'used' as a reason for not communicating at all, as was the case in the 'integrated' team when the newcomer shared very little of his knowledge of patients with others.

In the following examples we shall examine the *differences between the integrative philosophy and assumptions of parallel working in terms of communication.* Where people were working 'in parallel', communication seemed only to occur on a 'need to know' basis. Note-keeping was separate, and few professionals assumed that there was a need to access the information within these notes in a consistent fashion. In addition, because this was a hierarchical understanding of multiprofessional working, the type and level of communication tended to be driven by medical diagnosis and treatment.

Within the medical ward, doctors would require information from others which pertained specifically to physical progress, such as the outcomes of monitoring particular bodily functions, and the results of specific investigations which had been performed. It was generally accepted that the nursing records were not examined during this process, except for documentation related to fluid intake, or general physical observations. Furthermore, few professionals were observed to offer verbal information or knowledge of other aspects of the patient's situation or progress.

Exceptions to this included one male nurse, and two nurses who worked in the high-dependency unit on that ward. For these professionals, putting forward not only the nursing perspective, but also that of the patient, was vital. For example, they had firm beliefs about the nurse's role as a patient advocate, which encouraged them to challenge the decisions that were made by some doctors. The male nurse was observed on several occasions to question decisions during ward rounds, particularly in relation to discharge timing. His challenge was based on his knowledge of problems associated with the patient's social situation, which needed to be pointed out to the consultant. He felt that speaking out would not only alert the consultants to the current situation, but might also encourage them to consider these aspects on another occasion. He commented that other nurses may well have accepted the decision and then had to manoeuvre other professionals later in order to comply with a consultant, or have kept the patient in until the discharge could be managed. Either way, the patient would have been confused by the change of events.

The male nurse associated his success in communicating with the consultants with the fact that he 'played the consultants at their own game'; he felt that he matched their assumed air of authority. The male nurse noted that some of the nurses had a problem with the consultants. The unwillingness of these nurses to voice their opinions in a manner consistent with those in positions of power compounded the communication difficulties in this setting. He commented that he talked to less experienced nurses about this issue and tried to raise their awareness of the need to challenge the consultants. However, his success in acting as a role model for others seemed to be limited, since there was evidence that he was 'used' by others on several occasions to obtain information from or to challenge 'difficult' doctors. Thus this nurse was an advocate not only for the patients but also for some of the nurses.

By contrast, the nurses in the high-dependency unit spoke about how their increased confidence had enhanced their ability to challenge others. This confidence was related to the specialist nature of their work in the unit, the skills they had learned, and the fact that they had accrued in-depth knowledge of their patients by operating a system of primary nursing. When dealing with other professionals, particularly the doctors, they believed strongly that they 'knew' their patients:

> I mean here we only have two patients per nurse, so you are acutely aware of what's going on with your patients on a day-to-day basis. And you are always going to have the same doctor, the same physio, whatever, so you always know what is going on . . . and you can really apply yourself to those two patients and at the end of the day you can feel that you've really achieved something. I've never really felt like that on the ward.
>
> (Staff Nurse)

These feelings were relatively new for these nurses, and it was evident that they were beginning to see how professionals *could* work together in a more collaborative manner. Their time in the small unit had enabled them to see other possibilities. Unfortunately, whilst this collaborative notion of multiprofessional working was reinforced by the doctors who worked in the high-dependency unit, the assumptions implicit in the following quote by one of them further highlight the problems inherent in working with others who regard themselves as intrinsically superior:

> They know about their patients, and they know what is going on medically as well as nursing wise. They ask us questions which are always sensible; they have a bit of initiative, they think for themselves, and it's unusual to get an unnecessary bleep from HDU because they know what is going on.
>
> (Senior House Officer)

Similar assumptions about working with others were held by some members of the PHCT, including most doctors, the district nurses and, to some extent, the practice nurse. In this setting, communication was expected to be brief, with messages being frequently relayed to other professionals in a series of communication books. These professionals regarded effective communication as passing on information rather than sharing ideas about patient management. However, most of the GPs were perceived to control the *flow* of communication. Requests made to them could be blocked without explanation, and challenge was effectively quashed. For example, in one meeting to which the practice nurse and practice manager were invited, the latter raised an item on the agenda regarding the possibility of obtaining locum cover for one GP's long-term illness. One of the senior GPs said that the GPs would discuss the subject between themselves, and this was agreed by the second senior partner. However, the one team-minded GP said that she was happy for her views to be known, and she supported the idea of providing locum cover. The senior partner maintained his initial stance, effectively inhibiting the junior partner's input and disallowing further discussion. The practice manager felt 'put down' by the senior GPs, and 'hamstrung' by their refusal to involve her in the discussion.

The differences in communication between the various professionals were frustrating for everyone. Many team-minded professionals believed that detailed communication enhanced their practice and benefited the client. They felt that interaction with most of the GPs resulted in communication which denied their knowledge and experience, and deterred them from sharing any understanding of where or how the GPs saw the practice developing.

For example, the HV 'attached' to the practice described how on one occasion she received a message from a GP to weigh a particular child regularly. This was done without her being given a reason, and without the suggestion of any prior meeting to discuss her own knowledge of the child. She commented that information about the context of the child's home environment and their past development would have provided the GP with a deeper understanding of the family situation (although of course she did not know what the doctor knew about this family, as there had been no opportunity for her to find this out). The HV also felt that further discussion would have enhanced team interaction through the inclusion and therefore recognition of the HV's particular skills and knowledge, and might have changed the way in which the GP managed the child's care.

What can we distil from these descriptions of the way in which different philosophies of multiprofessional working shape the way in which individuals communicate with each other? First, they highlight the complexities of the term 'communication'. The literature on multiprofessional teamworking often uses the phrase 'effective communication' (e.g. Field and West, 1995). What is clear from our study is that individuals may identify the fact that they engage in 'effective communication' without comprehending that this may not tally with other people's understanding of the term. Furthermore, without a comparison of the outcome of employing different approaches to communication within similar settings, we cannot say with certainty that briefer communication necessarily leads to less effective care for patients or clients. However, we can identify that, in our study, where individuals came together with different understandings about the nature of communication, or where the culture of the setting was generally to liaise as was seen to be appropriate, then there were many missed opportunities for communication. More importantly, it could be risky in terms of decision-making practices. Decisions based on incomplete knowledge may only result in minor irritation for patients, but they could actually result in incorrect therapy or treatment.

Where should this direct our thinking with regard to student education? In terms of communication it seems that:

> Students would benefit from understanding the various levels of communicating within a multiprofessional context, and the ways in which differences in beliefs about employing those different levels can influence *team* patient care.

Furthermore, students need to maintain the belief that their own professional concerns for the patient should be the guiding principle in determining their communication with others in the team.

The next section will examine the way in which roles are understood to contribute within the multiprofessional team and, in relation to that understanding, how they are valued.

Understanding and valuing others' role contribution

We mentioned in Chapter 2 that, like communication, understanding how other professionals' roles contribute to the work of the team has several levels of meaning. When we talked to professionals in our study we were frequently told about other people's work in a way that suggested only a superficial understanding of what they did. In the context of understanding the role of others whose work does not immediately relate to one's own, this may be sufficient. However, people were often making referrals to team members with whom they were expected to be working closely. What differences would having only a superficial understanding make to teamworking? We mentioned in Chapter 3 that there may be organisational reasons why professionals in a team do not have the *opportunity* to develop an understanding of other people's contributions. In this chapter we argue that individuals may hold *beliefs about teamwork* in which the meaning of role contribution, what it is necessary to understand, and what value is placed on their own and others' roles, all differ.

If we consider the beliefs associated with the 'integrative' philosophy, then here there is an assumption that *an in-depth understanding of other people's contributions is required for effective multiprofessional collaboration*. This means that there is a basic understanding of the tasks that are incorporated into a particular role. In addition, it means knowing what that role involves in practice – the pattern of actions that a role encompasses and the constraints on that role on a day-to-day basis. It is also deemed important to gain insight into the nature of the boundaries between roles – whether and how they can overlap for the benefit of the patient. Finally, it is seen to be important for team members to develop a knowledge of the rationale underlying the actions of another professional.

The director of the rehabilitation team described how understanding the way in which individuals contribute to the work of the team can create an interweaving of roles – not a dilution or blending of roles, but a situation where each role maintains its own specialist core, and the edges of the role are flexible. It is this flexibility which enables continuity and consistency of care through the exchange of skills and knowledge. An example from this team clearly demonstrated how this practice could enhance care interventions. It involved a man who was dysphasic, and who also required physiotherapy to his lower limbs. The PT needed to elicit some communication from the man, so she asked the SLT to join her for the session. By using cueing strategies (e.g. helping the patient to say the first letter of the first word), the SLT was able to encourage the man to respond when this was required, thus helping the PT to work with the patient more effectively. In addition, the PT learned the cueing strategies herself for use in subsequent sessions with this patient, thereby ensuring 'carry-over' in the absence of other professional input.

Similarly, several of the nurses in this setting had developed an understanding of the physiotherapy approach to rehabilitation in which developing the quality of a movement was as important as developing the function of that movement (a further discussion of this physiotherapy model and its relationship to nursing models of care can be found in Chapter 5). The nurses had watched how the PTs moved the patients and encouraged the patients to move themselves, and had learned these techniques in order to ensure continuity over the 24-hour period.

This type of understanding of others' contributions led to beliefs about not only valuing the skills with which each team member performed their tasks, but also valuing the professional knowledge which underpinned their decisions to undertake particular actions. This was perceived as 'working with' other professionals in a way that allowed the roles to integrate to some extent. Furthermore, willingness to learn from others not only aided individual professional development, but also created a pool of team skills and knowledge.

Those who held 'directive' philosophies of multiprofessional teamwork had a *more limited understanding of the contribution that other people made to the team*, more in terms of the tasks which would be assumed by other professionals, from a particular diagnosis. Where a professional had status and power, this was translated as other professionals 'working for' rather than 'with' them. The philosophy assumed that roles lower in the hierarchy were valued for their service to the powerful role, rather than for having intrinsic worth.

This is illustrated by an example from the 'fragmented team' in the medical ward. One of the registrars was noted for his 'team director' approach. He would show role flexibility by offering to help nurses if they were busy, and he was observed to assist a patient in getting off a commode and into bed. As a result of his actions he was extremely well thought of by the nurses. However, his stated beliefs belied his actions, bringing into doubt their underlying motive. He also believed that other professionals 'worked for' him. His assumption was that he would be 'in control of the team', but of a team in which he said he valued other professional input. 'Value' in this context again seemed to relate to the tasks which others performed within the 'team'. For example, he spoke about the proficiency of the nurses in the high dependency unit in monitoring oxygen saturation levels and adjusting oxygen input accordingly. What he did not mention was the particular perspective which nurses could bring to the care of the patient on the basis of their own body of knowledge. Value did not seem to be related to this or other bodies of knowledge which might inform other professionals' judgements and actions.

For this registrar, and for several other professionals who held the same beliefs, valuing role knowledge was only ascribed to those deemed to be in a similar position in their hierarchy of professions. This was evident in that the registrar did not show any awareness that he could learn from other professionals. When interviewed he had spoken about a 'brilliant ward sister' and her response when there was a cardiac arrest on the ward: 'She knew exactly what I wanted, where everything was, and was willing to run around and get it while we sorted this chap out' (Registrar).

This comment suggested that the ward sister's perceived status was one of a service to the professionals, who did the important work. This view was later reinforced in interview when the doctor was asked about those from whom he had learned. He cited his seniors as the source of his professional learning *and* his learning about multiprofessional working. This closed approach to learning from other professionals was observed in all those who expressed 'directive' beliefs.

Those who subscribed to an 'elective' philosophy were also seen to have *a limited understanding of others' roles, that related more to job description.* They also had a *strong sense of their own role boundaries.* For example within the child development assessment team, the clinical psychologists had clear ideas about what they would and would not undertake as part of the team process. Although part of this rationale was related to time constraints, they opted not to take part in the joint assessment process, where their input could have been extremely valuable. One situation developed which illustrated how maintaining an isolationist stance could hamper other professional input. Two members of the core group in this team were attempting to work with a child with severe behavioural problems. After a joint assessment had been made they developed a strategy of action which proved to be unsuccessful in keeping the child focused on the therapy session. By chance they discovered that one of the clinical psychologists had also been working with the child and could have informed them of more suitable behaviour-shaping tactics to use. As suggested in the previous section with regard to confidentiality issues for those who held an 'elective' perspective, the clinical psychologist's closed professional working and lack of role flexibility constrained the beneficial outcome of this team's intervention. Furthermore, team members were neither able to learn about the clinical psychologist's practice, nor to learn strategies from this professional to assist their own practice.

The beliefs held by the clinical psychologists in this team shared much in common with those of the newcomer in the 'integrated' team, and of one psychiatrist and many of the CPNs in the 'fragmented' CMHT. While many professionals, whatever beliefs they subscribed to about teamworking, identified that role clarity was important for professional esteem and effective team function, having tight role boundaries was not regarded as helpful. For those who held this belief, encroachment of those boundaries was not readily entertained. This attitude left no room for negotiation, and ensured that they would be free to manage their own work without recourse to others.

A further example of the difficulties that this approach incurred was observed in the CMHTs. In Chapter 3 we discussed the effects of the introduction of the CPA on the roles of the CPN and the social workers. With the change in emphasis on caring for people with severe or long-term mental health problems, this changed team expectations of the CPN role, particularly among the social workers, who now wanted the CPNs to be more flexible about the way they worked, which would reflect the complex nature of mental illness. This encompassed dealing with the problems of those with 'antisocial' behaviour who were living in the community and finding it difficult to maintain accommodation and work placements. As with members of the rehabilitation team, many social workers believed that teamwork should include willingness to extend skills and knowledge in order to provide better continuity, and that the skills required by *all team members* should include addressing social aspects of care.

Few of the CPNs talked in this manner, and some, in contrast to the social workers, felt that their own role should be preserved. They did not regard it as appropriate that they should move away from their 'nursing role' of therapy and monitoring the effects of medication: 'but I still don't see that as my role; I'm not trained to do it, and I don't want to be trained to do it . . . I shall resist it to the nth degree' (CPN).

This unwillingness was partly related to resistance to change. Many CPNs had invested time and energy in developing their skills, and did not want to dilute these by involvement in social intervention. However, the unwillingness also related to a belief that multiprofessional working was about maintaining tight role boundaries, where each professional was clear about what they contributed to the team. Certainly all of the CPNs in the study were clear about their role, but many of them also knew what they did not want that role to be.

Within this setting it was clear that the different perceptions of role led to professional defensiveness, which became problematic for clients. This was exemplified in one team meeting where a client had been assessed in the day hospital by a nurse, who had identified that the client needed a key-worker to take on negotiation of his accommodation and funding. However, there was no response to this from the CMHT. In Chapter 3 we described how the lack of social work resources had resulted in social workers being unwilling to keep taking on a key-working role, even when the emphasis of the work might be social rather than psychiatric treatment. This meant that the nurse in this case was looking to the CPNs to take on the role. In the meeting the discussion became very strained, and one of the CPNs said: 'well, my time is valuable, I can't do it'. Not surprisingly, this response made the nurse feel unsupported:

> It was as if she was saying that my time *wasn't* valuable, and that made me angry. I got less than a sympathetic hearing at the meeting and I felt quite despondent. People were making me feel like a fool; that I didn't know my job . . . and when [the CPN] said that, I thought 'am I part of this team or aren't I?'. I felt really bad.
>
> (Staff nurse)

In this situation, professional role protection appeared to override patient focus. This mismatching of role expectations was fundamental to this team's dysfunction and arose specifically out of different perceptions of teamworking.

What about those who work in 'parallel' and their understanding of role contribution? As we have suggested, here there is an understanding of a hierarchical approach to patient care (i.e. the medical model). However, in contrast to the 'directive' philosophy, there are *not assumptions that the medical profession necessarily acts as a 'team leader'*, but rather that it is *the apex of the decision-making process.* This can also apply to both clinical and non-clinical aspects of teamworking, as is demonstrated by the following scenarios.

In the PHCT, the practice manager resigned after a long 'battle' in which she had felt undermined. She had come from a practice where she had a position of 'respected partnership' with the GPs. She spoke about having regular meetings with them and other members of the PHCT, in which team strategies would be developed. Furthermore, she was expected to devise and explicate business plans with the GPs. Her perception of her position in *this current setting* was very different. Here she felt disempowered because the GPs 'hold the reins so tightly' and 'keep me in the dark'. Evidence of this was observed, in relation to the employment of a new counsellor. The manager had not been involved in interviewing for this post, nor did she receive much feedback other than that someone had been appointed. In a meeting with the GPs she pointed out that she had been unable to draw up a contract for the new counsellor because she had no information about the basis on which she was being employed. This was not acknowledged by the senior partners.

She believed that the GPs in the current practice regarded her role as that of an administrator, in a position between themselves and the practice staff and simply carrying out whatever tasks were delegated to her. Interview and observational data reinforced this view and provided evidence of similar mismatches with regard to most of the GPs and their perceptions of the practice nurse, the HVs and the midwife. In all of these cases there was a belief that the GPs delegated tasks, rather than other professionals having intrinsic value due to their contribution to the PHCT.

A second example demonstrates how making assumptions about working within a medical model, where others work to a diagnosis as given by a member of the medical profession, can lead to perceptions of secondary status among some professionals and thus constrain their input. As was suggested in Chapter 2, there were some tensions between the therapy groups and several of the nurses in the 'integrated' team. Here the majority of the team members assumed role parity with regard to team interaction. By contrast, some nurses behaved 'as if' they had secondary status. What encouraged this perception? It was clear that, while many of the therapy groups had a high level of confidence in their team contribution, some nurses felt unsure about their role. They knew what they did, but they were unsure about their *specific* contribution over and above general patient care and being (as they put it) 'a therapy helper'. In addition to the lack of role clarity, this seemed to result in the perception that their input was less valuable than that of others. This related to the view that it is difficult to define a role in rehabilitation which is sufficiently demanding and challenging. This has been noted by other researchers (Fokke, 1994; Johnson and Fokke, 1995; Nolan *et al.*, 1997). Some of the nurses felt that their skills were diminished by working within the rehabilitation environment. The feelings expressed by the nurse in the following quotation reflect this:

> The medical knowledge needs to be there, to the extent that people feel confident in your knowledge and your skills, your abilities, basically they have got to trust you, that is what your fellow professionals look to you for. It's a bit difficult here because you are out of the mainstream of a medical model of care, therefore you can't help but miss out on a lot of what is happening in terms of the application of knowledge in procedures, etc. There's nothing like having to do a procedure to reinforce your knowledge base. It's difficult here because you don't do a lot of procedures.
>
> (Nurse)

It seemed that overarching this perception was a more diffuse uncertainty that they *could* practise outside the medical framework. The rehabilitation setting lacked the highly technical skills which might have helped the nurses to gain confidence as professionals. The double impact of being unable to express professional prowess through skills demonstration rather than knowledge sharing, *and* of having been socialised in an environment where those of higher status appeared to value that former aspect of nursing, seems likely to have created problems of role uncertainty. Whereas the therapy groups were operating autonomously at one level, this did not apply to some members of the nursing group, who seemed to feel the lack of reference from above. This appeared to be similar to the way in which nurses were traditionally socialised to accept that the medical model, and those within it, prescribed their actions to some extent. This is not to say that the body of nursing knowledge would not prescribe its own actions with patients, but that the point from which this would be developed would be the medical diagnosis.

The outcome of holding these beliefs for some of the nurses in the rehabilitation team was that they did not value their own contribution to the rehabilitation process in the same way as other professionals in the team. As will be seen in the following section, this had repercussions for their beliefs about team learning.

Clearly, in view of the nature of current working within the NHS, understanding one's own and others' contribution to the team is vital. However, understanding what happens at the boundaries of those roles has also become highly relevant. The requirement for professionals to be role-flexible is fundamental to services which have to be provided under such fluid circumstances. Furthermore, it can be argued that multiprofessional teamworking demands that professionals are flexible at the boundaries of their roles in order to develop team knowledge and skills and therefore maintain continuity of team care. Those who hold beliefs about roles which result in their being protected despite this process being demonstrably ineffective for patient care are swimming against the tide.

> Students entering multiprofessional health care teamwork will need to consider not only the way in which different professional roles contribute to the process of patient care, and to value them, but also to know how those roles can interweave at their boundaries in order to provide continuity of care.

As well as understanding others' contribution to patient care within a team context, we have spoken about the way that holding particular beliefs shapes the value which is given to other roles in the team. This has ramifications for individuals' willingness to learn from and teach others, and thus to share knowledge and skills. This final section will examine further how particular beliefs can enhance or inhibit this process.

Teaching and learning from each other

We suggested earlier that where individuals hold 'integrative' beliefs about teamworking there is an assumption that a professional *can teach – and learn from – others*. This relates to sharing specific professional knowledge which can give particular insight into patient or client care, and to the sharing of skills that are seen to be more peripheral to each role. Through this process a body of team knowledge and skills would develop which could be used to enhance patient care. It is the reciprocal nature of this learning that is a fundamental aspect of this set of beliefs. This type of teaching and learning was only seen in the 'integrated working' of the rehabilitation team, and in the core groups of the 'core and periphery' working (i.e. the diabetes team and the child development assessment team).

For those who held 'directive' beliefs or who engaged in 'parallel' working, teaching and learning was largely a one-way process (within a hierarchical context). Those who were at the top of the hierarchy would teach, while others would learn. Within this framework it was accepted that learning from one's own more experienced colleagues was appropriate. Learning from other professionals was possible, but only at certain stages of professional development. Within our study, some nurses spoke about their instructive role with the very junior doctors, but stated that this 'only lasted a few weeks, to get them on the road'. After this period, doctors increasingly, learned from their own profession. However, it was evident that this instructive period did not include learning about nursing skills or knowledge, but rather about the correct employment of certain medical procedures, and the ward routine.

For those who subscribed to an 'elective' approach to teamworking, learning from others was similarly a monoprofessional pursuit. However, the difference in this case was that there was no assumption that teaching others was important. It was considered more appropriate to maintain skills and knowledge within one's own professional domain. Given this description, it is easy to imagine the frustration that occurred when individuals with different ideas about sharing knowledge and skills came together in a team.

In the following examples we shall examine *how perceptions of the importance of learning from others differed depending on the philosophy that was held*. In the rehabilitation team, where many professionals subscribed to an 'integrated' philosophy, there were tensions, as has already been suggested. These existed between the therapy groups and the nurses with regard to perceptions about who could teach and who would need to learn. This seemed to relate to some nurses' perceptions of their own role within a hierarchical, 'parallel' way of working, and is reflected in much of the literature on relationships between nurses and doctors (Tellis-Nayak, 1984; Cambell-Heider and Pollock, 1987; Porter, 1991; Busby and Gilchrist, 1992; Mallik, 1992; Whale, 1993).

For those nurses who saw themselves to be of 'lower status' and operating within this way of working, it was common for them to reinforce this by acting as 'receivers of wisdom' in the team. The effect was to encourage them to behave 'as if' they had little of value to impart to other team members, even where they worked within an 'integrative' culture where learning from each other was part of general team practice.

This did not mean that there was not, in general, a two-way flow of information and knowledge. Some nurses were frequently heard giving medical advice to therapists, and feeding back details of patients' emotional state or social difficulties. However, it was the emphasis on therapeutic *prescription of practice* which some of the nurses perceived and interpreted as undermining their standing in the team, inhibiting them from involving therapists in patient care, and from holding sessions with therapists in which they could impart nursing knowledge and skills.

For these nurses it is possible that the physiotherapy-led ethos of the team (see Chapter 5) had created a 'proxy medical model' whereby some nurses believed that the direction of education would be from therapists to nurses. The therapists were aware of the nurses' dilemma and sensitive about the need to be diplomatic when showing them new skills or passing on new knowledge. However, despite these attempts, skills or knowledge teaching was not observed to have been reciprocated by the nurses, and indeed was not identified as a common phenomenon. In their difficulties in defining their skills and knowledge as equals, it seemed that the legacy of working in an environment where 'parallel' working assumptions would be prevalent played a part in undermining their professional confidence. By contrast, the therapists were keen to learn from each other, but this was accepted in the knowledge that they could teach others. In general, the nurses did not appear to feel that they had a teaching role, because they did not think the therapists would be interested in details about continence or skin integrity. Thus the knowledge flow remained largely a one-way process.

One nurse who did not espouse the assumptions made by some of the other nurses had attended a specific rehabilitation programme of education, which gave her a clearer understanding of the role nurses could play, and thus of the way in which they could teach others. She was able to reflect more comprehensively on her contribution and to see herself as a 'rehabilitation nurse' rather than a nurse who did rehabilitation – a difference which gave her confidence in her role. Unlike some others, she felt able to express her knowledge to other team members. Unfortunately, since the beliefs held by some nurses were reinforced by the head nurse, her ability to construct her contribution to learning in a more consistent manner, and the opportunity for it to become part of the nursing contribution in general, were inhibited.

The result of the tensions between some of the nurses and the therapists was a partial breakdown in continuity of therapeutic input in the absence of the therapists. Although, in general, the level of continuity and consistency of care was seen to greatly exceed that in general wards, this hiatus between the nurses and the therapists was still perceived to hamper the progress of patients. As will be seen in the following chapter, it is likely that only the unremitting efforts by therapists and some nurses to devise strategies for overcoming differences in managing certain patients ameliorated this situation.

The issue of reciprocal learning was also encountered between members of one of the core groups and those on the periphery. In the child development assessment team, the 'integrative' SLT had attempted to share learning through developing joint practice with some of the physiotherapists. She perceived that it had not been due to want of trying that she had been unable to do this. She had attempted on several occasions to establish this process, but these attempts had not been very successful. This contrasted with the work in her previous team, which had made her appreciate the way in which professional knowledge could intertwine in order to maximise the benefits for the children, and how it enhanced her own understanding of the contribution of each set of skills. She described how, in that setting, they had developed combined sessions in which both physical control and speech development could co-occur. The PTs would facilitate maximum physical control, which then enabled her to work on aspects of speech. At the same time, the PT would learn language and communication tasks that could reinforce their work. For both professionals it was about recognising that: 'when you are working on a PT task, children can't achieve their optimum cognitive skills, and when you are working on their cognitive skills, they can't achieve their optimum physical skills' (SLT).

This mirrors the way in which the PTs and SLTs worked in the rehabilitation team. The lack of ability to draw the PTs into learning with her in her current setting was extremely frustrating for the SLT. She felt that part of the problem related to the PTs' apparent beliefs about teamworking, especially their beliefs about sharing knowledge and skills:

> They have a closed way of working. We've got a physio department where there's a philosophy of doing the physio, but not imparting their skills and knowledge . . . you know we should be asking the physios do they feel able to describe what they are doing and why they are doing it as they are doing it.
>
> (SLT)

In the 'fragmented' teams, shared learning was relatively rare, although the desire for it to occur was not. The problem for 'integrative' professionals who wanted to share knowledge and skills was finding that a sufficient number of like-minded others was difficult. In the CMHTs, for example, only the OT and two of the three social workers expressed this wish. The social workers were both very experienced and felt that monitoring the effects of certain drug regimens (traditionally a CPN role) could be included in their role. Like many members of the 'integrated' team the social workers viewed learning as a reciprocal venture – they and the CPNs would learn from each other and form a 'safety-net' for clients. This did not mean that the social workers were necessarily advocating the introduction of a generic mental health worker, but rather that they saw the need for greater flexibility at the boundaries of both roles, where some skills and knowledge could be jointly used.

However, as was suggested earlier, many of the CPNs were not prepared to work in this fashion. For them, neither teaching nor learning from others seemed to be an appropriate part of their day-to-day work. Again, where two philosophies – the 'elective' and 'integrative' – met, differences in beliefs about what should and should not be possible or desirable were evident.

In this section we have proposed that only one set of beliefs, namely the 'integrative' approach to multiprofessional teamwork, appears to create the potential for shared learning. This relates to an acknowledgement of the benefits of various levels of communication for patient care, where each professional is encouraged to contribute not only information about particular patients, but also insights from their experience, and reasoning from their own professional body of knowledge to decisions about care and treatment.

Shared learning also relates to a widening of professional roles, overlapping to provide a 'team role'. This would allow patient care to be provided at some level by all of the professionals in the team, thus enabling them to provide continuity and consistency of care. Finally, shared learning relates to the development of a fund of 'team knowledge' about each patient. Since time is fundamental to the latter process, this aspect is naturally only possible with regard to long-term patient management such as elderly care, rehabilitation, and care of the chronically ill.

In uncovering how these different philosophies approach the sharing of skills and knowledge, we have discovered the possibility of providing, in a team, patient care that exceeds the sum of the various professional inputs. This is an important aspect of teamworking that students need to understand.

Students also need to see that sharing knowledge and skills facilitates individual professional development for the benefit of the patient.

Before we move on to Chapter 5 (the final chapter on clinical teamworking), it is helpful to draw together the ramifications of professionals holding either similar or different beliefs. First, it would be possible to predict that where a group of professionals hold similar beliefs about teamwork, this would result in a situation with reduced conflict of interests. It has the *potential* to move team practice towards effective functioning, and to provide identifiable benefits to patients or clients. Because different approaches to teamwork may be appropriate in different environments, this research makes no recommendation that any one approach is necessarily a predictor of better 'hard data' patient outcomes than another. Different levels of communication and role understanding may be sufficient under different circumstances to provide effective service delivery.

Where an 'integrative' philosophy was held, a major component of this philosophy was the development of joint working practices. Within these practices, discussion and debate in which it was possible to challenge the status quo were an important aspect of this approach to teamwork. Only through this type of communication did professionals believe that 'team' development could occur and the most informed decisions be made about patient care. Both of these factors would be predicated on an understanding that all members of 'the team' have an equally important contribution to make to patient care, and that their individual perspectives bring a unique piece of the jigsaw of information and knowledge to the decision-making process. Furthermore, role flexibility whereby professionals could extend their skills and knowledge through learning from each other, was deemed to be fundamental to effective working. It may only be possible to sustain teamworking based on this philosophy where there is a higher level of stability and predictability of service provision. It is noted that where the whole team, or core groups, had developed 'integrated' working, the team was dealing with long-stay patients, or was managing those with chronic illness or disability within an appointmented system. Those on the peripheries of the core groups were expected to spread their time across both these teams and the more fragmented acute sector.

If a whole team has beliefs that a 'directive' philosophy is appropriate, how would this affect teamwork? Superficially this would appear to entail a shared set of beliefs about communication and role understanding. Furthermore, these may lead to similar outcomes for patient care. However, because of the nature of this approach, in which one person directs the decision-making process and has the power to control communication made by others in the group, it is potentially limiting to professional input. In addition, because there seems to be a different interpretation of role (that is, that the person directing the team may assign value to the tasks rather than the rationale for action), this approach could be regarded as professionally undermining. Role overlap may occur, but could be viewed as 'helping out' by those directing, and to some extent in the gift of the 'helper', rather than a systematic pattern of role extension. Finally, because of the hierarchical nature of this approach, although professionals may learn from others, this is more likely to be a 'top-down' than a 'bottom-up' effect, which may preclude others from having the opportunity to share their knowledge and experiences. The hierarchical nature of this philosophy, together with the assumptions made by its existence within a medical model, may therefore hinder those who subscribe to it from maximising the benefits of multiprofessional teamworking for patients and clients.

Those who shared an 'elective' philosophy would not seem to fit a concept of multiprofessional teamworking, as essentially it appeared to be inward-looking in its relationship with the patient or client. Communication between the professional and others in the team *could* be informative but not generally discursive. Challenging others' opinions may not be viewed as appropriate because of the acceptance that each professional offers their own particular contribution from a standpoint of role clarity and confidence. This approach may well promote a sense of professional worth but, because of its perception of the need for impermeable role boundaries, does not accommodate change readily. As a result of the limited communication and closely guarded role boundaries, the opportunities for learning between professionals who hold these beliefs would be limited.

Finally, the assumptions that underpin *'parallel'* working represent a way of understanding teamwork based on long-held approaches to health care working. As such, they combine the hierarchical nature of the 'directive' approach with the professionally (rather than individually) bound understanding of working together of the 'elective' approach. By this we mean that instead of placing the emphasis on a one-to-one relationship with the patient or client, a professional group will share responsibility for those they care for. Again this would seem to result in limited communication. Assumptions about care will fall out of the medical diagnosis, and each profession will develop a plan of care for the patient based on that diagnosis. However, this does not seem to be done with a concept of the multiprofessional team. Role boundaries may be breached, but in general this relates to tasks which other individuals higher up the hierarchy are prepared to let go. Within this framework, again it appears as if professionals do not maximise patient or client care.

Having summarised the effects of whole teams subscribing to one or other of these philosophies, it is not difficult to imagine the problems that arise where individuals hold different philosophies within a team. Where professionals hold an 'integrative' philosophy and meet any of the other three approaches, expectations of being able to communicate in depth, challenge others, be role flexible and learn from others may well be confounded. Not surprisingly, where we observed this situation professionals were extremely frustrated and to some extent demoralised.

For those who subscribe to an 'elective' approach, meeting these professionals would be problematic because of expectations that they would discuss and debate issues, but more importantly that they would be role flexible. In our study, the subsequent development of *professionally defensive behaviour* was seen to be detrimental to patient or client care. Where the 'directive' or 'parallel' approach meets the 'integrative' and/or 'elective' approach, threats to *professional judgement* would be prevalent. Overarching all of these difficulties there would be an inability to develop a *shared vision* of the type of service the multiprofessional teams want to provide, how to provide that service, and in which direction it will be moving.

In this chapter we have seen that there are clear implications for the education and training of professionals in order to prepare them for this type of working.

Overall we feel that it is important that students entering the health professions develop an understanding of the fact that individuals have different understandings of multiprofessional teamworking. Furthermore, students need to understand how those different perceptions can shape interprofessional relationships. Finally, they need to understand how these affect the potential of the team to develop practices which maximise patient or client care.

This chapter and the previous one examined the external and individual factors that influence how a particular team operates. In Chapter 5 we shall examine aspects of group structure and process that will be shaped by both of these forces. We shall consider 'the way things are done' in the teams – that is, the cultures that develop, be they team cultures or the meeting of different professional cultures. We shall also highlight how the *norms of being and becoming a team member, the historical context, power and leadership, and the meeting of models of patient care* all help to shape the way in which teams are able to communicate, learn about each other's roles, develop team allegiances, and establish a shared focus for patient care. Again we shall compare the nature of these influences and how they affect team function for the three different types of working.

Group processes and their effects on teamwork

5

INTRODUCTION

The discussion in the last two chapters demonstrated clearly that collaborative multiprofessional working may not be easy to achieve. Organisational structures and processes may affect the stability of a team and hence their opportunities for effective communication and observing and understanding how each person contributes. In addition, the management structures may militate against the support of collaborative practices. Furthermore, individual understanding about the purpose and benefit of teamworking may differ widely, creating the potential for interprofessional resentment and frustration, and the obstruction of patient care. Thus both the organisation and the individual can have a major influence on the way that a group of different professionals can develop teamworking. Assuming that each member of a team is highly skilled and competent at what they do, these two factors will influence whether they can be brought together successfully.

With regard to the organisational influence, this will relate to the way in which *power and authority* are ratified within the organisation. Although most teams of individuals from the same profession will have their own hierarchy of power and authority, this is based on a system of accreditation through education and experience. Where a multiprofessional team is brought together, this system is no longer applicable, and other frameworks are employed. Much as many professional groups would like to see themselves as having parity within the NHS, the persistence of the medical model encourages the continuation of medical power within multiprofessional teams (Sinclair, 1997). In turn, this will impinge on *leadership processes*, and thus on decision-making within the team.

The organisational context will also relate to the way in which team membership is achieved – that is, whether availability as a team member is enabled or inhibited by organisational structures and processes. Finally it will relate to the 'ways of being' that a team develops around its practices for patient care, and whether opportunities for joint working are possible (even if desired).

With regard to the individual, we have identified that beliefs about teamwork may be largely bound by each team member's *professional culture*. Assembling a team which includes a number of different professions will bring together people who have already been socialised into their own cultures. In effect their allegiance will be to their own profession, and their identity as professional members will be well formed. Their situation in a particular profession will not only lend a particular identity, but that identity will have status and power, through organisational (and societal) recognition of a knowledge hierarchy. Thus each professional culture will reflect the power and status accorded to it in the 'ways of being' that it develops.

Becoming a member of any group requires that a person takes on these 'ways of being' – that is, the *norms and values* of that group. This socialisation process ensures the continuation of the group status quo, and thus enables it to fulfil the purpose for which it was formed, in the way that is recognised by the group as appropriate (Brown, 1988). We see the result of this process in the very different attributes and ways of working that are found in the professions which constitute health care services (e.g. Soothill *et al.*,1995). When we ask members of different professional groups to collaborate as a team, then we are asking them to step outside their own cultures to some extent, and to engage in the development of a *multiprofessional team culture*. In this context it is possible that very different 'ways of being' will develop. To enable this to happen, professional allegiances need to shift from a position where professional group membership is paramount, towards also viewing the team as an important reference point. In addition, it is important that the power and authority vested in certain professional groups do not undermine the efforts of other team members to engage in collaborative practices.

Since collaboration as a multiprofessional team is the direction in which professionals are expected to be moving, we have already suggested that this term assumes that professionals are able to communicate effectively. We have also suggested that they have a clear understanding of how their roles contribute to team patient care, and that they develop a shared focus for their work. In Chapter 3, sharing a focus related to the diversity of the patient group which the team served. In the group context it relates to the purpose of the team's service to the patient (i.e. the way team members see they offer the best care). In thinking about the interactions between team members, we would also add that to maintain motivation towards collaboration, team members need to feel that their roles are valued.

In order to understand how professional culture, status and power influence collaborative teamwork, we therefore need to examine 'how things are done' within teams. This relates to the following aspects:

- what it means to be a member of a team;
- what kind of environment for communication and role understanding is developed;
- how leadership is defined;
- how the team understands other role contributions;
- the basis on which the team develops a focus;
- how new members are incorporated into the team.

In this chapter we shall explore how the different types of working demonstrate different configurations in relation to these aspects, underpinned by differences in the extent to which a *team* culture is achieved, and the way in which power differences are managed.

What it means to be a team member in the context of multiprofessional working relates directly to the degree to which each professional feels they are part of a team in the first place. Where the degree of team cohesion is small, then professionals will (not surprisingly) feel more of a member of their own professional group. In the 'fragmented' teams there was little evidence of any sense of 'team belonging'. In the 'core and periphery' teams, 'team belonging' applied only to the core groups. Only in the 'integrated' team was there a more unified perception of belonging to a team. From these perceptions, therefore, it is clear that aspects of team function such as communication, developing a focus, and understanding each other's roles will be influenced to a large extent by where allegiance is situated.

The *kind of environment for communication and role understanding* which develops in a team is partly influenced by the extent to which professional cultures remain distinct or whether a team culture develops, and how well that culture encourages the incorporation of different members' views and opinions. In the 'integrated' team, there was a strong *team* culture, which evolved through the input of most professionals, in which an environment for communication and role understanding was facilitated through a wide range of structures and processes. This was considered to be a 'safe learning environment' in which people could learn from each other readily. In the 'core and periphery' teams this was also true, but only for the core groups. In the 'fragmented' teams, because allegiance remained primarily to the professional group rather than to the team, their own culture heavily influenced their communication, governed to a large extent by the overriding medical perspective. In these settings it was often considered 'unsafe' to communicate and thus to learn from others in this way.

The *style of leadership* in our study relates to the mix of professionals within the team, since by dint of status within the organisation, some professionals are more likely to take on that role than others. In the 'integrated' team, leadership was facilitative and regarded as a role model by other team members. This relatively cohesive team was the only one that was not medically 'led'. In other teams, leadership by members of the medical profession was seen to be problematic. Where 'core and periphery' working was observed, membership of both core groups included doctors who worked in an integrative fashion with other core members. However, one, operated in an autocratic fashion towards peripheral team members. Where we saw 'fragmented' working, autocratic behaviours, although not necessarily leadership, were again observed. Although other team members did not necessarily accept this position, the status of those who 'led' ensured that this was still a major influence on teamwork.

When we examine *the nature of other team members' role contribution*, we need to consider two factors – first, the *differentiation of roles*, and secondly, the way in which *non-task-based roles can develop*. In the 'integrated' team, with few exceptions, professionals were confident and clear about their role and were able to identify aspects of their role that could be shared with others. However, some of the nurses were less confident about a role which was more diffuse, and which they felt was less valued. This undermined their belief that they had knowledge and skills which others wanted to share. In the 'core and periphery' teams, professionals may have had a clear understanding of their role and valued its contribution to the work of the team, but this was not always shared by others. Where we saw 'fragmented' working, different professional groups contested their role contribution and beliefs that roles were given different values were common. As a result, professional defensive behaviours were evident.

With regard to non-task-based roles these were seen in the case of 'core and periphery' working. Here certain members of the teams had developed 'bridging roles' in which they attempted to overcome the gap between the core groups and the peripheral members.

The *basis on which a team develops a shared focus* is very much bound up with the culture of the professional groups represented in the team, and the purported role of the team. Where particular professional groups are brought together who may have very differing perspectives about how to manage a particular patient group, there can be tensions about developing a shared approach. Such tensions were observed in the 'integrated' team, and in one 'fragmented' team where there was cross-organisational working. In the 'integrated' team, differences in the underpinning rationale of rehabilitation caused some dislocation between the therapy groups and the nurses. In the CMHT, differing ideologies, such as the social work view of 'client rights' versus the health service understanding of 'duty of care', exacerbated an already difficult working situation.

How new members are incorporated into a team depends on the extent to which the multiprofessional team exists as an entity (i.e. whether a team culture has developed). In the case of 'integrated' working, because there was a cohesive team, incorporation was a *team* issue rather than a *professional group* issue. This would have ramifications for newcomers who might not be prepared to share the team's 'ways of being'. Similarly, this applied where peripheral members of the 'core and periphery' teams were unable or unwilling to find a means of entry to the core, or were not accepted into this group. Where 'fragmented' working was seen, incorporation was into the professional group, rather than into the team. In this situation the process was only visible where incoming professionals had expectations that they should be incorporated as a *team* member.

WHAT IT MEANS TO BE A TEAM MEMBER

This section will examine the way in which the experience of being a team member differed across the various teams in our study. *The more integrated the team, the more they shared a set of beliefs about 'the way things are done', and the greater was their allegiance to the team.* From the evidence in the previous two chapters we can begin to see that developing a sense of belonging to a multiprofessional team requires the presence of both external support and individual motivation. Where these come together, the opportunities for developing a team to which professionals have an allegiance are enhanced. The notion of allegiance to the team is important in terms of group process. When we aspire to belong to any specific group of people, it serves as a standard by which we evaluate the appropriateness of our attitudes and behaviour. As a result, that group becomes a reference point for us (Newcomb, 1965; an old but classic study of group process). The underlying assumption here is that the group is an important influence on the way we think and act, affecting our own beliefs. This means that individual members of a group will be more likely to produce a desired behaviour, whatever that may be, when, not only do they hold beliefs which would support that behaviour, but it is subsequently reinforced within the reference group. In the case of multiprofessional teamworking, the difficulty is in bringing together and then encouraging professionals to develop a sense of allegiance to a group in which a multitude of different attitudes about patient care and teamworking itself exist.

Within our study, only members of the 'integrated' rehabilitation team had shared norms and showed a high level of team allegiance. There was also largely a whole-team culture, as opposed to professional cultures existing side by side within the team. Despite some tensions between the therapy groups and some of the nurses, there was a strong sense of team cohesion. As might be expected, when a group is cohesive it is more likely to exhibit higher levels of communication, and thus desired beliefs can be strengthened. Within this team it was of paramount importance that individuals 'fitted in', and the beliefs to which people were expected to adhere were those which ensured a high degree of collaboration between team members. It has to be remembered that this team had a long history, with many members having been in the team for 10 years. As will be seen later, the historical context of a team is vital for understanding where it is currently situated. In the 'integrated' team, there was a core of these long-term members who, because of the strength of their convictions about collaborative working and also the stability of their influence, ensured that those who subsequently joined the team would be prepared to follow suit.

One of the most striking features that distinguished the majority of the members of this 'integrated' team from others in our study was their highly developed *awareness* of being a team, and the *values* which they all held to be important in order to function effectively. Being a 'team player' was seen to be almost as important as being a skilled professional. It was considered important not only that individuals espoused the beliefs, but also that they put them into action in every aspect of their work. This basic assumption was evident from the first selection interview, where the director and heads of the various professional departments would explore newcomers' understanding of teamworking: 'She asked me, about where I was working before, were there issues around role divisions in the team, and was there a lot of overlap among the professionals, and how could you get round the issues' (OT).

'Fitting in' also related to the degree to which individuals were likely to be open and frank communicators, and would be prepared to reflect on themselves and their practice on a consistent basis. The director identified the following:

> It is vital for me that I can assess how open they are likely to be; to look at their aplomb in dealing with emotional issues. I like to test that out

> because it is important for people to be able to let off steam at meetings, so I ask them questions they might think are off the wall about themselves as people.
>
> (Director)

'Fitting in' also meant that professionals were expected to respect and value both each other and patients within the unit. Failure to do so was met with disapproval by all concerned, as was clearly observed when the newcomer mentioned in the previous chapter joined the team. As with many aspects of what it meant to be a team player, individuals felt that they articulated these feelings more strongly when they had someone in their midst who was obviously displaying non-team behaviour. For most team members, however, the way in which they spoke about fellow professionals emphasised how much they valued them:

> It's an ability to talk to somebody, if you are having problems with somebody, or the good things; sharing everything, sharing the knowledge, and being willing to help other people . . . , this is teamwork . . . and you act as an advisor, as say a *companion*.
>
> (PT)

In addition, 'fitting in' meant that professionals were required not only to subscribe to the system of joint practices, but also to reflect on team practice and to find ways to improve it. The 'system' was perceived as constantly evolving, and all staff were expected to offer advice and opinions on how to change things if they felt that they were not working for the benefit of all. For example, a junior therapist had joined the staff the previous year. After attending the rehabilitation planning meetings on a few occasions, she noticed that it was possible for one person to hold 'centre stage' for long periods without any decisions being made, and without sufficient input from the other professionals. She raised this issue at one of the meetings, it was discussed, and a tighter agenda for speaking in turn was devised which was not only popular, but was also considered to be a more effective use of people's knowledge and time.

A final requisite of 'fitting in' was that professionals would share their knowledge and skills with others and that these would be actively sought by all:

> If you work on your own you can get stuck into your own role, and your own ideas, and you don't learn from it, and so learning from others . . . and their help with the patient's progress, there's always something you can do to assist one another. So with speech therapy, if the SLT knows that it is short sharp commands and short sentences that a patient understands, then you're not going to talk and talk in long sentences and ask loads of questions in physio.
>
> (PT)

It was expected that while the skills and knowledge base would essentially remain the province of particular professions, sufficient would be shared to enable all members of the team to have a large area of common ground. Many staff spoke about their main function being as 'enablers of the patients', rather than wanting to promote their own specific input to patient care. For this reason they felt that whatever was required of them, if it was beneficial to the patient then professional divisions of knowledge or skills were not appropriate:

> We all need to come towards the patient, not all take a little bit away from that patient and work on it individually. And that's one of the main things that I like about here, and I don't know how easy I would feel fitting into another unit where that didn't happen.
>
> (PT)

There were two main outcomes of this culture that could be regarded as beneficial to both the professionals and the patients. First, there was the growth of team knowledge, both in relation to the patients and about each other. Secondly, there was the assumption of a learning environment, which was seen to support professional development. Acquiring knowledge about other team members' personal attributes, skills and expertise encouraged a high level of professional and collegiate trust among many professionals.

Being a team member for other teams in our study was a different experience. In the 'core and periphery' teams there was certainly a sense in which a *'team' culture had developed within the two core groups*, and where the experience of being a team member was similar to that of many individuals in the 'integrated' team. Peripheral members were not able to enter this culture for either organisational or historical reasons.

As with the 'integrated' team, the core group in the diabetes team had a long history of working with each other. This group had developed in a specific way that differentiated it from other members, and its history created a barrier to the coalition of these beliefs with others. With the additional input of a dietitian (long since moved on), this group had become involved in the *evolution* of the diabetes team – they were founder members. Although all of them had an extensive understanding of diabetes, they had attended conferences and given papers together in order to improve and maintain their knowledge. Furthermore, they had developed education in order to help other professionals to become acquainted with the problems of managing diabetes in the hospital and community settings. Indeed, they had helped to establish satellite diabetes clinics in general practices locally.

This process had involved a great deal of initial and ongoing discussion about the practicalities and the philosophy of the diabetes team. Through the process of team development they had gained an in-depth understanding of each other's strengths and weaknesses. As a result they trusted each other's judgement in circumstances where they themselves were not available. This was borne out by the gradual extension in the roles of the diabetes specialist nurse and the podiatrist. For example, the diabetes specialist nurse was able to start patients on insulin and would adjust the dosages of this drug accordingly. In addition, although she did not actually want the role, the consultant had been very keen for her to perform fundoscopy examination at the Yearly Review Clinic. The podiatrist made the following comment:

> They trust me to do the right thing, right or wrong. I think my scope of practice has changed quite a bit, like admissions. If I see a patient who I think needs admitting, I'll pick up the phone . . . and get them admitted there and then. But that takes time to raise your credibility stakes 'cos they have a need to know who they are devolving responsibility to. They need to know that person is OK who is doing it.
>
> (Podiatrist)

The dietitian had been promoted out of the team, but the three remaining members of this group still felt as if they were pioneers. The diabetes specialist nurse acknowledged her feelings about the strength of team cohesion that still existed for the 'triumvirate':

> I think we do make that mistake, we do sometimes forget other people I have to confess. We just think sometimes there's this triangle of [the podiatrist, the consultant] and me and it's wrong.
>
> (Diabetes specialist nurse)

For the other professionals in the team, despite the fact that they shared many of the core group's beliefs about teamworking, they were seldom given the opportunity to express these. As a result, for these individuals, being a team member was an undermining experience in which they felt that their skills were undervalued and they were not being heard. Unfortunately, this situation was compounded by the abrasive behaviour of the consultant. As was suggested in Chapter 3, his belief that all team members should be specifically designated and therefore able to give '100% to the team' was not met in the input of the chiropodists and dietitians.

In the child development assessment team, again being a team member was a different experience depending on whether one was a core group member or not. The culture in this core group also displayed many similarities to those of the rehabilitation team and the core of the diabetes team. Although they did not have the historical background of the other groups, several members had previous experience of working in teams with similar beliefs about teamworking, which they were able to transfer to their current setting (in the core group). Through their ability to focus on a shared client group, they had been able to make small, in-house changes to the organisation of their time. They had developed a system of assessment sessions and feedback forums, and a number of other forums for debate specific to case review. The assessment sessions incorporated the use of 'agreed' notes, in that discussion at the end of sessions facilitated the writing of notes which did not conflict, and which could be put together as a joint report for parents. Like many members of the diabetes and rehabilitation teams, they recognised the need for professionals to feel equally valued and able to demonstrate their skills and knowledge in order for each to learn from the others.

For the peripheral members of this team, being a team member was different again. In the diabetes team, peripheral members were frustrated by their exclusion and would gladly have joined the core group. In the child development assessment team, beliefs about teamworking outside the core group varied. A large number of team members were clearly aware of the need for a collaborative multiprofessional approach to patient care. They also recognised the benefits to patients identified by members of the rehabilitation and diabetes teams, and with one or two exceptions they were willing attenders at 'away-days' which addressed issues related to team practice to improve patient care.

For these professionals the reasons for their non-inclusion in the core group were largely organisational, as was discussed in Chapter 3. However, again there was an historical context that inhibited some professionals from being core group members. For some of the PTs, there had been a legacy of difficult relationships with members of the core group, fostered by perceptions of 'domineering' physiotherapy behaviour and unwillingness to collaborate (see Chapter 4). The PT supervisor described an incident that had occurred prior to the employment of the playroom teacher, when two nursery nurses had run some play sessions. Neither of them had specific training in the management of children with physical problems, and the supervisor perceived that the sessions 'were not functioning well'. The PTs took it upon themselves to help the nurses to learn about handling children who had conditions such as cerebral palsy. The details of these teaching sessions are not known, but evidently they had not been received well. Indeed, in an apparently direct response to this situation, one nurse had resigned her post. As a result, the PTs had been treated as 'black sheep' for some time.

As will be discussed in a later section, the style that professionals employ when sharing knowledge or informing others can inhibit involvement in the communication process and thus compromise professional development. However, this one incident would not have been sufficient to create a long-lasting effect, and it would need to be set in the context of an ongoing perception of such behaviours. This appeared to be the case. Others in the centre still described some of the PTs as 'bossy' and 'domineering', citing further evidence of a continued abrupt manner when dealing with other professionals, and with parents and children. Because the PTs did not work regularly with the core group, it is possible that earlier perceptions of the old behaviours became established as a barrier to developing ways of coping with this style.

We shall now consider the other teams which were more 'fragmented', and their understanding of being a team member. The degree of fragmentation that was experienced by these different groups of professionals would make it extremely difficult to form what could be defined as a team – that is, individuals who share a common goal and are working *together* towards that goal. For the medical ward in particular, it was difficult to identify themselves as being members of a multiprofessional team, as this shifted according to the composition of the patient groupings. Lacking a sense of 'teamness' meant that their own professional orientation was strong, and their attention to group processes was also monoprofessionally focused.

As was suggested earlier, the degree of awareness of any group as an entity would determine the level to which members would associate themselves with that entity and so be affected by its dynamics. For example, if the professionals working in the medical ward had a sense of 'teamness', then integration into that 'team' would have been an important issue for them. However, 'belonging' in that situation was primarily to one's own professional group. To a large extent this was true of both the CMHTs and the PHCT. All of them operated from a professional 'them and us' position, and the group issues discussed in this chapter need to be seen from that standpoint. With regard to the CMHTs and the PHCT, the former were organisationally defined as a team, and the latter had been, historically, but it now seemed to be a looser formation. All of the groups had several foci, which resulted in only some professionals sharing a goal, rather than the groups as a whole. Furthermore, where goals were shared, there were often different understandings of how they would be reached, as the different philosophical stances of the various professional groups were not resolved. Conflict and/or distancing mechanisms were rife.

Because of the distanced nature of their interaction, the beliefs and values of the separate professional groups in the medical ward were not accentuated through being brought into conflict or agreement with each other. (However, the assumption of primacy in decision-making among the medical profession and its effect on other professionals will be discussed later in this chapter.) They rarely interacted in a way that made these beliefs visible. The CMHTs, despite their fragmented activities, at least had an *organisational* awareness of being a 'team'. They were geographically located together, they were defined in documentation as a team, and they met weekly as 'teams'. However, to all intents and purposes team members operated as distinct professional groups. Since these groups were required to interact regularly (e.g. at team meetings), the nature of their separate 'ways of being' was more readily visible. These affected both 'team' relationships and the way in which clients were dealt with.

This section has examined the way in which being a *team* member, as opposed to simply a group of professionals who work separately but liaise with each other, incorporates the development of similar beliefs, which then inform team practice. Those who are outside this 'team' will have very different experiences of 'team membership'. The implication for student education is therefore as follows:

> Students should have an understanding of group process, in which they appreciate how group beliefs can develop, and the team culture which will 'fall out' of that development.

The following sections will examine more closely how individual beliefs held largely within professional cultures can affect team practice, and will look at the possibilities for multiprofessional working where a whole-team culture is achieved. In addition, the influence on team function of power and authority invested in certain professional groups will be explored.

THE TEAM ENVIRONMENT

In Chapter 3 we considered how *opportunities* for communication could be created or not. In Chapter 4 we identified the fact that individuals were *motivated* in different ways to communicate. Within the group situation we saw how *the culture (or cultures) within the team* defines the environment in which communication and role understanding do or do not flourish. Furthermore, the degree to which the team environment is perceived to be safe or unsafe will influence the success or otherwise of collaborative practices. To a large extent this will reflect the degree to which there is an agreed and valued set of beliefs about communication and role understanding. The alternatives to the team as a whole having an agreed set of beliefs may be either that one professional culture sets the pace for team practices, or that different professional cultures bring alternative (and potentially conflicting) beliefs.

Within the 'integrated' team we have identified the fact that a number of joint practices had developed through the team holding specific beliefs about being a team member, and in which there was a safe learning environment. It was expected and agreed that all team members would communicate openly and in depth with each other. It was also expected that they would be willing to understand *what* each member contributed to patient care, and *how and why* professionals practised in the way that they did. Fundamental to the development of these practices was the expectation that professionals would learn both knowledge and skills from each other in order to provide continuity and consistency of care. The outward display of team values such as openness, directness, reflection and respect reinforced the team's culture both to existing members and to new members of the team.

The joint working practices included dedicated times for clinical discussion and practice development, joint note-keeping, and joint clinical procedures such as assessment, problem identification, monitoring, therapeutic intervention and evaluation. However, it was acknowledged that the development of these practices was only the first step towards effective teamworking. For example, one feature of the team's working week was a regular one-and-a-half-hour clinical case discussion in which a systematic review of a percentage of the patients was discussed by all of the professionals assigned to those patients. This seemed to be a useful vehicle for ensuring effective communication. However, it simply represented the bare bones on which the team had to put the flesh (i.e. commitment to the process). Implicit in that process was the fact that *all* relevant professionals attended and contributed information about a particular patient. Challenge to the status quo was considered appropriate both at a specific clinical level and in terms of more general aspects of practice relating to patient care. These expectations implied that each professional's contribution was worth hearing, exploring and acting upon if this was agreed. The team attended not only to the primary reason for the meeting – that is, communication on specific patients – but also to team dynamics, ensuring parity of input, learning from each other, and responding to others' input. All of these factors were felt to support the motivation to communicate. The way in which this team functioned on a day-to-day basis thus had two components, namely providing effective patient therapy and care, and maintaining the team as an entity.

Communication in these meetings demonstrates how, through sharing professional perspectives, a more holistic picture of the patient could be constructed. This was associated with personal disclosure and the way in which some professionals may be able to obtain sensitive information from patients that can then alter their management. It derives from the particular relationship which professionals such as nurses are able to develop with their patients or clients, given that they are available to them during quiet, reflective moments and intimate situations when the disclosure of certain aspects of feelings and thoughts is possible. The way in which the nurses in the 'integrated' team were able to listen to patients in this way was described by one therapist:

> [They] are very good at picking up people's moods, whether they think somebody is depressed, so they would notice, and particularly recently they are the first ones to say that they need clinical psychology input of some sort, antidepressant or whatever.
>
> (SLT)

The following scenario illustrates how the nurses also extended these skills to the relatives of their patients. They operated a primary nursing model of care so that only a few nurses were responsible for a specific patient. In this way they came to know their patients extremely well. They were also available for carers and relatives who wanted to unburden themselves of particular concerns. In one clinical meeting a nurse was talking about a patient who had been taken back into hospital after having had a major fit which resulted in a considerable reduction in his cognitive skills. She described a long conversation she had had over the weekend with the man's wife, who had wanted to express her feelings about the impact that this event had had on her. For example, she was worried about her decision to take a holiday. After hearing about this case, the director decided that he would telephone the patient's wife and ask if she would like an appointment to see him. This was arranged, and the director was able to help the woman to reach a decision, and suggest to her a strategy for addressing this subject with the patient. Respite care in the unit was arranged and the patient's wife was able to take the holiday without feeling that she was 'abandoning' her husband at this difficult time.

Being prepared to explore these aspects of patient care, and then to discuss them in an open forum where individuals expected to be heard, enabled the team to develop an understanding of the patient in the context of therapeutic and care interventions, their relationships outside the unit, and their future life after discharge. As a result it was seen that far more 'accurate and appropriate decisions' could be made with regard to the rehabilitation process.

With regard to understanding roles, members of the 'integrated' team would identify that this demands that professionals are prepared to display what they do, and to talk about how they are practising, and why. Within a hospital setting many professionals work behind closed doors (or bed curtains). In the rehabilitation setting, much of the work was undertaken in open areas such as the gym. This could initially be quite intimidating, but there were several perceived benefits to this way of working. Team members felt that it could provide a quick means of learning about other professions' practice, so enabling professionals to understand how they could 'slot into' programmes of therapy. It could also increase the confidence of new members, as they would be able to learn skills appropriate to their own profession. In addition, it could enable patients to see professionals combining their skills and expertise not only in their own case, but for other patients as well. One SLT, despite her early qualms about having to be regularly on display, was clearly convinced:

> I mean what are you actually assessing when you are on your own, if you don't have a physio there who can facilitate the physical responses, pointing or whatever. Or in physio if they are working on learning the components of an action, and that client can't understand them or can't remember them, and it looks like they just can't do it physically, then what is actually going on here? You can't see it unless you've got different disciplines involved, different bodies of knowledge.
>
> (SLT)

Within this environment of openness of communication and practice and willingness to be observed, it had to be safe to ask questions and to express ideas that might be felt to be 'irrelevant' or 'silly':

> You are allowed to make mistakes . . . you are given a lot of responsibility as for example in 'how long is this person going to need'? or whatever. But you know that when you give your opinion, that later if you want to revise that opinion you can, and people won't say 'oh, you got that wrong' . . . . As long as you have got reasons for things then that's OK. You *are* allowed to do that, and you *feel* that you are allowed to do that.
>
> (SLT)

Where professionals felt able to learn from each other, had watched others practice, and had developed programmes of care and therapy that had positive outcomes for the patient, there was a high level of trust. The one exception to this level of learning safety occurred when the new clinical psychologist joined the team. As has already been stated, he surrounded his practice with secrecy, much to the disappointment, frustration and ultimate resentment of other members of the team. Such was the tension between most of the team members and this professional that eventually he left.

In the 'core and periphery', working across the whole teams there were various competing cultures. A team culture, within which learning from each other was expected, was limited to the core groups. Within the teams as a whole, the problems already identified in Chapters 3 and 4, and in the earlier section on the historical aspect of team membership, all had a bearing on the development of a learning environment.

In the first of these, namely the diabetes team, the status of the consultant in the core group, and his use of power to control communication had the effect of stifling input from peripheral members. For example, weekly meetings were held which were supposed to be weekly case reviews. However, in the course of our study this agenda was not pursued. Instead the meetings were used by the consultant to 'talk at' other members. It was observed that if one of the core members (e.g. the specialist nurse) was absent, the consultant conducted a monologue, virtually lecturing all of the others about new research findings, for example. Often the only other voice heard was that of the senior registrar, with whom the consultant 'sparred'. When the specialist nurse was present she was able to challenge the consultant, as was noted by the podiatrist:

> [DSN1] knows that if there is anything [the consultant] has said that is unpalatable, she'll challenge it, it won't fester, and she'll say 'exactly what do you mean?'. She makes the communication.
>
> (Podiatrist)

Because of her challenging style, the specialist nurse was able to steer the conversation towards other issues, but it was still difficult for other members of the team to make an impact. In these situations the specialist nurse was regularly left to contribute to the conversation in order to attempt to make an entry point for others. Communicating under these circumstances became safer and easier to do by letter, which was a common occurrence.

The division between the two groups of team members was sharply focused by this difference in communication. The extent to which it could limit exchange knowledge and information could be damaging, given that this was the only time set aside for formal case discussion. Members of the core group pursued the discussion during clinic sessions, but lack of core membership inhibited others from taking ad hoc opportunities in the same way. Consequently, other members of the team relied on the specialist nurses for their channels of communication (this bridging role will be discussed further in a later section).

In the other 'core and periphery' team, namely the child development assessment team, the emphasis was different. Here it was the lack of preparedness on the part of peripheral members to communicate that caused dislocation between the two groups. For example, there were tensions related to sharing information and knowledge with the clinical psychologists. As suggested earlier, confidentiality was put forward as one reason why they did not share with others. This left other professionals, who were caring for some of the same patients, unaware of aspects of *their* patients' progress, unprepared as to how to deal with difficult behaviour, and lacking in understanding of what clinical psychology actually contributed to the team. This situation gave rise to an environment of distrust and secrecy, where core members in particular became extremely wary about even attempting to communicate with the clinical psychologists. As with the diabetes team, information was sent and requested by letter, with core members perceiving that this was not only unsatisfactory, but further limited what they *could* know of these professionals' role. As a further outcome, others interpreted the secrecy with which the clinical psychologists operated as undervaluing their own professional integrity: 'We're all professionals here, I don't understand what they are going on about, we all have to abide by the same principles; what's so special about their knowledge?' (CD).

In Chapter 4 we commented that all professionals within health care and social services expect to enter into a confidential relationship with their patients or clients. In the case of clinical psychology, it could be argued that the main purpose of any such service should be to meet the needs of the client, and that failing to protect disclosures made during therapy sessions would *not* meet their needs, unless it was related to the safety of a child, for example. However, most of the professionals, particularly those in the core group, complained that they had little or no feedback, even though they had been directly involved in the referral. The concept of a degree of team knowledge being allowable within the confines of confidentiality did not appear to be tolerated by the clinical psychology group. This level of knowledge guarding obviously impacted on how other professionals would be able to co-ordinate their service, but it would also compromise their own input to a particular child or family.

In all of the 'fragmented' teams there were professionals who considered there to be 'unsafe' environments in which learning from one another, either about patients or clients, or about each other's contribution to the team, would be difficult. This related either to the wielding of professional power, or to the meeting between different professional cultures that gave rise to professional defensiveness, or both. As we have suggested in Chapter 4, the increasing emphasis on teamworking within trusts would be likely to increase professional defensiveness among those for whom rigid role boundaries are important, and where the importance of communication is limited to giving information on a 'need to know' basis.

Within the PHCT, the way in which some of the GPs chose to limit information and to control who attended meetings effectively created a 'divide and rule' environment. This type of approach gave rise to circumstances where, for example, professionals could be dismissed from meetings in order for others to discuss clinical or business issues. This comment from a practice nurse illustrates the effects of operating in this fashion:

> I've been invited to a couple of the meetings, and one time I was sent out of the room because they were discussing something they didn't want me to hear. I found it all quite upsetting . . . it's happened to the practice manager as well. It's like treating you as a child and I feel very strongly about that. At the end of the day we are all here for the patients and that goes a bit out of the window.
>
> (Practice nurse)

This was perceived as unnecessary secrecy by several members in the team, and it gave rise to feelings of resentment because it constrained what could and could not be voiced by others. In this way roles could also be contained, as the distancing of professionals from each other in order to discuss their practice would inhibit opportunities for practice development and thus for collaboration.

Of the 'fragmented' teams, the least helpful environment for learning was seen in the CMHTs. In this setting not only did the consultant psychiatrists use their power to stifle communication, but as already discussed in Chapter 4, many of the CPNs subscribed to beliefs which were antithetical to teamwork. These two factors together constitute the worst possible combination of both use of power and differing professional culture, which can preclude others from learning from and developing an understanding of other team members. The use of power to inhibit a learning environment will be discussed further later in this section. However, the way in which some of the CPNs operated had a major impact on their communication, on the management of feelings related to dealing with more problematic clients, and thus on team practice.

The differences between several of the CPNs and the social workers and OT caused misunderstanding between these two groups. During the period of this study, there were many changes to the 'teams', including reorganisation into smaller groups, removal of some members to another area, and the transfer of the remaining members to a new site. Both managers and consultants were blamed for the way in which the changes were handled, and the CPNs and social workers were anxious and angry as a result. However, the social workers and the new OT expressed their feelings openly, as they did about many other aspects of their work. The CPNs also expressed anxiety and anger, but seldom in the open arena – instead they chose to speak among themselves. The different approaches had different interpretations. As the social workers and the OT were in general very vocal, often discussing their feelings about a particular client and the management of the case, they obtained support from other team members. However, this was sometimes interpreted by the CPNs and their manager as 'spilling out' inappropriately. Indeed, some individuals felt that this vocalisation was unprofessional.

By comparison, the CPNs' apparent silence within the team was interpreted by the social workers as apathy. The CPNs were regarded as neither challenging the status quo by themselves, nor being prepared to act with the social workers and OT. Thus their response was viewed as frustrating, and was perceived as a lack of support on issues common to all professional groups within the team setting. Furthermore, the CPNs' silence was sometimes interpreted by the social workers as deferral to the consultants (the consultants' behaviour having often prompted the anger in the first place). If the social workers expressed their feelings openly to the consultants in meetings, the CPNs felt that this was damaging. Neither professional group felt that open debate of feelings was 'safe'. The CPNs coped by remaining silent, and the social workers (finally) by removing themselves from weekly meetings. The subsequent lack of unified response across the social work and CPN professions may have been an important factor with regard to the problems of communication with the consultants.

Newcomers to the teams, such as social work and CPN students, noticed the way in which professionals maintained separation from each other: 'People come in, work and sometimes that [their distanced behaviour] is shown in lack of eye contact; they want to get to their desk, head down, that's it, no discussion' (Social work student).

When professionals *did* meet to talk about clients, this was done in a manner reminiscent of a stereotypical ward round in which one person asks all of the questions and others simply respond. In the context of a learning environment, it was clear that the consultants' input suppressed that of others, and therefore restricted what could be learned. During observation sessions in this study several meetings were seen where challenges were made by some social workers to decisions made by the psychiatrists. One was considered to be more overtly dismissive than the other, and during his meetings outright but unresolved conflict occurred between himself and other professionals, particularly the social workers. It was considered 'a dangerous place to be'. Those who held very different ideas about how teamworking should be developed, such as the social workers and the OT, found the meetings 'destructive' both in terms of progressing client care and on a personal level. As suggested above, and as a mark of the extent of their feelings, social workers opted out of many of the meetings. The OT chose to stay, but felt invisible because of the way in which the psychiatrist effectively controlled the nature of the meetings:

> I haven't even been given permission to put my referrals down on that piece of paper . . . and it's like I'm not even there; I'm not allowed to get my people down on to the patient list so I don't exist; my work doesn't exist.
>
> (OT)

Such an environment is the antithesis of that seen in the 'integrated' team and the core groups of the 'core and periphery' teams. The difficulty for those who would wish to see different and more collaborative patterns of working is that they may be lone voices in the wilderness, either because of lack of willingness on the part of others to join them, or because of frank distaste for this approach. It begs the question of why it should be *possible* for some professionals to constrain the development of greater collaboration in a multiprofessional team. Again this has implications for student education.

> Students need to understand that teamworking demands the sharing of knowledge, and can benefit from the sharing of skills, and that this can be done in a way which is not detrimental to the specialist role of each professional.

Having examined the culture of the teams in our study we shall now look more closely at the way in which some of roles in the teams contributed to the level of multiprofessional collaboration. We shall begin with the leadership role and the ways in which different leadership styles may facilitate or inhibit collaborative practices.

LEADERSHIP STYLES AND THEIR INFLUENCE ON TEAMWORK

The way in which a team brings together the different aspects of its work and makes decisions about the management of patient or client care relies on the ability of a person, or persons within the team to take responsibility for co-ordination, or bringing the decision-making process to a conclusion. The ways in which this is achieved vary widely, and we do not intend to make any judgement ourselves about the relative benefits of one approach over another. However, in this section we want *to differentiate the notion of leadership from the mere use of power*. We shall demonstrate the way in which *different approaches to leadership did or did not foster collaborative working*. The implications for all professionals in terms of those who lead and those who respond to that leadership will be examined, and the considerations which therefore need to be given to education processes to enhance collaborative working will be made clear.

Other than co-operative groups, all teams have some form of leadership. This can refer to one person taking that role by dint of status (i.e. the power to lead resides in the role). Alternatively, it can occur where a person is chosen for some particular skill or expertise that they have (and this can relate to different people taking a lead role by dint of the task involved). Whatever form it takes, the term 'leadership' is used to denote a wide variety of behaviours, ranging from the more democratic and facilitative (or transformational) to the more autocratic (Bass *et al.*, 1996). All of these may be appropriate for different teams, at different stages in their evolution, and for different tasks. However, within this framework, the motivation of other team members to subscribe to a particular type of leadership relies on this person being viewed as worthy. Their actions need to be seen as enhancing the work of the team, and in a way which keeps team members 'on board' (e.g. Hersey and Blanchard, 1982). In this sense, simply using the power which may reside in a particular role to push through decisions which prove unsuccessful or unpopular will do little to foster allegiance to a 'leader'. Nor will using power in a way that undermines personal interactions between the 'leader' and other team members assist in effective working. Leadership theory (Hersey and Blanchard, 1982; Schein, 1985) suggests that support for leadership must be earned. Where it is imposed, there is the potential for subversive or defensive behaviour.

What types of leadership were seen in the different types of teamworking observed in our study, and what influence did that leadership have? Within the 'integrated team', the director was perceived as an 'inspirational leader'. Bass and colleagues (1996) describe a form of leadership known as 'transformational' in which the leader: 'creates new scenarios and visions, challenges the status quo, initiates new approaches and excites the creative and emotional drive to individuals to strive beyond the ordinary to deliver the exceptional'.

The director was viewed in this way by almost all team members. Together with the heads of the professional groups in the team he was seen to have been instrumental in creating and ensuring the continuation of a team culture which promoted highly effective teamwork. Unlike 'leaders' in some of the other types of teams (and reinforced by other research; see, for example, Poulton and West, 1993), he did not simply pay lip-service to the notion of multiprofessional collaboration, but worked continuously to promote a collaborative culture. Comments similar to the following were frequently voiced by team members: 'He's the kind of ultimate role model of how we should be working' (OT).

The director felt that the approach he had developed stemmed partly from his previous experience of working with 'difficult' groups of adolescents and, through his training as a social worker, his understanding of the group process. He recognised that although a team may develop structures and processes which could ensure effective communication and encourage individuals to learn about each other's roles, the *manner* in which this occurs must support their continued development. Simply providing the space and time for people to discuss patient care or talk about the development of practice is not sufficient to ensure that this is done effectively. Nor is it sufficient to put into place joint processes for practice. *People need to see their relevance and feel motivated to adhere to them.*

The director's keyword was openness, and many other aspects of the team's culture sprang from this value. Other team members commented on how strongly this had permeated the team: 'you have to communicate, go and talk to someone face to face, deal with it there and then, don't put things off, don't give mixed messages, be direct, be honest, be straight with people' (PT).

He recognised and put into practice strategies for encouraging openness in difficult circumstances, and he provided practical and emotional support to help resolve problems related to both patient care and team relationships. In order to do this, individuals in the team felt that he had 'acutely focused antennae' which quickly detected problems. Having done this he was seen to respond and to discuss potential courses of action, letting team members see that their opinions and ideas could result in changes to practice. His preference for openness encouraged the sharing of information and knowledge, and the voicing of concerns, both related to patients' conditions and to professionals' feelings of pleasure or inadequacy in dealing with them.

For example, in a meeting that included members of all professions and the director, a therapist was talking about a patient who was becoming upset at her lack of progress. The therapist was also finding this situation difficult to deal with, and she became rather distressed. She said 'how do you comfort someone who is making an accurate statement?'. The director agreed that it was difficult, but that one of the worst things would be 'to pat her on the head', as it was not an honest way of dealing with people. Another team member agreed that the patient's feelings were not easy to manage, and offered a strategy for enabling her to share her emotions by saying 'you could reflect back to her what she is saying to you and let her talk about her feelings'. The director added that it might be useful to 'keep success and failure out of the conversation', and he gave an example of how the situation could be dealt with in a more neutral manner. The therapist thanked those who had contributed ideas and said 'I don't feel so bad now, because I know that you feel the same; I don't feel it's just me now'.

This scenario was particularly useful for showing how the expression of anxieties and the fostering of coping strategies were encouraged by the director. This reinforced his position as an integral member of the team, and someone before whom people felt safe displaying these feelings.

In addition to providing an appropriate role model, the director encouraged a democratic team process. Although he was aware that he could have the final say in decision-making, he understood that many decisions had to be owned by the team in order to facilitate establishment of actions. Indeed, since he had no clinical skills (in terms of therapy or nursing), he could not have acted alone. One of his strongest attributes, as perceived by others, was an awareness of his own limitations – he knew what he knew, and he did not hesitate to ask for guidance and advice if he was unsure. As such, he 'set the pace' for people to ask questions in order to expand their own knowledge. Because of this self-awareness there were no qualms among the professional groups about his assessing patients for admission. People felt that they could trust him to call upon their professional opinion as required.

Despite the universal acknowledgement of his leadership abilities, some nurses in the team rued his lack of medical expertise, almost as an umbrella encompassing their own role. The wish for a consultant to lead the unit may also have been related to their perceived lack of nursing support and the way in which the medical cover provided by local GPs was considered to be both ineffective and a source of antagonism. However, it also highlighted the interdependency which nurses have with the medical profession, and indeed the less autonomous nature of some nursing practice – both factors which related to the effects of medical leadership in other teams.

Many aspects of leadership such as was demonstrated in the integrated team, have been identified as important in fostering effective teamworking (Tappen and Touhy, 1983; Goldenberg, 1990; Pearson and Spencer, 1995; Onyett *et al.*, 1996). There was no doubt that, *for the type of specialism in which this team was working*, this person's approach had promoted the development of a highly collaborative and effective team. Furthermore, this was done in keeping with a stated philosophy of a problem-focused, multiprofessional approach to patient care (i.e. he directed the team in its practice, and helped to provide structures and processes which would make the philosophy manifest). As was suggested in Chapter 2, the benefits that we identified for patients were only seen consistently in this setting, and this was reinforced by records of progress made by patients over time, matched to accurate predictions of progress by the team members.

Although this director used ascribed power – that is, power situated in the role – it was also felt that he did so having earned credibility as a leader – that is, power situated in the person. His credibility as a leader, and through that the willingness on the part of other team members to follow his direction, was not found elsewhere. A more common scenario, particularly among the 'fragmented' teams, was one where the most powerful team member made decisions, but did not act as a leader. Alternatively, the most powerful team member acted as a leader, whether this was deemed appropriate or not by other team members.

The perpetuation of the 'medical model' in many secondary and primary care settings fosters the assumption of primacy in decision-making by senior members of the medical profession. Since some members of the medical profession seem to perceive that they still carry the ultimate legal responsibility for patient care, it is not surprising that they should continue to view themselves as being in this position of indispensable leadership. A comment from one of the senior house officers in the medical ward illustrates the cultural divide with regard to perceived responsibility. Nurses were seen as having limited, dispersible responsibility, whereas doctors would carry an ongoing burden of care – the patients they looked after were indeed 'their patients':

> It's because nurses work set hours, they go for their coffee breaks, they go for their lunch breaks, and they go home and they hand over to someone else. I have no one else to hand over to at five o'clock. I go home and there's an on-call team, but they are only there for emergencies.
>
> (Senior house officer)

However, the fact that one professional group perceives itself to be responsible for making decisions does not mean that this needs to be done in a way which alienates, suppresses and undermines other members of the team. Previous research has shown however that this is often the case (Busby and Gilchrist, 1992; Mallik, 1992; Whale, 1993), particularly where interactions between doctors and nurses are being explored. Despite changes in the education of nurses, and some moves to change the emphasis of medical training (General Medical Council, 1997), it seems that shifting the prevailing cultures of both professions is more difficult to achieve. In our study, evidence of and collusion with these behaviours was common. They were identified where we saw 'fragmented' working, and in one 'core and periphery' team, where interaction between peripheral members and the consultant was problematic.

In all three 'fragmented' teams the use of medical power without actual leadership was seen to be detrimental to aspects of teamwork such as communication and developing a shared focus. For example, in the medical ward, the visiting consultants expected their decisions to be adhered to, without necessarily having taken into account the input that other professionals would have regarded as important. This unilateral approach was often spoken about and observed with regard to the discharge process. In this setting a consultant would come to the patient's bedside and tell them that they could go home. This would be said without consultation with nursing or other staff to ascertain whether they, too, considered that it would be appropriate for the patient to leave hospital. Whilst to make this statement to other team members is acceptable, as it may simply be expressing the view that *medically* the patient is ready for discharge, to say it to the patient assumes an end-point of that decision. Behaviour such as this presumes that only this decision is worthwhile, and it can therefore be a source of much frustration to other professionals.

This behaviour was also accompanied by a style of communication that compounded the frustration. Although, in general terms, the nurses were the professionals who commented most frequently about this issue in our study, members of other professional groups such as physiotherapists and pharmacists also made comments about the 'closed attitudes' of some consultants, which they felt disallowed their contribution. These 'closed attitudes' could be translated into intimidating behaviour. One senior PT noted of a consultant that he frequently 'snapped the heads off' her colleagues when they 'dared to suggest alternative ways of doing things'. Other professionals' ability to deal effectively with senior doctors was also limited in this setting.

The image of the abrasive consultant has not disappeared, and while new intakes of medical students may acquire more comprehensive communication skills, and a different perception of their role in the multiprofessional team, they still have the role model of their consultants to follow when they first practise. It was acknowledged that intimidating behaviour was seen in some junior doctors, a typical statement made by others being 'you can see what sort of consultant they are going to make when they first arrive, some of them are so arrogant'. Nurses' responses to these behaviours were mixed. In the medical ward, 'fighting fire with fire' was deemed by some experienced nurses to be an acceptable response to more junior doctors who displayed such behaviour. As we have already mentioned, one male nurse continued to behave in this relatively assertive manner with the more senior medical staff, believing strongly that he was required to contribute as the patient's advocate. More commonly, however, nurses and other professionals felt unable to respond in a way that helped them to communicate comprehensively. They felt too inhibited to give *all* of the information they had gathered, and unable to express their professional opinion. This can have the effect of restricting the development of a wide-ranging picture of the patient's progress (i.e. 'team knowledge' through the sharing of professional perspectives).

During medical ward rounds in our study, knowledge required by doctors from other professionals about a patient related specifically to their medical condition, rather than other factors which might impinge on that illness. This information-gathering process, as defined by the consultant, rather than a multiprofessional input of ideas, has been reported in other research (e.g. Busby and Gilchrist, 1992). Decisions about patient interventions are made on the basis of this limited input, and should other professionals disagree, it is not always easy to make their case. For example, nurses spoke about the way in which their assessment plans, and the progress that the patient was making in relation to those plans, were not taken into account by consultants. In general, the consultants' interest was in the latest physical observations, and in the results of any medical investigations. The nurses felt that the ongoing nature of their input gave them the opportunity to observe and act upon subtle changes. They also had an awareness of the psychological factors contributing to health. In combination, this gave them an understanding of the patient's specific response to their illness, and how psychological factors might have contributed to the illness in the first place. However, in all but one of the ward rounds we observed, enquiries from the consultants or other medical staff did not include such aspects of patient progress. The nurses *could* have put forward their own views but, since several of the senior medical staff were seen to be abrupt and 'dismissive' in their behaviour, this was not easy to achieve.

'Standing up to the docs' requires considerable stamina, and it may be that

nurses simply accommodate to these behaviours, whilst continuing their own paths of care. Unfortunately, this is seen to reinforce the lesser value attributed to them by many doctors (e.g. Adshead and Dickenson, 1993). In the case of the CMHTs, this collusion with the emphasis on medical input to decision-making was recognised and resented by other professionals such as social workers in the team. One might imagine that the transposing of the medical profession from the acute setting, where 'life and death' medical decisions may well necessarily reside with that profession, into the community, where this does not automatically apply, would change the power imbalance. However, this was not the case. Both consultant psychiatrists made arbitrary clinical decisions, like many of the consultants in the medical ward, wielding power without necessarily leading the team.

Weekly meetings of one of these CMHTs were extremely uncomfortable. During these meetings, a list of clients derived from the consultant's most recent out-patient clinics, together with new discharges from the in-patient facility, would be used as a source of 'discussion'. Despite other professionals identifying that they had other clients to talk about, the consultant expected that only people on 'the list' would be discussed during the meetings. Furthermore, as with many consultants in the medical ward, this professional's communication style was felt to be brusque. Interactions between this person and several other members of the team were reminiscent of the medical ward consultants' rounds. The CPNs in general responded to the consultant by offering only the information that they felt would be listened to (i.e. they tended to 'play the game'. They often kept their counsel and, as was suggested earlier, their silence was sometimes construed by the social workers as deferral. The social workers were generally more vocal and attempted to make known their views and beliefs about how a particular client should be managed.

This lack of ability by other professionals to make it known which clients *they* would like to discuss has clear implications for the effectiveness of teams such as CMHTs. Without a systematic review of clients who are being seen by all members of the team, it is possible for people to 'fall through the net'. The manner in which this consultant used his power to influence the nature of these meetings was undoubtedly detrimental in terms of the team being able to offer comprehensive care that reached all of the relevant clients.

Meetings of the second CMHT in this study were also problematic because of their consultant's behaviour. This team did have a more systematic approach to client review (incorporating discussion around new referrals, monitoring of current clients, and specific problems from the previous week). However, this had not been developed as an all-encompassing system, where all professionals' clients were regularly discussed. Despite the consultant's espoused ideas about team leadership, he attempted to achieve this by autocratic rather than democratic means. As was mentioned in Chapter 4, he was renowned for making decisions on behalf of others without prior discussion with either the professional or their clients. The situation in which he was informing clients that their CPN would no longer be visiting them, without discussing the matter first with the CPN, had been occurring for some time.

Although to a large extent the CPNs in this team colluded with the consultant's behaviour, their anger at his actions finally caused one of them to challenge him. His lack of helpful response and his apparent inability to comprehend how this might have affected the relevant CPNs highlights the fact that, despite his avowed beliefs, as far as he was concerned teamworking did not include valuing other professional input.

The level of professional autonomy that is still retained by members of the medical profession, harnessed to a position (although not necessarily reality) as clinical team leader, can create great problems for other team members with regard to developing a shared approach to team care. For example, many professional roles within the PHCT, such as the midwife, HV and district nurse, while they have some autonomy in their patient or client management, exist within a trust framework of general strategies for action, such as protocols and guidelines. If we set aside the argument that these may limit professional judgement (e.g. Scholes, 1998), they are intended to ensure that specific standards of care are adhered to, that the most efficient and effective use of professional resources is made, and that the amount of ambiguous advice and information being given to patients is minimised. Where these are developed as cross-professional processes, the opportunities for developing shared approaches to patient care are enhanced within a team.

Although the advent of clinical governance may alter circumstances, GPs may have no such clear expectations made public of their treatment or the management of their practice. Indeed, in our study they were perceived to have no specific direction for their practice within the PHCT at all. With one exception, they responded to the needs of their patients, but without considering proactive strategies that could be implemented with other professionals, in keeping with trust guidelines. These could have included topics such as the treatment of head lice or the management of breastfeeding. Despite the fact that GP involvement in these matters is often minimal, their lack of acknowledgement or adherence to procedures defined by the trust had left other professionals unsure how to proceed with regard to certain issues, and unclear about their role as part of the PHCT.

Evidence from senior trust management across a number of trusts supports the notion that doctors are often loath to follow prescribed guidelines. For example, in the development of integrated care pathways (ICP), doctors have been perceived to absent themselves from relevant meetings. Not surprisingly, this has given rise to negative perceptions of the potential success of a particular strategy:

> We have used a stroke pathway throughout the winter emergencies initiative to provide the framework for the stroke team. We've got evidence locally that it can work. But getting the medical staff on board has been difficult. It is frustrating and I have tried every which way in.
>
> (Manager 3)

The inertia shown by some doctors with regard to identified trust processes may stem from threats to their autonomy within that framework. However, it also attests to the continued strength of their power despite organisational changes to reduce it. The ability to use this option to remain distant from structures and processes to which others are bound does little to enhance collaboration, and thus to promote teamwork. Yet many doctors are still the assumed leaders of multiprofessional teams and, as we have seen, this was not viewed positively by many other members of the teams that we studied.

By the same token, some professionals have responded by colluding with this behaviour, in the sense that they avoided conflict by keeping quiet at times when they could have been ensuring that a wider basis for decision-making was provided. Those who did challenge this behaviour, such as the male nurse in the medical ward team, and the OT and some social workers in the CMHT, had some limited success in influencing the decision-making process.

One other professional was seen to overcome such behaviours. This was the diabetes specialist nurse in one of the 'core and periphery' teams. It was clear that in this situation, and despite his alienating behaviour towards the other team members, the consultant in this team perceived himself as a friend and professional equal of this nurse. In turn, she saw that discussions with the consultant were as likely to include specific clinical discussion as professional support. She felt that the experience she had developed in day-to-day management of diabetes was listened to and acknowledged by the consultant; he came to *her* for advice on particular areas of patient care. She was seen to 'cut through' the consultant's communication by changing the subject, disagreeing with him, and being an advocate for other team members. Her position of parity in the core group had developed partly because of the particular historical context and partly because of her experience in the management of diabetes. However, it was also related to her skills in challenging. As in the case of the male nurse, the social workers and the OT, she believed passionately that her contribution was vital for the well-being of her patients, and she was prepared to 'fight fire with fire' in the same way as the nurses identified earlier in this section challenged the more junior doctors.

The lack of response to powerful others in a team has been noted among overseas nurses who come to work in the UK, as have their 'scathing [comments] about home-grown nurses' refusals to question doctors' decisions or to take responsibility' (MacKay, 1993, p. 122). This difference in approach has been related to socio-cultural and historical factors in the UK which have influenced the relationships between the medical and in particular the nursing professions. However, the adversarial nature of medical education and the hitherto largely unreflective nature of nursing education have also played a part, and both need to be considered if collaborative working is to become established as part of health care.

> Students from all professions need to understand the benefit of developing communication styles that maximise all professional input into the decision-making process with regard to patient care.

They also need to understand that powerful roles within a team can undermine others' role value in the team. Communicating consistently and assertively in order to have a voice in the team is a vital skill to learn.

This section has shown that nurses and other professionals still need to find ways of ameliorating the emphasis on medical-led care, and by implication medical input into discussion and decisions about patient management. The assumption of medical power within the multiprofessional team, and the effects of communication style by some members of this profession, have been shown to limit nurses' and other professionals' contributions to those discussions and decisions. Reflecting on the collaboration within the 'integrated' team, we can see how a leadership style which encourages contribution, through an awareness of the value which each team member brings to decision-making, promotes team motivation and support. However, the level of discussion that was enjoyed in this team may not be possible or indeed desirable for all teams in every situation. For example, in a critical-care setting, the need for one person to be making swift decisions for team action would, of necessity, rule out lengthy debate. However, underpinning any effective leadership should be recognition of how best to develop a team culture in which collaboration is sustainable, and which assumes that all members are valued. This relates, not only to what they do in the team, but also to the body of knowledge and skills which their profession represents.

Our study demonstrates that unless doctors are willing to engage in genuinely collaborative teamwork, it will not happen. Nurses may represent the largest number of clinical staff in the NHS, but it is universally acknowledged that the dominant professional group is the medical profession. For example, Soothill and colleagues made the following comment:

> Doctors enjoy undoubted supremacy in the management and direction of the health care team. Without doctors' goodwill to listen, the contributions of other professionals can be marginalised. Interprofessional working, in other words, is a question of the redistribution of power in health care. Other than in the interests of patients, there seems little reason why doctors should accede to demands to power-share. Why should one professional group embark on a process of decision-making which reduces its power and makes decision-making a slower and more laborious process?
>
> (Soothill *et al.* 1995, p. 8)

Soothill and colleagues believe that changes in the NHS will compel doctors to change. Government initiatives to improve efficiency and cost-effectiveness, changes in both management structure and the type and style of manager, and pressures for accountability (currently manifest in clinical governance) will all tend to diminish 'medical supremacy'. Yet, as those authors identify, these changes and pressures might indicate that this is the worst time to bring in further changes in working practices. More optimistically, they comment that attempts to improve interprofessional collaboration and teamworking 'may well be the antidote to the disorienting changes in the NHS' (Soothill *et al.*, 1995, p. 10) as different professionals come together in adversity. It would seem that this has yet to happen – indeed what has been observed more frequently is people striving to maintain the status quo in times of stress.

From the discussion in Chapter 3 on the organisational issues that may constrain collaborative teamworking, this is all too evident. Bed-management policies, resulting in a spread of working across many wards in acute care, heavy workloads and shortages of staff, militate against such collaborative practices. However, it is possible that new policies such as Integrated Patient Care, practised by closely collaborative teams, would be effective in bolstering morale, assuming that the will is there. This is a crucial point. As suggested earlier we noted that some members of the medical profession have sabotaged the instigation of care pathways (e.g. by opting out of the evolution of the process). Managers face the dilemma of how to bring unwilling professionals into the collaborative arena. Yet the various professional bodies, including the General Medical Council (in a response to the research team), seem to support the notion of collaborative working:

> We believe that making the best possible use of the skills and abilities of both doctors and nurses contributes significantly to good patient care and the effective use of resources. These objectives can be achieved only where all professionals work together and understand and respect each other's roles and abilities. Indeed, we have already taken some steps towards encouraging doctors to work constructively with nurses. We believe that good interprofessional relationships should be established as early as possible in the training of doctors, and this is reflected in our guidance *Tomorrow's Doctors* and *The New Doctor*.
>
> (General Medical Council, 1993)

This recommendation for medical training seems helpful. However, more radical steps may need to be taken to encourage medical students to understand other professional perspectives and rationales more comprehensively, and to enhance their willingness to listen to others' input. It is possible that their inclusion in a shared learning process with other professional groups, as part of their initial education, could produce these outcomes.

Having identified the contribution of one specific team role (i.e. the leader), we shall now move on to examine other professionals' role contribution in the team.

TASK AND TEAM ROLE CONTRIBUTION

As members of a multiprofessional team, *the roles that professionals take on within that context may be both clinical and serve a group dynamic function*. In this section we shall examine two aspects of role as part of the group process. The first relates to *role differentiation and how this shapes individuals' perceptions of their own value to the multiprofessional team*. The second aspect concerns *ways in which some professionals can develop roles that bring together various other team members* (that is, they play a *bridging role* within the team).

We shall begin by looking at the way in which *lack of clarity of role* may prevent some professionals from seeing the importance of their own contribution to the team. Implicit in the concept of a multiprofessional team is the fact that each profession has its own specific and unique contribution to make. Other research (Iles and Auluck, 1990; Gibbon, 1992; Field and West, 1995) has shown that in order to achieve 'effective teamwork', not only do individual professionals need an appreciation of other members' roles and their contribution to patient care, but they also require a clear understanding of their own role in the team.

We have spoken at length in previous chapters about the development of role understanding as an important feature of teamwork. Knowing what team members do and why they do it enables professionals to determine how roles within a multiprofessional context fit together to provide patient care. However, this presupposes that each professional has a clear understanding of exactly how their *own* role contributes to the process of care, and within that understanding, an appreciation of the *importance* of that contribution within the multiprofessional context. In our study those individuals who felt that they had this clarity of role also perceived their value to the function of the multiprofessional team. However, as will be seen, these role perceptions were not evident among all professional groups. For example, some nurses were unclear about their role, and about its value to patient care. Furthermore, despite the fact that some other professionals had a clear understanding of, and valued their own contribution, others in the teams did not share these views.

As an example of the former case, members of the 'integrated' rehabilitation team in general had very clear ideas about their roles, and the confidence to perform them. This confidence ensured that negotiations related to tackling specific aspects of patient care or therapy did not degenerate into debates about who was responsible for a particular action. It also allowed members to identify areas that could be shared. Many professionals in this team were prepared to be flexible at the boundaries of their roles. They knew exactly what they did and why they did it, which gave them an awareness of those aspects of their role which were at the core of their professional specialism, and those which were more peripheral. In this way the peripheral aspects could be shared with and learned by others. However, we have already identified a dislocation between some of the nurses and the therapists. In part this may well be regarded as a structural problem – communication between a large group that works a shift system and a small group that works nine to five will have the potential for communication gaps. Yet some members of both the therapy groups and the nurses were convinced that lack of a clear role – and within that, lack of confidence in terms of role value – gave rise to communication difficulties for the team. In this situation, the lack of value in the *clinical* nursing role was not felt by the therapists, but by some of the nurses themselves. However, all of the professional groups were ambivalent about the value of nurses *educating* other professionals within the team.

For the therapists there was a universal wish to see *all* of the nurses working with the same degree of closeness that they shared between themselves and with some of the nurses. The importance of the nursing role was acknowledged, but therapists commented on its diversity and how that might pose difficulties in terms of role clarity. Despite the therapists' agreement about the wide-ranging 'jack-of-all-trades' nature of the nursing role, there was little discussion about a specific therapeutic role that nurses may play.

This contrast between the very specific input of the therapy professionals in the rehabilitation process and the rather diffuse role which was perceived was a problem for some of the nurses. Nurses have been likened to the 'glue' that binds the other professional contributions together, an all-encompassing role which has greater continuity than others (Johnson and Fokke, 1995). However, some nurses were ambivalent about this definition. They could see its benefits to the patient, but many of them could not see its value for themselves. Some felt as if they were playing a supporting role in a therapist-led environment and were simply 'part of the furniture'. One particularly disaffected nurse commented that the role could be 'anything you can perceive it to be; helper, or substitute therapist, waiter, slave – you name it, the perception's there.'

These negative role perceptions appeared to be related to feelings of low confidence and self-esteem among some of the nurses:

> But it's because we are carrying on their therapies whereas they don't actually want to know what nurses do because it's not pleasant is it . . . and that is quite hard to accept sometimes, especially when you are coming from a low position, and nursing is still here.
>
> (Nurse)

One therapist acknowledged that some therapists may have operated with the nurses in a way which might reinforce such feelings:

> We kind of call on them to say 'come and have a quick look at this transfer here' or 'can you just go and get blah-di-blah out of the nurses' station so they can have a quick look at this?'; and that's not how I work with the other therapists. When I work with them it's 'let's plan a session' or 'let's book in a whole hour together to look at that, and let's talk about it afterwards'. . . . Nursing is almost kind of like they are disposable, which is not nice.
>
> (OT)

There was not consensus among the nurses regarding the degree of negativity of this perception. However, it was shared by the head nurse. She was viewed as a good role model for nursing in the team, but she did not seem to provide a role model as a 'rehabilitation nurse'. In this context, we mean one who could identify how plans of therapy and care *could* include nursing leadership. We stated earlier that the team used a holistic problem-solving model in which any of the professional groups could have steered the care and therapy of the patient. Therapists assessed patients, drew up a plan of therapy and then, using the problem/goal orientation, their actions defined team practice (i.e. all team members were expected to help in implementing those plans as and when appropriate). As all therapists would draw up their own plans and have similar expectations of other therapists, any 'carry-over' they were required to do in their own sessions was not perceived as a problem – it was simply part of the therapy process.

The nurses also assessed patients and drew up plans of care and treatment. However, their plans only defined nursing practice. The therapists did not generally take part in those aspects of care, a fact that was noted by both therapists and nurses, but with some puzzlement on the part of the therapists. In many ways the nurses' position with the therapists could be identified as similar to the nurses' position in the medical model (i.e. administering and carrying out treatment on behalf of the therapists). Further to this, since the physiotherapy principles of Bobath (see later in the chapter) defined many carry-over techniques, the direction of education was also perceived to be from therapists to nurses. All of the therapists spoke about 'getting the nurses together to talk to them about . . . '. This type of interaction was not observed to have been reciprocated by the nurses, and indeed was not identified as a common phenomenon because of the emphasis of the unit.

The situation whereby nurses did not take a lead role in care interventions could have been altered. For example, if a client was perceived to have difficulties with regard to changes in body image which had led to feelings of low self-esteem, and thus to an unwillingness to participate in therapy, nurses with counselling skills could have taken the lead in helping to unravel that particular problem. However, despite suggestions from the director that these skills would be a beneficial addition to the nursing role, these were not taken up by the nursing group. Given the difficulties experienced by some of the nurses in this setting, this would seem to be a potentially useful avenue to have pursued, as it would have provided them with a specific 'rehabilitation skill' which could then have led to their teaching input to the team.

However, not only did nurses not take a lead role in care intervention, but it also appeared that some of them did not approach problem definition in the same way as the therapists, which would then determine which professionals did what in the pattern of care. This related to the specificity of problem definition and its antecedents, and the way in which these were analysed. This may have been associated with differences in training, given that few nurses had benefited from training using specific problem-solving models. Since one nurse raised the issue with the researcher, it was felt that highlighting the analytical discrepancy may only have reinforced some nurses' more negative feelings about their professional standing.

From the orientation package provided for new nurses, it appeared that a self-care deficit model of nursing was used. However, this was not clearly articulated by the nurses themselves in terms of how it steered their practice. Furthermore, it did not seem to match the problem-solving approach that was used by the therapists. The lack of an explicit nursing model seems to have fostered ambiguous perceptions of the parameters of the nursing role and problems with defining nursing practice. Without such a model, some of the nurses felt themselves to be in a similar position *vis-à-vis* the therapists as they were with the medical profession – that is, practising in the service of that profession, rather than having a case to argue from their own standpoint. The subsequent perceptions of some nurses of their reduced value to patient progress could therefore be associated with both the lack of a specific 'rehabilitation role' and differences in analytical skills. The development of these two aspects could have enabled the nurses to identify the importance of their role in a way which they themselves could value, and allowed them to contribute more comprehensively to the interprofessional teaching and learning process in the team.

In the other teams we looked at, particularly in the acute care setting in the medical ward, nurses did not appear to identify this lack of value *vis-à-vis* other professionals in the same way. *Lack of value in other contexts was less self-defined than defined by others*. This also applied to professions other than nursing. Lack of value with regard to the chiropody role was identified in particular in one of the 'core and periphery' teams, and lack of value of the social work role in one of the 'fragmented' teams. In these cases there was a perception *that they were seen to be of secondary status, and that their skills were 'wasted'*.

In the diabetes team, the core group had no doubt about each other's contribution, exactly how their colleagues' reasoning had led them to their conclusions, and the value that their expertise brought to the process of patient care. Others in the team, particularly the hospital chiropodists, were not able to share those feelings. One was part-time and rarely seen in the centre, but the other regularly attended clinics and education sessions with new patients. During her 2 years in post she had become resentful of her treatment in the diabetes team. She felt that the consultant often sidelined her opinions and gave work that should have gone to her, to the podiatrist (a core group member) instead. The chiropodist was confident in her own expertise, although she had no specific grounding in diabetes. She believed that this expertise was being 'wasted' in the team because it was so rarely sought by the consultant. This was corroborated by observation, but it raises an interesting point. Why was it apparently only possible for the chiropodist's role to be validated by the consultant? She had a reasonably good relationship with the specialist nurses, regularly discussing specific cases and giving her opinions about patient management. Would this not have been a way for her to have developed credibility as a team member?

The main problem for this chiropodist, was her lack of standing as a *diabetes* chiropodist, and in this she could not – and did not – want to compete with the podiatrist. Consequently, she was likely to remain less of a team member, because her role contribution was deemed by the core group to be (in that sense), less valuable. In the context of diabetes care, it was clear that role value was ascribed to those within the core group. Since others outside the team were perceived to have less motivation with regard to this specialism, it seemed that their value to the core group was compromised as a result.

In the CMHTs, there was an assumption by some health professionals that their input made the most important contribution to the team's work, with the social workers perceiving that they simply provided 'housing and finance' needs. There were differences in balance between professionals' perceived required input that generated tension in meetings. As was suggested in an earlier section, the way in which clients were brought up for discussion within both of these teams tended to be related to in-patient discharge and out-patient appointments. The social workers felt that this excluded a large number of long-term community-based clients for whom they had responsibility. In addition, it was evident that changes in the social work role had reduced the amount of specific therapeutic input that was given by the social workers, leaving them mainly their statutory work (which was not necessarily related to the clients cared for by the teams) and finding the task of accommodation and financial support. As discussion around the key-worker role (see Chapter 3) demonstrated, this aspect of their role was not regarded by some of the CPNs as commensurate with their own therapeutic role. This was reflected on by one of the social workers:

> A CPN said to me whilst in a team meeting, 'I'm not quite sure what level to pitch it at when I'm talking to you about therapy'. And I just thought 'that's quite frightening'. And another person said 'I know nothing about housing', as if it was something so incredibly crass and stupid, and it dawned on me that the team was just chronically shut into that way of thinking.
>
> (SW)

For both the CPNs and the social workers, having to give up a therapeutic aspect of their role was a cause for concern. The CPNs felt that they were currently fighting hard not to have their therapy skills diluted by being required to take on the social aspect of mental health care. For the social workers, the increased amount of statutory work and the lack of resources meant that therapeutic work had been eliminated almost completely, leaving some of them feeling undervalued as professionals.

> I just think we're being deprofessionalised, and I don't think we are given credit for what we know. I mean I did a Masters in social work. I did a very thorough intensive training, working with families, family therapy, but here my work is pen-pushing, applying for money, statutory duties, and waiting for cases to blow. And it is frustrating.
>
> (SW)

Not only was it possible that social workers could have brought an added dimension to the therapeutic input of the team, but the emphasis on the social aspect of their role was felt by some social workers to be minimising the likelihood of their opinions being listened to in meetings. This perception was reinforced numerically. Often they were the only social worker represented and, as one of them said, they did not feel 'as if we are part of this family in many ways'. In this situation, because support from CPNs was uncommon, social workers found it difficult to maintain an argument with the consultants. As discussed earlier in this chapter, interactions between the consultants and the social workers could be heated, but with little resolution as far as the social workers were concerned. Their perceived inability to shape decisions made in the CMHTs highlighted for them the lack of value that was placed on their input to the team. The potential impact for their clients was noted earlier in Chapter 4.

Where roles are not valued and are therefore identified as being unable to offer direction to patient care, or where changes to roles have apparently reduced the input that professionals *could* make to a team, then it seems that opportunities for comprehensive care may be lost. Collaborative teamworking, where it is assumed that equal weight is being given to professional input, would seem to provide the greatest scope for effective patterns of care to be developed.

All students need to consider the way in which some expertise within the multiprofessional team may be valued differently, and how this impacts on some professionals' abilities to contribute to team problem-solving and decisions made on that basis.

This discussion also has implications for post-registration education. The way that some nurses in the 'integrated' team setting had difficulty in perceiving the value of their contribution to rehabilitation (rather than simply their contribution to nursing the patient), and in perceiving an educative role in the team, merits consideration. Although nurses may currently be educated to employ greater analytical skills, some of those in this setting did not apply an analysis to their practice *within the multiprofessional context of problem-solving*, as did the therapists. Opportunities for professionals to continue their education and thus to develop their practice need to be taken in all specialisms by large enough numbers of individuals to impact on clinical practice.

The final part of this section will examine *ways in which professionals can serve other non-clinical roles in the team that can act to bridge the gap between different groups within the team.* Not surprisingly, this was observed in the 'core and periphery' working, with professionals in both teams attempting to act as conduits of information 'smoothers' in contentious situations and motivators for peripheral team members.

As we have suggested on several occasions, the existence of a 'core and periphery' structure in a team causes problems in communication and understanding. In the diabetes team, the specialist nurses in combination helped to overcome the divisions to a certain extent by creating communication pathways. The specialist nurse in the core group of this team was confident and assertive, and because of her standing with the consultant, she experienced little difficulty in coping with his rather abrasive communication style. Because of the trusting relationship she had built with the consultant, she was able to discuss with him aspects of care, or questions raised by the other professionals. Since this route was used by the 'peripheral' nurse specialist, *she* could see how this worked:

> They are aware of each other's good points and bad points, and they both appreciate the expertise of each one, so they are able to communicate

> on the same level really. I mean they have got a good working relationship, they both understand each other very well and so they know how far they can go. I mean they argue sometimes, but that's not a bad thing.
>
> (Diabetes specialist nurse)

As a result, the core group specialist nurse was able to some extent to act as part of a bridge between the consultant and peripheral professionals, and she did this in tandem with the 'peripheral' specialist nurse. The results of discussions between the core group specialist nurse and the consultant would be fed back to the 'peripheral' specialist nurse. The latter had worked in the team for several years but, unlike the core group nurse, she had developed a close working relationship with the hospital-based professionals. Consequently, she was better placed to pass on information and requests to them. Furthermore, she was considered by the chiropodists and the dietitians to be a good listener, and to be willing to give them time to express their difficulties in meeting the consultant's requests, as the following quote from a dietitian suggests:

> Well, she is good at listening. If you want to talk about a patient you know that she will let you say what you have to say and give your opinion properly. I feel on the same level as her somehow. She also gives out more than is really necessary and that makes you feel that you can go to her if you need to for assistance or to talk about a patient. But then she will fill in other details about his life that may be helpful, or she will say well he has tried so and so and hasn't been successful, little things that might not seem necessary, but help to make things easier between us.
>
> (Dietitian)

This professional was a gentle, shy person who had also found it difficult to deal with the consultant, but for the hospital-based professionals she was a natural ally. After discussion with other peripheral team members, she was able to give feedback to the core group specialist nurse, and so to the consultant. By this rather tortuous route, communication was achieved and, one hoped, it would be possible to develop an understanding of the problems as perceived by the hospital staff.

A similar role was seen to be performed by the HV in the child development assessment team, although not in the sense that she helped to smooth over communication rifts. Rather, she offered a collating and information dissemination service. These were specific aspects of her role, but they had been envisaged as providing a link between community services and the Centre. For example, she would be expected to contact community HVs to ensure that they had information about the Centre's activities and were passing on information about children in their case-loads who might need attention. However, she also developed a stronger link between several hospital-based staff, such as the dietitian and the ward nurses, and members of the child development assessment team, by regularly visiting these professionals, discussing new cases, sifting out relevant information and passing on what she had found out.

In her approach to her work *within* the child development assessment team this professional was also seen to facilitate more effective communication. With the help of the core group consultant she had developed a system of case review in which *all professionals* were expected to provide her with a list of all relevant children. From this, she drew up a list of children to be discussed at a weekly meeting chaired by herself. All members of the core group and an OT assigned to young children attended this meeting. Although the HV was unable to persuade the clinical psychologists to attend, or to supply information, she was persistent in her attempts to encourage the PTs to attend regularly. This involved her visiting the PTs when she was in the main hospital, and asking them which patients they were seeing who could potentially be discussed at the review.

The OT identified above, perceived herself and was also regarded by core group members as 'moving towards the core group'. She felt that her attendance at the case-review meetings had improved her interaction with them. It had enabled her to engage in regular discussion relating to specific children, and to demonstrate the usefulness of her input. On one occasion, the OT's observations about a child had created a better understanding of his condition, and led to a change in the programme of care that the SLT in the core group had devised. It was hoped that the PTs' attendance at the meetings would facilitate a similar experience for them, and thus bring them further into this group.

These examples suggest different interpretations of the term 'bridging'. The first example simply involves a link between two bodies of the team without necessarily ensuring an integrating outcome. The process appeared only to facilitate communication. The other example demonstrated a degree of incorporation of a peripheral member – potentially a more useful process. This may reflect the effects of training on the professional involved, as it had given her an understanding both of herself in relation to her work, and of the group process. Her subsequent work as a community HV had encouraged her to be a negotiater and a collator and disseminator of information to a wide variety of professionals. Together, the training and practice experience might have enabled her to assume this bridging/incorporating role more readily. This has obvious implications for future student education.

> All students need to understand the non-clinical roles that members of the multiprofessional team can use to help to overcome divisions between professionals or professional groups. Strategies for facilitating and linking others may be extremely useful tools for managing problematic group dynamics.

This bridging role may play a part in bringing together professionals who have very different views – not about teamworking, but about the best way to manage patient care.

CONFLICTING MODELS OF PATIENT CARE

One of the problems in bringing together professionals from different cultures concerns their potentially differing beliefs about how to achieve the optimum patient care – that is, the model of treatment, care or therapy to which they subscribe. In two types of working ('integrated' and 'fragmented') we saw how bringing together these different models created tensions for the development of a shared focus for care. We are not arguing here that this necessarily constrains patient care – the evidence was not available for us to reach that conclusion. What we are saying is that bringing together individuals with different beliefs about patient care can create difficulties for the development of team practice as a result of their having different approaches. By implication this may mean that members of a team provide conflicting input to patient care, which could compromise outcomes for patients.

In our first example we shall examine how *two different models of rehabilitation* caused some strained relationships between professionals in the rehabilitation team. From its days under the leadership of a PT, the rehabilitation unit had retained a leaning towards this profession as its primary therapy (in keeping with evidence from other research on rehabilitation units; e.g. Fokke, 1994; Johnson and Fokke, 1995), and the principles of therapeutic intervention embraced by all professions, to some extent, were physiotherapy based. Within this context, many professionals had employed the principles of Bobath (Lennon, 1996) to pursue the best outcomes for their patients. The goal of the Bobath approach was to provide patients with as normal (as opposed to functional) a range of movement as possible given the limitations of their impairments. This meant reducing muscle tone where damage had caused it to increase, and helping the brain to make new links with affected muscle. Part of the process of using the Bobath principles was therefore to prevent patients from extending muscles in a way that might achieve a functional movement, but would also increase their muscle tone. Although functional outcome was still an overarching goal, the quality of the movement was an important consideration.

For other professionals, especially OTs and nurses, independence had always been the primary goal – the manner of that independence being considered less important than the fact of it. Since it took some time for the Bobath approach to demonstrate an effective outcome, these other professionals often felt that it was more important for the patient to be able to go home within a reasonable length of time, and to be able to operate as independently as possible, rather than being able to do less, but do it more 'normally'. However, the OTs had now to a large extent incorporated the principles into their practice, and this was facilitated by the fact that their head of department was Bobath trained. This may have been an easier option for the OTs, as their therapy sessions were conducted within purpose-built accommodation such as the gym, the workshop or the kitchen. By contrast, the nurses were required to extend the use of Bobath principles into their 24-hour patient care in small, often fairly cluttered patients' rooms, and in tiny bathrooms. While they were 'always willing to try' to accommodate therapists' wishes, as several nurses pointed out this was not always easy:

> One of the things that can madden all the nurses, trained and untrained, is if we're given something to carry over which is not very practical, and the favourite one is the low transfer, and we're trying to do that with someone who needs their trousers pulled down, when you are trying to get them on the toilet . . . it's not practical. They have to stand up to do that.
>
> (Nurse)

In order to achieve effective carry-over, the nurses were involved in ongoing sessions with the PTs to learn the basic concepts and strategies for transferring and positioning patients. However, taking these into their working practices often seemed inappropriate, as was suggested above. As a result, there had been conflict about the interpretation of the principles. Negotiation was sometimes successful and sometimes not so. The therapists appreciated the nurses' difficulties, and had attempted to compromise the principles with regard to carry-over techniques. In so doing they had spent time with the nurses, teaching them useful strategies to help them to overcome their limited circumstances. However, the carry-over of the Bobath principles still caused problems for some nurses. Not only were they constantly faced with need to make pragmatic decisions about moving and handling patients in different contexts, but they also *believed* that functional independence was more important.

The result was that, in some situations, communications about specific procedures were perceived to have broken down, as it was felt that some nurses were continuing to manage patients according to their own beliefs about independence, rather than following supposedly agreed patterns of care. Furthermore, as a result of the communication gap, some PTs felt that they were unable to proceed with their therapy in the way that they might have done because of the consequent increase of patients' muscle tone.

Since this team operated in a more integrated fashion than the other teams observed in our study, it was evident that the issue was at least raised regularly, and means to overcome the differences between the two models were addressed. Indeed, as was acknowledged by many professionals in this team, the level of agreement between the professionals in this regard was comparatively high compared to people's experiences elsewhere. However, it is clear that where there are such differences in beliefs, then there is the potential for existing divisions within multiprofessional teams to be reinforced further.

The second example concerns the *health and social care divide* in the CMHTs. Although it is acknowledged that some CMHTs have adopted a more comprehensive psychosocial model of mental health (Onyett *et al.*, 1996), within the CMHTs in our study there were two significant differences between the health and social models of client care. The first difference related to the rights of the client. Social workers in the teams believed that clients had the right to decide whether or not to have medical treatment for their severe mental illness. They saw it as their duty to promote the client's right to choose for themselves by advocating on their client's behalf and supporting them in the community.

This they would achieve by offering more secure housing, obtaining financial support, and the input of other community workers. The second point was that this was underpinned by a belief that mental illness has its roots in social structures, rather than in biological deficits, whereby the provision of more supportive structures would enable the client to maintain as independent a lifestyle as possible. If those options failed, then social workers would hope to persuade the client to go into in-patient facilities *voluntarily*, rather than being detained under a Section of the Mental Health Act.

In contrast, the medical model would tend to argue that a range of mental illnesses have a biological basis, and can be treated with medication. This underpinned what could be termed a benevolent patriarchal belief that psychiatrists have a 'duty of care' for patients. This belief assumes that health care treatment *should* be given to clients until the client has recovered to the point where they are able to make judgements on their own behalf. In order that treatment could be given, this path would then arguably be more likely to lead to people being detained under the Mental Health Act.

This cultural, attitudinal difference has been noted in other research (e.g. Wilmot, 1995), and we have presented it as an extreme polarising of beliefs. In the reality of our study team members' beliefs were not so black-and-white, as each group of professionals was able to acknowledge the other's argument. Nor were the two positions always at odds in terms of whether a person required in-patient care – both the social workers and the psychiatrists commented that they could be in agreement. However, the social workers felt that the emphasis on 'sectioning' in order to enforce medication was more frequent than was necessary.

The adherence to the medical model was also queried by some of the CPNs who subscribed to a more psychosocial model of care, indicating perhaps that they had started to develop more common values with the social workers. Some of them proposed that diagnostic and medicating decisions were based on an uncertain understanding of the causes and processes of mental illness, and they conveyed a picture of psychiatry as to some extent 'stabbing in the dark'. It would seem that the confidence with which decisions were made by the medical profession may have *needed* to be tempered by other input from the multiprofessional team.

The ways in which these differences were manifested were frequently apparent in team meetings, where there could be heated interactions about the 'right' approach to managing care. As such, the social workers' beliefs about their clients' rights were a direct challenge to medical power. In order for a client to be detained, both the social workers and the psychiatrists made an assessment under the Mental Health Act, with the social worker making the application to 'section'. Thus the social workers needed to agree with the medical opinion in order for sectioning to occur. The differences in beliefs underpinning the roles of the two professions in this decision therefore had the potential to lead to conflict. Furthermore, the action that social workers took as a result of their different orientation may have been perceived as a challenge to consultants' professional autonomy. This then spilled over into other interactions between the social workers and the psychiatrists.

For example, in one team meeting a client who, in tandem with her mental illness, had a severe alcohol problem, was mentioned by the consultant. This client was currently being supported by a care worker in the community. The psychiatrist wanted her to go to the day hospital for therapeutic input. The social worker felt that the client's alcohol problem was not being dealt with in a comprehensive fashion. She suggested 'why don't we get some advice from the alcohol team psychiatrist?'. At this point the psychiatrist became angry and simply said 'no'. The social worker attempted to soften her suggestion by saying 'I didn't mean to imply that your treatment wasn't right, I just thought it might be helpful.' The consultant remained angry and said 'but it's like me saying "I'm going to refer her to another social worker"'. The social worker commented 'but you do that already; you refer people to the rehab social worker when people are seeing me, and without telling me, and that's OK, I don't mind because it gets another perspective in.' Another social worker in the meeting joined the conversation and supported her colleague. However, the consultant dismissed the idea outright. In this situation it is possible to deduce that the social worker would have been attempting to advocate on her client's behalf for the most comprehensive input to his care. However, the consultant's response disallowed this.

Unlike the culture that existed within the 'integrated' team, where discussion and debate helped to smooth the edges of the differences between professionals, in the CMHT such behaviours was rare. Opportunities to discuss and debate team practice were almost non-existent during the time of our study. Social workers were seen to challenge the decisions made by the psychiatrists, but these challenges often met with little shifted ground. As a result, it was uncommon for there to be collaboration in which both beliefs about client management could have been aired and a negotiated path found.

It is not our intention that the comments in this section should imply that all professionals should necessarily all hold the same views with regard to patient care. Indeed, one of the potential benefits of multiprofessional working is that different perspectives can be brought together to provide a more detailed picture of what could be achieved for the patient. However, it could be argued that professionals should be prepared to negotiate the issues and respect each other's professional viewpoint. This could lead to a more cohesive approach that incorporates or modifies different perspectives.

If we consider the culture within the 'integrated' team, where it was *expected* that feelings would be expressed, discussed and managed, and where these were listened to and acknowledged, we can see how the development of a team culture construed by all as 'safe' could help to overcome differences of opinion and any resentments. In that team, differing viewpoints were raised and debated until a resolution was reached which suited most members. It was appreciated that dissension was the norm with regard to multiprofessional interaction, but that the way forward was open discussion in which all professionals' views were valid. Where there is no challenge to the status quo stagnation can occur, and where the status quo is dictated by only one professional group, oppression can result. Neither of these options would seem to be helpful to the development of 'effective multiprofessional teamwork'.

Students need to appreciate the differences between professional cultures in terms of approaches to care in order to understand how these could impact on the patient or client.

In the final section we shall examine how people may become members of a team. This is a twofold process, and accordingly we shall first look at how new members act in order to be incorporated, and then we shall consider the ways in which the current team brings people into it.

BECOMING A NEW TEAM MEMBER

We discussed earlier in this chapter what it means to be a team member, and we identified the way in which 'team belonging' (i.e. a sense of allegiance to a team) depends on individuals taking on the norms and values of that team. If this occurs then, in effect, it can shape the way in which those people think and behave in that context. In the multiprofessional context, this socialisation process therefore requires a redefinition of what a person is outside of their own professional group. However, socialisation into a team as a new member is a two-way process. Not only does a person experience changes in order to become a team member, but the team needs to accommodate that person. Two aspects of this process need to be considered. First, how does the new member demonstrate his or her willingness and suitability to be part of the team? Secondly, what strategies do the team use which support the process?

The concept of joining a team does assume that there is a 'team' entity which is sufficiently cohesive for it to have developed norms and values that an outsider would be required to take on. Where this is not the case, as in the 'fragmented' teams in our study, then it is possible that a professional may simply join other similar professionals in 'the team'. Alternatively, as in the 'core and periphery' working, it may be that joining the team does not mean that a professional has joined 'the team' at all (i.e. the core group within the team).

In this example we shall examine *the process of incorporation of new members where the team has a well-structured and supportive approach*. This was the rehabilitation team. We have spoken earlier about the way in which being a team player was an important attribute for membership of the team, and that individuals were actively recruited on the basis of their willingness to demonstrate how good they would be at behaving as team players. This was not an option for people coming into the team – such was the strength of feeling in the team that this was 'the way to do it', that newcomers who were not prepared to demonstrate such behaviour would not be accommodated: 'and you've got no choice either. It's not like you can either do it this way or that way; this is the way you do it and this is the way it works' (PT).

Apart from the active selection of team players, there were a number of ways in which current team members attempted to incorporate new people into the team. In the course of our study, three new members joined the team.

Two of them were junior members of their professions and one was an experienced professional. For the first two, this process appeared almost to be seamless. In common with others' perceptions of the integration process, both of them felt that people 'reached out to me to make me welcome'. This 'reaching out' was both formal and informal. New members were involved in an induction procedure to discuss their work in the unit with the head of their profession. They would also attend a series of meetings with the other professional groups to discuss how each of them slotted into the rehabilitation process, and the expected working relationships between the roles. In both of these processes it was anticipated that the newcomer would be prepared to discuss how they themselves would fit into the process of joint working practices.

At the same time, opportunities would be provided early on for the newcomer to demonstrate practising with others. This served a twofold purpose. It showed that the person was prepared to take on the ways of the team, but it also gave them an opportunity to demonstrate their skills and knowledge, and it enabled others in the team to determine how well that person would contribute to patient care. Since much of the work in the team was highly visible, this could be achieved rapidly. For example, one new and junior therapist had previously worked with comatose patients and had learned coma stimulation response techniques. She described how the team used her skills to help a non-responsive patient to communicate:

> It's with the patient who is not communicating at this stage, so I have talked with an SLT about the work that is going on at [another rehabilitation unit], and how to establish a yes/no response. And we have been going through the process of establishing a yes/no response, and we have gone through the assessment form. I have been able to give them some information on coma stimulation procedure, and the assessment they would need to go through. . . . It has been really nice because we have done some joint sessions, and they have said 'is it OK if we do a little bit more, and you observe us, or help or feedback?' that sort of thing.
>
> (OT)

This process not only allowed the newcomer to demonstrate her skills and knowledge, but it also enabled other professionals to learn new techniques themselves.

In addition, the director was instrumental in the integration process. He regularly asked for new members' opinions, and would encourage discussion as to whether new action needed to be taken as a result. The behaviours of current team members were identified as giving newcomers a feeling of value. They felt that they were listened to and had their suggestions acted upon, 'as if' they were already accepted team members with established credentials of expertise.

The learning environment that had been created in this team therefore allowed both newcomers and current team members to benefit. The latter were also comfortable about acknowledging their own lack of information or understanding in front of new members, in order to encourage them not to feel inhibited about asking what might be construed as 'silly questions':

> I think it's important as well, that it isn't just the juniors that are seen to be doing the asking, it needs to come from the seniors; I have to ask quite a lot. But that will then encourage anybody who is new to do that, because they will think 'oh well, they are as daft as I am'.
>
> (Nurse)

This type of disclosure was observed on many occasions during the study, both across and within professions, and from the director himself. One final aspect of this integration process was the assumption of new members' inclusion in the team's social life. Many members of the team had regular evenings out together as a group, bowling or going to the cinema, and both of the new junior members were asked to join in these occasions.

Despite the various ways in which integration into the team was devised, it was decidedly unsuccessful on one occasion. In this example we shall examine *the way newcomers play their part in the incorporation process*. The recruitment of one particular newcomer to the team had been a longed-for achievement, but team members soon realised that he might not 'fit in' with the team. This newcomer's beliefs about teamworking have already been discussed in Chapter 4 and in an earlier section of this chapter. His beliefs were so different to those of the team that he was seen to have created significant disturbance for other team members. During the early months of his being in post, team members offered the same means of integration as they did to all new members. There were several 'uncomfortable' meetings with the various professions, where they spoke about their roles and asked the newcomer about his expectations of 'slotting in'. His response was seen to be 'frosty' in that he would not define ways of interacting with other team members, and he declined to watch various groups working together. Team members were not only angry at this person's behaviour but also, given their predilection for reflecting on and evaluating practice, they began to ponder on the nature of their team interaction and how a non-team-player could have been appointed to the post – a matter on which the director himself reflected:

> There was no consensus view about his employment; I did it. I'm the one who spent the money, and if it screws up then it would reflect on me . . . that [the goodwill] will only run for a while. If we can't get it to work, then we'll have to think again.
>
> (Director)

This situation illustrates nicely the way in which integration is a two-way process, as the current team members were all willing, and indeed persevered for several months, to draw the newcomer into the team. However, he was unwilling to change and the team was unwilling to compromise their behaviour as a team. An impasse ensued which finally led to this professional leaving the team.

Where multiprofessional groups have a less well-defined sense of 'teamness', those who express their contribution in a different way may well be contained more readily, because they will not be impinging on such an evident set of team beliefs and values. Moreover, a newcomer to such a multiprofessional group may be able to practise in a way that is far less visible if collaborative practices are not so highly developed. This situation was observed in the 'fragmented teams', where integration was largely into a professional's own group, rather than into the team as a whole. In the PHCT and the medical ward, people operated at such a distance from each other professionally that integration was a meaningless concept in multiprofessional terms. However, for the CMHTs, because of their geographical proximity and the fact that they had developed some of the symbols of 'teamworking' (e.g. meetings as a team), integration *was* an issue, albeit a negative one.

Incorporation into teams where professionals 'go their own way' may be extremely uncomfortable for newcomers, particularly where they themselves are showing willingness to become a 'team member'. During our research with these two small CMHTs, several new members arrived. Two of them were permanent staff and two were students on 3-month placements. Although it might be expected from the transient nature of the students' position in the teams that they would not be likely to feel a sense of belonging, in fact *none* of the newcomers found it easy to feel part of the team. The new CPN said that she was 'floundering' after having been in the team for 3 months, and the new OT felt 'isolated'. Both of these professionals expressed a willingness to work in a collaborative fashion, the OT in particular having come from a team which she felt was integrated and effective. These professionals had the opposite experience to the newcomer who caused problems for the rehabilitation team – that is, they were willing to collaborate and many other team members in the CMHTs were not. However, the reasons for their negative feelings had similarities and differences.

In the case of the CPN it might have been supposed that she would have been welcomed as a fellow professional by other CPNs, and shown the 'way it is done'. She attended CPN meetings in which she would have learned about the structures and processes *for the CPNs in the team*. The OT was on her own, so she had no peer group to tell her what it was like to be an OT in the team. However, both of these new professionals found it difficult to learn about other professionals' structures and processes, because they were largely hidden from view.

During the course of the study there was no way in which others' professional practice could be observed. Weekly team meetings in one CMHT in particular were perceived by new professionals to be unproductive due to the lack of facilitative structure, the rationale for the inclusion of specific clients for discussion being difficult to fathom. As a result, it was not easy for newcomers to know how or when to raise relevant issues. Both the CPN and the OT were commonly heard to ask – after the meetings – when they could or should have said or asked something. However, as was identified earlier, such was the nature of the team environment that they felt they could not raise these issues *in* the meetings. For the OT, because she was regarded as a 'last resort' for referral of clients, rather than an integral part of a team process, she felt that she was unable to demonstrate the range of her skills and knowledge. If we consider the rehabilitation team, there the nature of team practice ensured that new professionals learned the process of patient care quickly, and learned how they could contribute to it, while it also gave them opportunities to demonstrate, comprehensively how effective that contribution could be. This may have been possible for the new CPN in her own professional domain, but not as a multiprofessional team member. With regard to the OT, her lack of involvement with others in the process of care made this extremely difficult.

Both new professionals finally came to accept the fact that there were no 'teams' to belong to, in the sense that there were two groups of people moving in the same direction with a uniting purpose. They felt separate from others and despondent about this fact: 'and everybody's in their wee box, it is definitely like that for me, and I don't want to be there, I want to burst out of this box' (OT).

Where we saw *core and periphery working, incorporation into the team was a different proposition to becoming a core group member*. However, to a large extent it depended on what the newcomers wanted to achieve with regard to how they practised. In both the diabetes team and the child development assessment team, there were currently individuals on the periphery who should have been, and wanted to be, in the core groups. Since *these* people had not been integrated, it is clear that a newcomer with similar beliefs could join the team without ever becoming a member of the core group. There were also individuals, particularly in the child development assessment team, who did not share the values and beliefs of the core group and therefore would not have wished to belong to this group in any case. Newcomers such as these would presumably have been similarly comfortable in that position. However, in our study the newcomers to both the 'core and periphery' teams recognised that becoming accepted by the core group *would* be their goal, as they saw that this was where their perceptions of collaborative teamwork could be realised.

For two dietitians joining the diabetes team, much greater effort was needed, but it was possible to see evidence of a shift in the potential for integration into this core group. The specialist nurse in the diabetes core group acknowledged that they had a reputation for being inward-looking and elitist. As stated earlier, historically they had been through a group development process that was very binding – the diabetes team was 'their baby' in many ways. Their amassed team knowledge and experience were unlikely to be shared with any latecomers except for the second specialist nurse, as the other professionals were not specialist in orientation or practice. Incorporation was going to be difficult for newcomers and would possibly require more proactive work on their part, rather than being a straightforward reciprocal process. The dietitians realised this and began to make a determined effort to attend meetings. This meant that they had to persuade their manager – a person who, after the development of difficulties in dealing with the consultant, had very definite ideas about maintaining a distance from the team. Since a comment was made by the senior diabetes specialist nurse to the effect that 'dietitians don't come to the meetings except when there's a rep and sandwiches are on offer', this change in practice had the potential to alter that perception.

In meetings that were not attended by the consultant they made a point of raising issues and suggestions with the specialist nurses. For example, they talked about having a social evening as a team, and in the face of a rather lukewarm reception they persisted in their efforts. The resulting event was nevertheless considered successful both by the dietitians and by other members of the team. However, the greatest barrier to their integration was the fact that they were not designated specialist dietitians – they still had other priorities in the hospital. For the members of the core group, this was a major obstacle to acceptance, despite willingness on the part of the newcomers to act as core group members, and the issue remained unresolved during our study.

The core group in the child development assessment team was far more open in terms of accepting newcomers. Although it did not have a definite approach to incorporating them, it was a welcoming and friendly group of people. However, in this team, because of the diversity of the client groups, newcomers would of necessity have to be oriented towards the core group's specialism in order to become members. Furthermore, competing priorities in other contexts made it difficult for newcomers to become core group members. However, the new HV was a proactive newcomer. Her work was largely autonomous, without the need for her to divide her time between various competing sites and client groups. Moreover, she saw that she had a role in the core group which, whilst it was not specifically related to language development, was extremely useful for the group. In the 8 months since her arrival in post she had quickly made her presence felt as a like-minded professional in the following ways.

First, she made it clear that she wanted to be involved by attending all case discussions. Since, as part of her role, she had dealings with a wide number of professionals both inside and outside the child development assessment team, she was gathering information about a large number of children. Consequently, she was often able to contribute in a meaningful way to discussions about children from a number of contexts. Furthermore, she was able to give feedback to relevant professionals in order to co-ordinate other meetings.

Secondly, she regularly joined play sessions, run by the playroom teacher, as a helper. This brought her into contact with other core group members and allowed her to meet the parents. She would engage in conversation with parents while the other professionals worked with the children. In this way, too, she was able to feed back appropriate information at a later stage to core group members.

Thirdly, her establishment of a case-review system was regarded by core members as a means of strengthening team interaction, and so earned the HV credibility as a 'bridge-builder' (see earlier section). Finally, she made a point of coming out of her office and talking to others, both in terms of *ad hoc* clinical communication and as a social gesture. She made a great effort to become a member of the core group, and since this group's perceptions of working were similar to hers, her incorporation into the group was relatively easy.

This section has examined how professionals may or may not be integrated into a team, depending on the newcomer's effort and willingness to be a team member, their accommodation and acceptance by current team members, and the influence of the organisational context. These are important aspects of teamworking for students to learn.

> Incorporation into a multiprofessional team has its own particular problems of which students need to be aware. These are related to the extent to which professionals in the team have developed or are able to develop cohesiveness as a team, with common beliefs and values. They also relate to whether those in positions of power are facilitative of newcomer integration. Finally, they relate to whether those entering a multiprofessional team, by virtue of their own professional culture or personal conviction, are able to demonstrate that they are prepared to take on the beliefs and values of that team (where this has become evident). If these beliefs do not marry, incorporation into the team will be inhibited.

If professionals join teams and have ideas about collaborative working that are not matched within the new team, is it possible for them to influence team practice? In this and the previous chapter, we have noted the problems experienced by several professionals who have tried to bring prior positive learning about collaborative teamwork into their current, less collaborative teams. For example, the HV in the PHCT, the SLT in the child development assessment team, and the OT in the CMHT. Both group and organisational issues made the transfer of their teamwork skills and knowledge difficult to achieve. The problems for them lay not in their motivation to pursue this type of working, but in either the reception of such ideas about teamworking, or the overarching organisational structures and processes which inhibited the setting up of such patterns of work, or a combination of both.

For the HV in the PHCT, the distant and separate practices of individuals within the team made it logistically and ideologically difficult for her to develop her approach to collaborative working. Only where she met a like-minded professional working in an area that was fairly discrete from other aspects of the team's work (i.e. the midwife) was she able to make a difference. This also applied to the OT from the CMHT. Her enthusiasm and motivation for teamworking could not be expressed because of the lack of openness to the concepts in her new team. For the SLT from the child development assessment team, her ideas had been accepted and had changed some professionals' practice in the team. However, her message fell on stony ground for other professionals, partly because of the organisational context. These examples raise important issues about the transfer of collaborative practices among professionals, and about the development of student education that might seek to promote multiprofessional working.

The professionals identified above had developed an awareness of the benefits that this working could provide for patients and professionals alike, and were keen to promote the same working in their current teams. They felt that they understood what was required in terms of facilitative structures and processes, and they discussed such issues with other team members. However, describing what could be achieved through this pattern of working, and how to change and develop practices to support it, did not appear to have sufficient impact to promote its development. Why was this? Several possible explanations could be put forward. First, the promulgation of a convincing argument for change takes dedicated time for team members to explore and develop understanding of new practices. Secondly, establishing processes of change demands a great deal of attention and effort. This extra effort on the part of a change agent may not be possible within a busy working environment. Thirdly, it was clear from the child development assessment team, for example, that working across different trusts was problematic when pursuing change. Where policies do not match, or management staff from the different trusts are not in communication, ideas may be stillborn and opportunities lost. Much organisational development research supports the need for all of these organisational factors to be taken into consideration when moving people towards a different goal (e.g. Harrison and Roberts, 1985; Pettigrew *et al.*, 1992).

Resistance to change within the team itself relates to issues linked to professional cultures and the power that resides within those cultures. For example, individuals entering a new team would need to find a sufficiently large number of professionals who were both open to the proposition *and* in a powerful enough position to be able to execute a change process. From our discussion of individual beliefs it is clear that current teams may well be divided about the best way to practise with other professionals. Both managers and team leaders would have to be open to such ideas and to help develop and promote collaboration among other team members. However, as we have also shown, those in positions of power can inhibit change. In a situation where several members are prepared to change, but those in positions of power in the team are not, the idea of moving practice on may be a lost cause. The implication here is that professionals would need to be supported by a 'collaboration-friendly context' in order to use their prior experiences in a particular setting.

This discussion also has implications for those who may in future be educated in a multiprofessional approach. How would they as new and junior members of a team influence others to alter their practices? For *students* entering a clinical setting, their chances of maintaining the motivation and skills to promote multiprofessional teamwork might be more easily be lost, as they would lack confidence and credibility. It would be both wasteful and demoralising for great effort to be put into a multiprofessional education process, only for the effects to be extinguished within an unsupportive clinical context.

In the next three chapters we shall take the implications for education which have emerged from the evidence of clinical teamworking and place them in an educational context. In Chapter 6 we shall set the agenda for future education based on these implications. In Chapter 7 we shall examine the current educational provision in order to compare it with what is implied from the clinical setting and what is on offer in higher education. In Chapter 8 we shall identify a model for future education based on the agenda described in Chapter 6.

Deriving an educational agenda from the realities of teamworking

6

INTRODUCTION

The exploration of multiprofessional working in the preceding chapters sets a clear agenda for education, in terms of the knowledge, skills and attitudes required by members of different professions who work in teams.

The promotion of effective multiprofessional teamworking is not the only agenda for multiprofessional education, but it is the one agenda for which multiprofessional learning can clearly demonstrate added value over any monoprofessional alternative. Shared learning between members of different professions offers a potential which is simply unavailable through other means.

The previous chapters have drawn out the lessons of the teamworking study as they relate to the organisation, the individual and the work group. Each of these chapters has identified implications for education which, although they take on a different priority at different times, are of relevance throughout the initial and continuing education process for all of the health care professions.

This chapter will explore the impact that these implications might have at various stages of the professional development process – identifying learning outcomes that give an effective lead to curriculum development. The means of achieving these outcomes, and the extent to which that achievement is dependent on the learning process as well as learning content, will be discussed in later chapters.

THE IMPLICATIONS FOR EDUCATION

Organisational issues

As was clear from the case studies, no team, however autonomous it may be, exists in a vacuum. The organisational context within which any identified group of health care workers functions is a major factor in determining both the potential for effective multiprofessional teamworking to develop and the pattern of teamworking which emerges. The majority of professionals will move through a series of health care organisations during their careers. They need to be aware that teamworking practices supported by policies, structures and processes in one organisation may not be transferable to another, where the organisation is less supportive. Equally, they need to be aware that within an organisation, policies may impact in different ways, depending on the specific clinical context. Education therefore needs to prepare professionals for the fact that it may not be possible to achieve best practice in terms of teamwork in all environments.

Equally, education needs to prepare professionals to cope with the fluidity of the organisations within which they work, and the resulting change in the context within which clinicians function. This fluidity may extend to the organisational definition of role boundaries. If professionals do not want changes in role boundary imposed upon them, it is likely that they will have to learn to take an active role in policy development.

Individual issues

It is also evident from the case studies that professionals come to the organisational context 'primed' in certain ways. However, the prior learning that individuals bring to the team is not confined to the knowledge, skills and attitudes they bring to the specific tasks of patient care. They also bring with them a set of attitudes to and strategies for the process of teamworking. Clearly this prior learning may have instilled conflicting teamwork philosophies and mutually exclusive approaches in individuals working in any given clinical area. Prior learning that is relevant to teamworking may result from the individual's experience within their monoprofessional team and the norms within that profession. It may also relate to previous experience of a range of other multiprofessional teams, which has exposed the individual to a range of working – from integrated to fragmented working, and from the democratic to the hierarchical. Currently, the knowledge, skills and attitudes to teamworking that are maintained by most individuals will have little if anything to do with a planned programme of education. They will have much more to do with what Snyder called 'the hidden curriculum' (Snyder, 1971) – that is, the real expectations held of student behaviour in the culture in which they learn.

What should education plan to do? During the processes of initial training and continuing professional development, education should aim to provide students with learning which they can use in any team, such as interprofessional communication skills, an understanding of group dynamics and leadership. It should also instil an understanding of the philosophy of teamworking and a recognition of the importance of all members of a team working to congruent models of and strategies for professional interaction and patient care.

In addition to the skills required of team members, education should provide the individual with those particular skills which are necessary for them to achieve team membership. These include skills of negotiation as well as general interpersonal skills. It should also enable them to recognise the existing team member who is best able to show them the ropes and 'sponsor' their membership. In addition, newcomers to a multiprofessional team (unless they enter as the designated team leader) need to identify the different points in their incorporation into the team at which it becomes appropriate to offer first, new ideas for patient care based on their monoprofessional expertise, and second, new ideas in relation to the multiprofessional team's way of working. The proposal and implementation of new approaches to teamwork require diplomacy and may well necessitate compromise. Any professional entering a new team (especially as a leader) needs to recognise that, however valuable their experience may tell them a particular teamwork approach can be, its benefit will be limited unless the team own the change.

Group issues

The incorporation of new members is equally an issue for the existing team members. As a multiprofessional (or indeed a monoprofessional) team develops a greater sense of cohesion, there is a danger that it may become impervious to individuals and ideas from outside. Long-standing members of the team may be unaware of the impression they give to newcomers, who do not share their history and may not understand their communication 'shorthand'. If the team is not to stagnate, it requires new blood. Education should enable teams to develop practices that facilitate new members in voicing their ideas and that promote the incorporation of those ideas into team practice.

The importance of an appropriate culture for teamworking is a recurring theme throughout the case-studies. The case study data showed that a culture of teamworking should be developed which promotes cross-professional accessibility of skills and knowledge within the team. Within such a culture, health workers can enhance their core professional skills and knowledge through in-depth interactions with other professionals, and subsequent reflection on their own practice. Equally, the team culture should support a high level of collaborative working, including structures and processes which regularly bring professionals together to discuss and make decisions on patient/client care (such as joint planning and evaluation and shared notes). When considering education towards such a culture, it is important to realise that the democratic model of teamworking may be the natural choice of some health care professions, but that it will run counter to the experience and expectations of others.

In the same way, the design of education for teamworking needs to take account of different perspectives on the development of a shared direction for practice through reflection and discussion, which are regarded as an important underpinning of the teamworking culture. Such a development may be viewed differently by groups who are actively seeking a say in the direction of practice, those who are being asked to 'give away' a degree of control over practice, and those who would much rather have practice directed *for* them by another professional group.

Communication and interpersonal skills are an important component of all initial programmes of professional education, but the tendency is to focus on interaction with patients, rather than with fellow professionals. The case studies identify an equally important educational agenda for the development of interprofessional communication skills. They demonstrate the value of developing communication styles which maximise the input of all professions into decision-making processes. In some cases this may mean assertiveness training, while in others it may suggest the training of high-status professionals to develop more facilitative communication styles. In either case, education should prepare professionals to communicate consistently with members of other professions.

Within any given clinical team, good communication is of the utmost importance for effective functioning and therefore quality patient care. Although good communication about patient care may have the most explicit value, the research study recognises that this has to be built on a foundation of informal, social meeting and talking (i.e. good interprofessional communication is built on good interpersonal relationships). It also identifies that the pattern of interprofessional communication may initially be limited to the grasping of opportunities as they present themselves, and that this should be augmented by regular, structured meetings. This will inherently move the focus of professional communication from discussion of particular cases to the development of common approaches to care. The development of appropriate strategies for formal communication is an appropriate focus for whole-team learning.

It is vitally important for the team that individual professionals are clear about their own role, and equally that they have an understanding of the roles of others. Even in the case of professions that work closely together and where mutual role clarity might be considered a natural consequence of clinical activity, education can enable individuals to grasp the core skills, knowledge and philosophies that underpin the observed professional behaviour. Where large sections of a professional role are not even observed by other professions, formal opportunities to gain an understanding of the role become even more important. Although education should provide health care professionals with an understanding of what differentiates professions, it should equally enable them to recognise what they hold in common, and to develop a sense of ease with the role overlap that is bound to occur at professional boundaries. This enables appropriate sharing of professional expertise and appropriate patterns of referral. Education aimed at providing a clear understanding of roles should equally recognise professional interdependence, thereby enabling individuals to value their own contribution to 'team knowledge' and to recognise what they have to learn from others.

THE STAGES OF PROFESSIONAL DEVELOPMENT

Whether or not health care professionals consider themselves to be part of a multiprofessional team, they almost all work within a multiprofessional context. This is as true of junior students taking their first steps in the clinical arena as it is of the senior managers of a trust.

Even before students become observers of or participants in clinical practice, they are aware of this context, and the relationship between the health care professions will have formed as salient a part of their media socialisation as the characteristics of their own chosen profession. Although the initial concern of students entering the clinical arena is to develop comfort and competence in their monoprofessional role, that role will almost certainly involve contact with other professions. This contact will either reinforce or modify their stereotypes of the individual health care professions and their interaction.

Typical student experience involves exposure to a series of health care settings and teams, offering a rich environment for learning about teamwork, but requiring the early provision of tools to enable the student to make effective use of these learning opportunities. Because of the short duration of their involvement, students may only ever gain 'affiliate status' in a multiprofessional team. However, once they qualify and make a longer-term commitment to working in a particular clinical area, they have the opportunity to become more fully involved as individual professionals. Taking that opportunity involves a further development of their teamworking skills, including team building and their own skill at involving new members. The necessary development may take place as a result of individual learning or as part of a whole-team learning process.

Senior professional managers in the NHS may need to learn to promote and manage multiprofessional teamworking at an institutional level but, as is apparent from the evidence of the case studies, they also need to provide an organisational culture in which 'shop-floor' initiatives in effective clinical multiprofessional teamworking can thrive.

The issues raised by the study have implications for education at every stage of professional development. However, the precise agenda varies depending on the learning needs, learning opportunities and professional responsibilities that obtain at each stage of development. The agenda is also dependent on the extent to which students are capable of seeing themselves as part of a multiprofessional team rather than a monoprofessional one. The model shown in Figure 6.1 (see overleaf) (Miller *et al.*, 1997) identifies the stages of entry into full multiprofessional teamworking. It shows the new team member initially focusing on their own monoprofessional role, developing their awareness of the multiprofessional context and working in the background to gain recognition for their own expertise. It is only at this point that they can become comfortable as a proactive player on the multiprofessional stage. This model does not deny that the most junior student, working in a multiprofessional health care context, is required to participate in professional interaction, but it recognises that (at that stage) they do so largely as a proxy for senior members of their own profession.

A number of broad stages can be identified in the development of the professional. The clinical roles that are undertaken at any given stage will clearly be profession specific but, although the stages will vary in duration, they are common to all. These stages of professional development will first be briefly described, then the remainder of the chapter will map out the

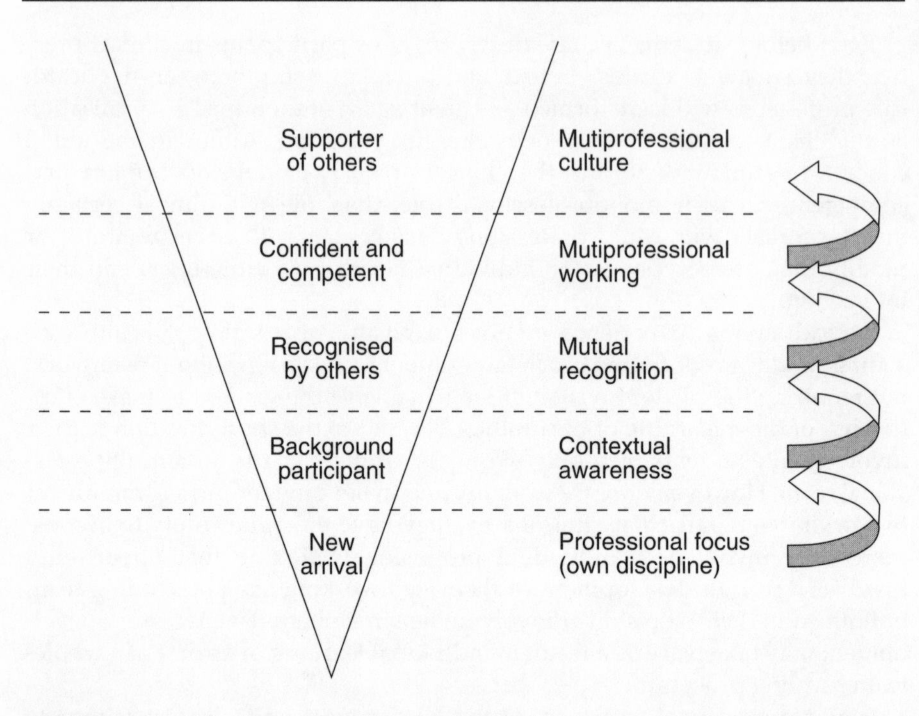

Figure 6.1 The stages of development from monoprofessional to multiprofessional working.

teamworking agenda for each stage and the learning outcomes that may be achieved.

The *preclinical student* is one who has not yet undertaken any clinical experience. Their initial theoretical instruction may take place in a multiprofessional environment, but any meaningful professional interaction is limited by their lack of knowledge of the realities of professional roles and their lack of experience of real clinical situations. The length of time spent in this stage varies considerably both between professions and over time. Student nurses have traditionally started ward-based learning after only a few weeks, although some courses now provide a much longer period of 'classroom'-based work. By contrast, medical students have traditionally spent the first 2 years of their training in a non-clinical environment, but many courses now introduce students to clinical practice, or at least to the influence of clinicians, at a much earlier stage.

As a *clinical novice*, the student is becoming familiar with clinical learning for the first time. However long the preclinical phase may be, theoretical study cannot fully prepare students for the reality of the clinical situation, either as a service or as a learning environment. At the beginning of this phase they recognise that they have a very limited command of their own profession's practice repertoire, and that the burden they impose on the monoprofessional team in terms of supervision and teaching outweighs the service that they provide. The student's first imperative is to equalise this balance by engendering trust among his or her colleagues (so reducing the level of supervision needed) and using the teaching they offer to become of service. Because of this imperative, their focus is almost entirely on the monoprofessional team rather than the multiprofessional one. Typically, the clinical novice develops their professional knowledge, skills and attitudes through a series of short clinical placements. Because much of what they learn in one clinical environment is applicable to the next, they enter each new clinical area with greater clinical ability and a more effective learning pattern.

As students develop a degree of comfort in their own professional role, they make the transition from clinical novice to *probationer*. The probationer is a senior student or 'intern' who is familiar with the clinical environment in general, but is not yet 'resident' in a particular clinical environment. Although their skill levels have increased, their accountability and responsibility are limited (often by law). As they develop ease in their monoprofessional roles and in their own professional persona, they become more capable of broadening their perspective to consider multiprofessional working.

To some extent, the difference between the probationer and the *practitioner* is one of organisational status. The practitioner is a qualified professional who practices in a particular clinical environment for a substantial period. They therefore have a commitment to and accountability for standards of professional care, and a responsibility for effective interaction with other professions. They are thus part of a multiprofessional work-force, which may or may not already function as a team. Equally, learning in relation to the teamwork agenda may continue to be an individual process for the practitioner, but may be at its most effective as a *whole-team learning activity*.

We have defined the *professional leader* in organisational terms as one who has overarching responsibility for the function of their profession in a number of clinical areas. The precise role varies from one profession to another. In medicine, the professional leader takes on those broader responsibilities in addition to maintaining an active clinical role. In many other professions, direct clinical activity gives way to a more managerial and supervisory role. In either case, the professional leader has a responsibility for developing or enabling the development of effective teamwork through individual or team learning strategies.

As identified in the previous chapters, our study raises issues in relation to the organisation, the individual and the group. All of these issues have implications for education. However it is managed, learning is fundamentally an individual process and, as has been suggested above, the new student is almost exclusively interested in their own individual development. It therefore seems appropriate to start by looking at the teamwork agenda as it relates to the individual, before moving on to look at the group and organisational issues on the agenda.

Pre-clinical learning

Clearly, our clinical teamwork study has implications for the education of health care professionals before they embark on their first clinical experiences.

It is, after all, the arena for which they are being prepared. It is important to consider the mind-set of students entering this clinical arena for the first time and the factors that mould it. This mind-set is largely the result of learning that has taken place prior to starting professional training, but the lay perspective and the stereotypes they bring with them can be either challenged or reinforced by their first experiences of health care education.

As has already been mentioned, students of some professions (e.g. medicine) may have a substantial preclinical component to their course. The majority of students from all professions will have a period of 'classroom' preparation before being placed in a clinical setting. For some, the preclinical phase of learning may be typified by a non-clinical educational agenda (e.g. the underpinning science), but even here the majority of courses will utilise clinical examples to contextualise and demonstrate the relevance of the basic science being taught. Most courses, including undergraduate medicine, will also recognise the importance of a preparatory agenda, that is broader than the basic sciences and which includes the instilling of a sense of personal responsibility for professional learning, and an understanding of the nature of the relationship between the professional and the patient.

Although a lack of clinical experience obviously places a number of restrictions on the relevance of the teamworking agenda for preclinical students, there are issues that can usefully be addressed at this stage. As identified above, some of these issues relate to the 'baggage' with which students enter their respective courses. Views of the health care professions are often stereotypical. These perceptions are based on the student's own contact (or that of their family) with the professions, and on the images (both factual and dramatic) portrayed in the media. Most students will have gone some way towards confirming or confronting the stereotypes they hold of their chosen profession before entering the course. Whether they have done so or not, there is a degree of automatic 'debunking' inherent in the professional education process. This debunking is unlikely to be as effective with regard to the views they hold of other professions, and the longer such views remain unchallenged the more consolidated they are likely to become.

The challenge to stereotypical views of other professions may be effectively started during the preclinical phase in multiprofessional groups, but it needs to avoid detailed consideration of roles. It can usefully focus on issues such as student understanding of the ethos of their own and other professions, and the different perspectives on the patient or client from which they work. As with most stereotypes, this is likely to involve a conscious recognition of the truth represented by the stereotype, as well as the misrepresentation (Hewstone and Stroebe, 1994). It can also bring in issues such as their reasons for choosing their own profession, and the way they perceive the relationship between their own profession and others. Although an appropriate focus for such learning is important, it may be that social contact, the development of good personal relationships between members of different professions, and the recognition of each other as individuals, rather than as a homogeneous professional group, represent as valuable an outcome as any other. Whatever the content, instruction provided by members of other professions, and especially by members of their own profession working in conjunction with other professions, will offer students a positive role model. Once again (with regard to the teamwork agenda) the content of such sessions is less important than the educational process.

During the preclinical period, courses should prepare students for the opportunities and constraints of clinical learning. This includes learning about the relationship between the health care worker and the patient, and the interpersonal skills through which this relationship is enacted. Students should also learn about their ethical responsibility as health workers to ensure that their learning 'should do the sick no harm' – that it should recognise the rights of the patient and their reason for being in a health care setting. This agenda can be extended to consider the worker–worker relationship and the professional and organisational context within which that relationship exists.

At this stage such learning can only be conceptual, because the students lack the clinical experience to make it real. However, they can learn the basic skills of working as a group through the experience of learning sets. The small group can also provide a context in which to start assertiveness/facilitative communication training. The development of such skills will enhance the acceptance of students into teams in the clinical setting, but students will also require more specific advice about how to negotiate entry into the team. Although such learning is clearly of value in a multiprofessional situation, this part of the agenda may initially be met within a monoprofessional framework. Since every student's first aspiration is to be accepted as a member of the monoprofessional team, this is entirely appropriate. Skills for negotiating entry into these teams will be transferable to the multiprofessional team at a later date.

By the end of the preclinical stage, students will:

- have a more realistic perception of their own profession and of the way in which professional approaches differ;
- have been given positive role models of interprofessional interaction;
- be able to communicate easily on a social level with students from other professions;
- have started to develop skills of assertive and facilitative communication which can be applied in the clinical arena;
- have developed skills of group working which will facilitate team entry.

The clinical novice

As students enter the clinical arena for the first time, the teamwork agenda starts to develop a more intrinsic relevance, but the focus is still on their own profession and the monoprofessional team. This is likely to be true whether the students have been in training for a few weeks (e.g. in nursing) or 2 years (as in the traditional medical school), because they have yet to be exposed to the multiprofessional context. Students at this stage judge the relevance of learning within a narrow frame of reference that is defined by the expectations held by themselves and others in relation to their own role (e.g. Lucas, 1990; Funnell *et al.*, 1992). Since they are still trying to develop their own basic competence and establish their own professional identity, they have little interest in making sense of the roles fulfilled by other professions. However, although the multiprofessional context of health care may be peripheral to their vision, they are constantly exposed to and acutely aware of it.

Within the clinical environment the health professions constantly interact, and students will see basic competence as being concerned with competently providing information to members of other professions, or competently carrying out the instructions of other professions, as well as being competent in their own profession's working practices. As novices, they have a limited sense of their own competence and will judge their professional performance on the basis of the approval of others. They therefore need to learn what other professions can legitimately expect of them. They are interested in learning how to respond 'correctly' to members of other professions, rather than being proactive, and in being able to offer information within predetermined and explicit parameters. They are therefore working within the multiprofessional context, but as 'part of the nursing team' or as 'part of the physiotherapy team' (i.e. the interactions are being determined by others). However, they are undertaking learning which will eventually enable them to play a fuller role in the multiprofessional team.

During the clinical novice phase, learning takes place in the theory or practice setting and may involve formal teaching, exposure to influential others within their own and other professions, or direct observation of the professions and their interaction. There are two specific questions about formal teaching that can usefully be asked in relation to this stage of the professional development process. First, considering the 'own profession' focus of the new student, what if any formal teaching about the multiprofessional context and teamwork is going to resonate sufficiently to enable quality learning? Secondly, what learning in relation to monoprofessional teamworking will, by its nature, be equally appropriate as preparation for multiprofessional work?

Although it is tempting to suggest that no formal teaching should take place in relation to the multiprofessional context until students have developed an appropriate level of comfort in their own professional role, this is to deny the fact that students are learning about other professions all the time. For example, a student nurse working with a staff nurse on the ward will learn about:

- the interface between their role and that of other professions: 'We are going to give this drug now because the doctor has ordered it on the drug chart';
- how their own profession views another profession: 'Typical! We can't give the drug because the doctor hasn't filled in the drug chart';
- how their own profession is viewed by another: 'You know the consultant

always gives this antibiotic post-operatively, so why did you have to get me out of bed to rewrite the drug chart?'.

Through these types of interaction, as well as more explicit passing on of opinions, the student develops a view of the professions involved in health care and of their professional station within the hierarchy (Hewstone and Stroebe, 1994). If students were only exposed to positive models of interactive working this would not be a problem, but this is clearly not the case. Even if they have gone through the preclinical preparation suggested in the previous section, the comparative strength of personal experience and clinical role models in professional socialisation means that negative influences may overturn the positive work that was undertaken in the controlled environment of the classroom. Even if the new student is not yet ready to learn about proactive involvement in multiprofessional teamwork, some sort of action will therefore be needed to ensure that they reach the point where such learning *is* relevant with positive views of the other professions, or at least with an open mind.

Brief formal teaching outlining the roles fulfilled by each profession and focusing on the interface and overlap at the role boundaries may be appropriate, especially as students become able to identify roles they have seen performed in the clinical area. More importantly, students may benefit from opportunities to reflect on and re-run critical incidents from their clinical experience – encouraging them to think more critically about received perspectives from fellow professionals and about the mental filter through which they observe others. Such interactive learning opportunities are probably only possible within the context of a multiprofessional learning group but, as suggested earlier, aspects of the teamwork agenda may also be addressed through monoprofessional learning.

Our clinical case studies identified a number of teamworking concepts and skills with which students need to become familiar. As was suggested in the previous section, students can embark on parts of this learning agenda before they move into the clinical learning environment, but such learning needs to continue into the clinical novice phase and beyond. Indeed, there are aspects of detailed learning about the skills of clinical teamwork (such as the development of strategies for securing entry and support) which would be difficult to consider without the opportunities that are provided by real experience. Although the concepts and skills are raised by the case studies in the context of the multiprofessional team, a number of them are equally relevant to monoprofessional teamwork. Students will observe considerable differences in the monoprofessional teams to which they are exposed, in relation to both structure and philosophy (e.g. those created by democratic, authoritarian or *laissez-faire* leaders) (Lippett and White, 1958). This will enable them to reflect on the rationale for and effect of different team strategies long before they are in a position to consider differents types of multiprofessional team (Øvretveit, 1995).

The monoprofessional team cannot be excised from its multiprofessional context, and students will be exposed to considerable differences in role boundaries. If these are explored rather than merely experienced, students may develop a more positive view of the differences in role boundaries. Rather than being a source of confusion, a comparison between roles and role boundaries in different settings may enable the student to identify the fluid periphery and (by differentiation) the core of the professional role.

One particular skill which our study showed that students need to develop as early as possible is that of gaining acceptance and incorporation into a team. Again, this is just as true of a monoprofessional team as it is of a multiprofessional team. The development of team entry strategies which started in the preclinical phase can usefully continue here. At this stage in the student's development, institutionally driven mentoring systems are particularly important, as new students are in greatest need of having someone 'to take them under their wing', but are least able to choose an appropriate mentor for themselves.

Students who started assertiveness training in the relatively safe, non-hierarchical (but often competitive) environment of the learning group will need to continue the development of their skills during this stage. Our study suggests that, in a multiprofessional context, assertiveness training may be particularly important for groups such as nurses, who view themselves as less powerful. However, observations of patterns of communication within medical teams (Sinclair, 1997) would suggest that junior entrants to 'high-status' monoprofessional teams may be just as much in need of assertiveness training as their counterparts who enter 'low-status' monoprofessional teams. Although this need might be universal, differences in the status of the various groups of junior students would suggest that training might still be better managed monoprofessionally.

If the agenda outlined above were to be followed, new students would enter the senior stages of initial training much better equipped to move from a monoprofessional to a multiprofessional learning focus. They should be less burdened by inappropriate professional stereotypes, have a clearer and better contextualised perception of the permanent core and fluid periphery of their own professional role, and have a clearer picture of the variety of teamworking models. Furthermore, they would have the appropriate communication and interpersonal skills for gaining acceptance within the multiprofessional team and for making an effective contribution.

By the end of the clinical novice stage, students will:

- respond to members of other professions with confidence, communicating formally within parameters and using channels determined or defined by the professions involved;
- reflect on the ways in which the health care professions view each other, and recognise the truths and fictions underpinning these views;
- recognise that each profession is a heterogeneous collection of individuals, and that individual members of a profession should be treated as such;

- have an outline understanding of the roles fulfilled by each profession and the ways in which these roles abut/overlap;
- demonstrate a clearer understanding of the solid core and fluid periphery of the role of their own profession;
- identify effective strategies for securing entry to and support from the monoprofessional team;
- observe different teamworking strategies within the monoprofessional teams to which they are exposed, and identify the factors that shape those strategies and their consequences;
- apply their initial assertiveness training when dealing with members of their own and other professions.

The probationer

Within the loose categorisation that was suggested at the beginning of this chapter, the probationer may be defined as one who has already gained sufficient experience within the clinical area to have developed a degree of comfort with their own professional role, but who is still being required to undertake set clinical learning in a number of different clinical areas. Their responsibility and accountability are therefore limited. Commitment to a particular area is also likely to be limited by the transient nature of the probationer's presence, and by the fact that the experiences were allocated to the individual, rather than selected by them.

The sophistication and accuracy of insight into the roles and behaviours of other professions may be dependent on the curriculum in the early part of the course, but all senior students will have had ample opportunity to observe other professions in the clinical area. They will necessarily have had some interaction with other professions through their own clinical activity, but this interaction is likely to have related to specific tasks being undertaken under instruction from more senior members of their own profession (e.g. responding to others or acting as a conduit for information).

The priority of students entering the probationer stage is still usually the demonstration of effective monoprofessional teamworking (Miller *et al.*, 1998). They will have some theoretical knowledge of multiprofessional working, but minimal experience of being a player in the multiprofessional team. They will have considered the roles fulfilled by each profession 'in principle', but will not have considered how those roles might 'play out' in specific clinical situations. They may well have been aware of conflicts arising from the different professional perspectives, but they are unlikely to have considered strategies for conflict resolution. They may have acted under instruction to enable a co-ordinated multiprofessional response (e.g. through agreed patterns of referral), but will not have been active in negotiating the multiprofessional response.

As the case studies suggested, these developments represent an important agenda. Qualifying professionals quickly find themselves without close supervision and therefore required to 'lead' for their profession in multiprofessional negotiation in relation to decision-making about clinical intervention. It is therefore an appropriate agenda for later years of initial training. Without encouragement, students are unlikely to look beyond the monoprofessional nest and start to prepare themselves for their role in the multiprofessional world. In the best team environments, this encouragement may take place automatically through appropriate involvement in effective teamworking strategies but, as was mentioned earlier, exposure to such teams cannot be guaranteed. A more planned approach to this learning is therefore necessary.

Appropriate planned approaches could be expected to revolve around an interplay between 'classroom' and clinical environments. Senior students will already have sufficient experience to be able to bring a realistic professional perspective to clinical teamworking problems translated into a safe (i.e. non-clinical) multiprofessional environment. This would give students greater opportunity to explore the rationale underpinning particular professional actions, rather than simply surface behaviours, thereby enabling them to explore the knowledge base and health care philosophy of other professions. This learning can focus on the interaction between the professions and the development of effective tactics for resolving conflicts and getting the best from the multiprofessional team. Clearly, any problems or cases (case scenarios) would need to be relevant to all of the students involved in their consideration (Knowles, 1984; Areskog, 1995). As students are using their monoprofessional experience to date as the basis for working on such problems or case scenarios, they should not relate to types of clinical area in which the students have not worked. The specific problem or case needs to offer all students the opportunity to work together (Silver, 1998) to contribute meaningfully to its solution.

The case studies suggested that problem- or case-scenario-based learning might be sequenced to manage the student's route through this complex agenda. Students may start with problems/scenarios where professional roles are clear and compatible and the focus of learning is on appropriate patterns of interprofessional communication. They might then move on to problems/scenarios where there is some uncertainty about which profession does what, allowing them to explore 'conflicts' over role boundaries. At a later stage in initial training, they may tackle problems/scenarios where the perspective of the various professions would lead them to favour different patient interventions.

The understanding developed through these classroom processes can then be used in the clinical area, thereby sensitising students to multiprofessional issues. This will enable them to observe multiprofessional practices with a more intelligent eye, and to engage more competently with members of other professions on an individual level. In gaining acceptance within the team, senior students are better placed than their more junior colleagues because of the more even balance of the increased service workload undertaken and the reduced supervision workload created for the trained staff (Cerinus and Furguson, 1994). Although gaining entry still means finding an appropriate sponsor within the team, their relationship becomes more collegiate than controlling. By the end of their initial training, students are likely to be required to find this mentor figure for themselves, a skill which is going to be vital to their continuing professional development.

During the probationary phase, students are also in the best position to explore teamworking models and strategies, to evaluate their effectiveness and to take ownership of those approaches they would wish to promote in monoprofessional and multiprofessional working. Compared to their junior colleagues, they are more aware of the activities of the multiprofessional team. They are also exposed to a number of different teams and thus have the opportunity to compare and contrast them.

The students' exploration of teamwork and of the differences in structure and process of the teams through which they pass will undoubtedly raise questions about how teams are shaped by their organisational context. The understanding they develop will make them more constructively critical of patterns of teamwork that they encounter in new environments. Understanding the organisational constraints within which their 'new' team functions may make it easier for students to recognise which of the teamworking strategies that they have developed through past experience can and cannot be appropriately utilised in the new environment. In a conducive environment, this might involve sharing collaborative strategies which they have found useful elsewhere. In a less conducive environment, it might mean invoking strategies which would at least ensure that they use any opportunities they find for multiprofessional interaction (i.e. we are not advocating that students act as agents for change).

In the 'real world' of clinical learning, equivalent student experience cannot be guaranteed. Some students will be exposed to team-orientated clinical environments and joint working practices such as shared notes and joint planning and evaluation. Group reflection will allow those students who have had such experience to share their learning with those who have been less fortunate. A discussion of the effects of such approaches and the different ways in which they are applied can provide students with an array of tools to take into their post-qualification role.

By the end of the probationer stage, students will:

- understand how the roles of the various professions translate into required action and interaction in a given clinical situation;
- be able to lead for their profession in negotiating an effective, co-ordinated multiprofessional response to a specific clinical situation;
- be able to identify successful strategies for conflict resolution between members of the multiprofessional team;
- demonstrate a growing understanding of the thought process underpinning clinical decisions made by members of other professions and what that process demands of them in terms of sharing information;
- start to engage effectively in dialogue with members of other professions in the clinical area, in both unstructured situations (e.g. bedside planning) and structured ones (e.g multiprofessional team meetings);
- understand a range of teamworking models, and recognise how they are shaped by the organisation and the clinical field;
- recognise whether teamworking strategies to which they have been exposed are applicable within a given clinical setting.

The practitioner

The newly qualified professional, in becoming a long-term member of the work-force in a particular clinical area, faces a massive change in role and responsibilities. Despite the fact that students have been training to take on the qualified role for anything from 3 to 5 years, research has shown that many of them still experience considerable 'future shock' when they leave behind the relative protection of student or probationer status. This relates partly to the new roles they are required to fulfil and partly to the new context of accountability within which they have to fulfil roles (Sinclair, 1997). The move may therefore create a situation in which the newly qualified professional experiences a reduction in confidence and competence.

For the first time, new professionals find themselves in a situation where they are stable members of a clinical environment and have an opportunity to take up full membership of a multiprofessional team. Full membership is gained in their own right as individual professionals, as opposed to the 'associate membership' that is granted through membership of their profession. Although team membership is now a possibility, it is not achieved automatically on qualification. As was demonstrated by the case studies, it is dependent on both the team and the individual concerned.

Some teams appear to be more reluctant than others to allow new staff full entry. A sense of trust between existing members of the team may have developed over a number of years through a shared history that can never be experienced by a newcomer. In addition, such shared experience leads to the development of a communication shorthand which further excludes the newcomer. In these situations, the difficulty experienced by the newcomer is to some extent the result of the cohesion of the existing team. In other situations, it may be the result of lack of cohesion. Cliques within a team make life very difficult for the newcomer, and their selection of a mentor (from their own or another profession) may make the difference between acceptance and non-acceptance.

In other areas, the existing professionals may simply lack the strategies to include new members effectively, and to make them feel valued. Where such difficulties are long-standing, these groups are clearly likely to suffer generally in terms of team function. The rate of turnover is likely to be high, and the team may consist of a number of 'generations' of unassimilated newcomers. Such groups can be melded through the development of joint philosophies and working practices. (The means for achieving this will be discussed later in relation to whole-team learning.)

Where the existing professionals in a particular clinical area can be termed a team, the new professional needs to refine and reapply the skills they developed as a student (gaining associate membership of a monoprofessional team), and develop new skills related to full membership of both monoprofessional and multiprofessional teams. The degree to which such skills are absolutely necessary will to some extent be determined by the degree of facilitation available, but they are always valuable. A team that needs to expend less energy in drawing in a new member is bound to be more positively disposed towards him or her.

For the first time, new professionals are likely to be in a clinical team long enough to experience change processes happening to the team, rather than differences between one team and another.

The case studies suggest that team members need help to come to terms with this experience of personal change, especially if it is perceived as change in professional roles or role boundaries. There may be advantages to such help being provided within the team, as others in the same situation will be aware of both external and internal factors relating to the change process, and they are also likely to be party to any negotiation over changing boundaries. Indeed, where such facilitation of new professionals is not possible internally, this might suggest that there is a need for whole-team learning in relation to strategies for managing and coping with role change.

As was identified previously, some degree of assertiveness training may be important throughout initial training, but this relates as much to functioning within the monoprofessional hierarchy as to any multiprofessional activity. The newly qualified professional needs to reapply those assertiveness skills in what may be perceived as a more threatening context. Current patterns of staffing mean that, in many clinical areas, the new professional is unlikely to have the peer group support (however tacit) that they enjoyed as students, or the direct back-up of a more experienced member of their own profession. They may be forced by circumstance into a position where they have to communicate across considerable variation in seniority *and* across the hierarchy of the professions. New learning of assertiveness skills is likely to be necessary for newly qualified nurses dealing with senior doctors, but it is also likely to be valued by junior doctors, who may feel very vulnerable in their dealings with senior nurses. Such learning may well be best provided outside the specific clinical area in which a new professional works. This provides a safe environment in which to test and refine interprofessional communication strategies without endangering long-term relationships.

Additional learning in relation to joint working practices and the development of common philosophies is vitally important to the new professional. Although the perceived advantages of joint practices may be taught didactically in the 'classroom' situation, specific joint practices and common philosophies need to be developed within the context of a specific team. They need to take into account the physical resource, the client base and the specific mix of professions involved.

Where a multiprofessional team already has well-developed, shared philosophies and joint practices, the case studies showed that these were likely to be effectively transmitted to newcomers. However, where the existing team members excluded newcomers from 'full communion', the transmission of a team philosophy could not be guaranteed. Where there is a need for development of a shared philosophy and effective joint working practices, a process of whole-team learning is likely to be appropriate. This will be explored in the next section. Developing the strategies and skills necessary to enable such learning where motivation exists, and to foster motivation where it does not, forms part of the teamwork agenda for senior staff, and this subject will be discussed subsequently.

As practitioners, qualified professionals will:

- demonstrate attitudes which facilitate the development and maintenance of effective multiprofessional teamworking;
- apply appropriate strategies to gain entry to the multiprofessional team, including the selection of an appropriate mentor from their own or another profession;
- respond to change processes in a multiprofessional context, especially in relation to professional boundaries, in a way that balances professional and whole-team considerations;
- demonstrate assertive and facilitative communication styles as appropriate in multiprofessional negotiation;
- select appropriate joint working practices from those with which they are familiar, and propose their adoption by the multiprofessional team.

Whole-team learning

Each of the individuals who together comprise a multiprofessional team may usefully develop and bring to the specific team context an understanding of other professions and their roles, with a raft of skills and attitudes which foster appropriate interaction. Indeed, the previous sections of this chapter have identified how such a learning agenda for teamworking might be structured and managed. Whether or not such learning becomes the norm, the issues raised by the case studies suggest that there is a further level of teamworking development that can only realistically be undertaken as part of a whole-team learning process.

An important aspect of the multiprofessional teamwork learning agenda suggested by the case studies relates to the development of shared strategies for clinical interventions and for professional interaction, and joint practices in note-keeping, hand-over procedures, etc. Whole-team learning strategies, in which not just all professions but all staff are involved, are an ideal means of meeting this agenda. They enable learning to be focused on the specific clinical context in terms of geography, organisation, resource and function. Interprofessional communication can therefore be learned in the context of everyday reality, rather than as an abstract concept, and the development of joint working practices can take effective account of specific constraints and opportunities. Furthermore, the shared learning process becomes an exemplar for the model of teamworking that is being promoted in day-to-day clinical activity. When the intention is to shift what may be deeply entrenched attitudes, the appropriateness of the learning process to the intended outcome is vital (Jarvis, 1988; Long, 1996).

Where do such whole-team learning processes take place? Clearly the material for much of the learning is to be found in the clinical area itself. Current practices – both satisfactory and unsatisfactory – can provide a springboard for continuing development of best teamwork practice. Poor teamworking practices may provide evidence of patient care problems that might have been prevented, or patient care opportunities that were missed. Satisfactory practices may bring to light new opportunities for the continuing consolidation and enhancement of teamwork. However, in-depth learning in the clinical environment is constrained by the primacy and urgency of patient care, the need to present a united face, and existing team practice, structure and hierarchy.

Whether an issue is one that needs to be brought to the attention of the whole team by an individual profession, or whether it is one which the whole team recognises, there may therefore be advantages to considering it outside the clinical area. As was discussed in previous sections, reflective learning is a useful means by which professionals can make sense of their clinical experience (Palmer *et al.*, 1994). Members of different professions may well have different perceptions of any given clinical event. Group reflective processes can help a team to share those perceptions and identify a common way forward, whether this is in terms of shared strategies, joint practices or changed behaviours.

Individuals who are familiar with reflective processes and are part of a group that is already functioning well may be able to participate in such group learning processes without the need for facilitation. When considering non-contentious issues, facilitation may be provided by a member of the team who has the necessary skills to maintain an even-handed approach. However, there are many group learning issues for which some sort of external facilitation is likely to be vital to a successful conclusion. For example, where a powerful individual from a high-status profession is reluctant to recognise a need for change, internal group leadership may be problematic. If that individual is also the leader, the problems suggesting the need for change may not even reach the agenda. Where two or more professions are in conflict, an external facilitator may be viewed as an impartial 'referee' who is able to achieve resolution, when an internal group leader would be regarded as an interested party. An external facilitator may also play a key role in encouraging those professionals who are not raising issues or challenging others to take a more active part in the group process.

The design of whole-team learning strategies, including decisions about the need for external facilitation, has to take on board the different entry behaviour of each profession – that is, the degree to which each is signed up to the idea that the development of joint approaches and working practices is desirable and should be achieved by democratic means. It is only too easy to bring to mind situations in which joint working strategies are desired by some professions and rejected by others. Unless the dissenters can be brought on board, the best that can be achieved is joint working among part of the team. If the dissenters are peripheral, the result will be a core and periphery model. If one of the key players refuses to 'play', the result is likely to be the continuation of fragmentary working. Depending on the power of the objecting profession, it may be that they are in a position to veto the development overtly or to undermine it covertly. If a belief in the importance of common purpose and direction is part of the definition of a team, then whole-team learning strategies need to be designed to facilitate this before they move on to a more substantive agenda.

There is also an assumption that the *individuals* concerned in whole-team learning – whatever their profession – are able to cast aside constraints on patterns of communication, interaction and decision-making which may be current within the clinical area. As was identified from the case studies, constraints may relate to the comparative status of the various professions, to the comparative status of an individual within a profession, or to their status within a team (e.g. founder member/newcomer, insider/outsider, central/peripheral). Constraints may also relate to a perceived risk in opening up specific clinical actions and decisions to scrutiny. It may be valuable to consider how such constraints could be affected by the following:

- the proximity of the learning environment to the clinical workplace;
- the 'ownership' of the learning environment (territorial advantage);
- the organisation of learning as part of, or separate from, a clinical shift;
- the organisation of learning in terms of 'a whole study day' or 'the odd hour';
- making whole team-learning a 'uniform' or 'mufti' activity.

There are very real organisational constraints on whole-team learning in most secondary care situations, created by the impossibility of closing down a 7-day service to enable all team members to meet at one time. This is likely to mean that all of the individual members of the team can only be involved serially in any learning/development process. Although many whole-team learning processes will, in any case, take place through a series of events, care needs to be taken to avoid the potential problems caused by inconsistent attendance.

Senior professionals form the interface between the clinical team and the larger organisation, representing each entity to the other. As such, they have a vital role to play in both encouraging and enabling the development of effective teamwork. Much of their role within the clinical team is about facilitation and leadership in the achievement of the learning agenda already identified within this and previous sections. Preparation for leadership in these activities suggests an additional learning process to those already described, if not a different content. The final section of this chapter will therefore focus on these additional processes and on issues raised by the case studies which suggest a specific teamwork agenda for the senior professional.

> In addition to their learning as individual practitioners, whole-team learning will enable professionals who work together to:
>
> - develop a shared team philosophy and culture which supports individual and collective responsibilities;
> - develop a multiprofessional team structure that will enable the team philosophy to be enacted in patient care;

- develop shared strategies for clinical intervention in given circumstances, identifying the roles of each profession and the means of ensuring effective interaction;
- develop patterns of communication which facilitate efficient interaction between existing team members, but which do not exclude new members;
- develop strategies for inclusion of new members which allow the sharing of team culture and philosophy whilst at the same time promoting openness to the new ideas and ways of working they bring with them;
- value the input of a neutral outsider in facilitating the development of effective team processes.

The professional leader

Senior members of any profession have a specific responsibility for the development of team processes. In terms of the management of change, they are key players. They have considerable influence over more junior staff through the role model they present, the professional opinions they offer, the organisational position they hold and the organisational decisions they make. Successful multiprofessional teams often rely on a high-level sponsor to lead the process. For example, in the rehabilitation unit case study the importance of the unit manager to the development of effective team practices was paramount.

Senior management courses will therefore need to alert professional leaders to a whole raft of issues relating to their role in creating a fertile environment for the development of multiprofessional teamworking and ways of responding constructively to teamworking initiatives that are developed on the 'shop floor'.

Generally speaking, all the management issues raised by multiprofessional working will have their monoprofessional counterpart. Creating an appropriate environment for the development of multiprofessional teamworking will share many facets of creating a fertile environment for teaching students, or for clinical audit, or for the introduction of named nurses. In the same way, the ability to respond to initiatives from the 'shop floor' is largely about management style, whether those initiatives are about instituting joint note-keeping or changing physiotherapy practices.

The required change in any senior management course would therefore be a reframing of existing content to reflect the increasingly multiprofessional environment of health and social care. This reframing would require the same awareness of other professions as was previously discussed in relation to the probationer and the practitioner, with a change in focus towards the organisational and management context within which each profession works. Courses need to enable the professional leader to avoid dissonance between their role as figurehead and spokesperson for their own profession, and their role as a manager for the organisation. Joint learning at senior management level will enable the development of an understanding of how the managers of different professions feel themselves to be either enabled or constrained by both the organisational context and by their own professional bodies.

At the level of professional leaders, simulation or modelling of alternative patterns of multiprofessional working can be a useful learning tool for the organisation as well as for the individual. It provides a vehicle for the consideration of service decisions, in which risks may be taken with limited consequences and in which less constrained thinking may therefore be safely employed.

If members of all professions were developing through the staged multiprofessional learning framework that has been described in this chapter, there might be little need to specify formal multiprofessional learning at this stage, as it could be assumed that the necessary levels of interprofessional empathy had already been reached. However, waiting for those 'changed' professionals to rise through the ranks is not an option. If the organisational context fails to encourage collaborative working, the learning which should support multiprofessional working may be extinguished in individuals before they themselves reach levels of influence.

Multiprofessional learning at a management level might therefore valuably precede the implementation of the suggested learning at more junior levels. Much of the teaching and learning of senior professionals already takes place in small multiprofessional groups. A shift in focus from common learning ('we all need to learn the same thing') towards shared learning ('we all have something to learn from each other') should be both achievable and effective.

As professional leaders, senior staff will:

- develop an understanding of multiprofessional working which will enable them to provide a fertile environment for the development of a shared culture and joint practices;
- use their professional expertise to respond constructively and critically to multiprofessional initiatives coming from the clinical area;
- have a clear understanding of the context created for each profession by the organisation and their management structures;
- balance their role as champions of their own professions with their organisational role in the promotion of effective health care in a multiprofessional environment;
- develop effective strategies for multiprofessional leadership within the organisation.

In this chapter we have described the multiprofessional teamworking agenda and what it would mean in terms of learning content and outcome at the various stages of professional development. Whilst recognising the importance of the organisational context in determining the potential for effective teamworking, it is clear that, although formal education in effective multiprofessional working may not be a *sine qua non*, it can be of considerable benefit in encouraging and enabling best practice.

The teamwork agenda and the nature of the required learning both suggest specific learning strategies, but these need to be implemented within higher education and health care organisations. The reality of the health care organisation as a context for multiprofessional learning has been described in the previous chapters. We shall now explore the current reality of higher education. What is the extent of multiprofessional education, and to what degree is it informed by the teamwork agenda? What are the barriers to multiprofessional learning, and to what extent have they been overcome? These questions will be addressed in Chapter 7.

7 Where we are now: the current provision of multiprofessional education

INTRODUCTION

The clinical case studies provided a clear picture of the varying and vital nature of teamwork in multiprofessional practice and the experiential learning which helped to shape it. They also gave an insight into the potential role of formal education in enabling professionals to work together more effectively. Multiprofessional teamwork in clinical areas provides an agenda for education, but education is shaped by competing and sometimes conflicting factors. Each set of circumstances is different, and educational solutions must take the differences into account; it would therefore be inappropriate to try to identify a single ideal model. However, it is possible to identify characteristics which would enhance a programme's value and facilitate learning that could not otherwise be achieved. The clinical teamwork agenda has implications for both of the following:

- the appropriate content of multiprofessional learning;
- the nature of the teaching and learning strategies employed.

THE CONTENT OF MULTIPROFESSIONAL EDUCATION

The nature of much of the educational content suggested by the case studies means that it is often impossible to separate the subject being taught from the teaching and learning strategies employed. However, some elements of programme content are not process-specific. There are also elements of learning about multiprofessional teamwork which could be equally well managed through monoprofessional learning. For example, learning about different types of team and their impact on the nature of teamwork, and how teams function within the context of the organisation, does not depend on a multiprofessional forum but could be delivered as lectures or small-group teaching. In either case, it might be most appropriate to start from a consideration of the monoprofessional team, before bringing in cross-professional complexities. For most learning that is needed to support multiprofessional teamwork, an appropriate teaching and learning process is as important as the specific content.

Students need to:

- be aware of different professional roles and to understand the type of rationale which underpins actions/decisions;
- communicate in an interprofessional arena, using assertive and facilitative communication styles across status differences;
- take on team member and team leader roles, depending on the nature of the problem, rather than the status of the professionals involved;
- recognise and value multiple perspectives on problems and differences in value/belief systems;
- be aware of the stereotypes they hold of other professions and their limited value;
- deal effectively with interprofessional conflict, learning to treat it as a positive challenge and using it to hone their professional skills.

The clinical case studies also showed that students need to:

- be aware of joint practices such as joint report/handover, shared notes, joint planning and evaluation, and their potential benefits for patient care;
- recognise that the team is a social as well as a functional entity, and that all of its members are needed to build and maintain it;
- learn to work flexibly within different team patterns and to deal effectively with change; role boundaries shift over time and in relation to specific contexts, and students need to understand their role in a given context, in relation to the 'jigsaw' of other roles, while keeping sight of their own professional core activities;
- learn the skills of being a newcomer and seeking a helpful team member to facilitate their acceptance, and develop the skills of incorporating other professionals into a team of which they are already a member.

THE PROCESS OF MULTIPROFESSIONAL EDUCATION

Most of the learning agenda identified above can only be effectively learned through interactive strategies. This suggests the utilisation of small multiprofessional groups that enable the sharing of experiences and expertise.

Many of the appropriate attitudes and skills are difficult to construe outside the practice environment, which suggests that scenario-based learning might be appropriate, utilising the skills of interaction in relation to specific problems. It might also facilitate interprofessional sharing if two students from each profession were included in each group, enabling them to discuss and refine a monoprofessional argument before proposing it to other members.

Although such learning might focus on patient problems, it is equally possible to conceive of exercises that focus on team problems, complex interprofessional communication and some of the joint activities already mentioned.

Scenarios would need to:

- enable the development of particular skills;
- ensure that all members had the opportunity to be a team leader and a team member;
- enable students to move from monoprofessional situations through collaborative multiprofessional situations before being faced with scenarios in which professional roles and opinions might be expected to conflict.

COMPARISON OF THE TEAMWORK AGENDA AND CURRENT PATTERNS OF MULTIPROFESSIONAL LEARNING IN HIGHER EDUCATION

The clinical case studies suggest that considerable benefit can be derived from interactive multiprofessional education. However, the survey revealed that little multiprofessional education was being offered, despite the rise in numbers of primary and community care initiatives since 1992 (Barr and Waterton, 1996). Moreover, little of the multiprofessional education on offer follows the pattern suggested by the NHS teamworking agenda.

Quantitative data from the survey include the distribution of current initiatives in terms of pre- and post-qualification education and categories of learning focus (e.g. biological science, research, interprofessional issues). Following the collection of the survey data, telephone interviews and follow-up visits identified factors that were constraining the provision of multiprofessional education, which may go some way towards explaining the mismatch between current provision and the agenda identified in Chapter 6.

THE NATIONAL SURVEY OF INITIATIVES IN MULTIPROFESSIONAL EDUCATION

The aim of the survey of educational institutions in the UK that offer pre- or post-qualification education programmes for health and social care professionals was to gain an insight into the extent, nature and purpose of multiprofessional learning, and to identify initiatives in which nurses, midwives and/or health visitors undertook learning with other professions. An initiative might be a whole programme, a module or a workshop/study day. The survey separated pre- and post-qualification education using the following definitions.

- *Pre-qualification education:* education leading to entry to a particular profession (e.g. programmes for nurses wishing to register as midwives, undergraduate medical education and pre-qualification house officer training, pre-registration physiotherapy).
- *Post-qualification education:* education for which membership of a profession is a prerequisite, or which is designed to serve health care professionals as one among a number of professional groups.

As well as providing an overview of national provision, the survey represented the first stage in the process of identifying appropriate initiatives for further study. Two questionnaires were distributed to all higher education institutions that were running programmes for health and social care professions. The first questionnaire sought information about the extent of provision and the second one explored the initiatives in greater depth. Questionnaires were distributed to all higher education institutions running programmes for health and social care professions. The response identified a wide spectrum of different types of initiative, which appears to be representative.

The first questionnaire included questions about the spread of health care professions taught within the institution, and whether they were taught at a pre- or post-qualification level. It asked respondents to list multiprofessional learning initiatives and to specify the professions involved. The second questionnaire was designed to collect information about the following aspects of each initiative identified:

- the professions involved and the number from each profession;
- status – when was it implemented, or whether it was still just a proposal;
- who instigated the development and for what purpose;
- the topic area, the nature of the teaching and learning process and the aims and learning outcomes;
- the length of the initiative and how it fitted in with the overall educational process for different professions;
- the financial and resource implications;
- the response of students, teachers and professional bodies.

The first questionnaire was distributed to a named person in each of 181 faculties/departments. It was not restricted to institutions offering nurse education. The response is shown in Figure 7.1. A total of 74 contacts identified multiprofessional initiatives running or under development, and in total 206 initiatives were identified, including 13 initiatives from one institution. The majority of them (68%) were in post-qualification education.

A second questionnaire related to each of the 206 initiatives identified; 95 of these questionnaires were completed and returned. In terms of pre- and post-qualification education, the profile was consistent with the first questionnaire; 65 (68%) related to post-qualification education, 27 (28%) to pre-qualification education and three (4%) involved pre- and post-qualification students.

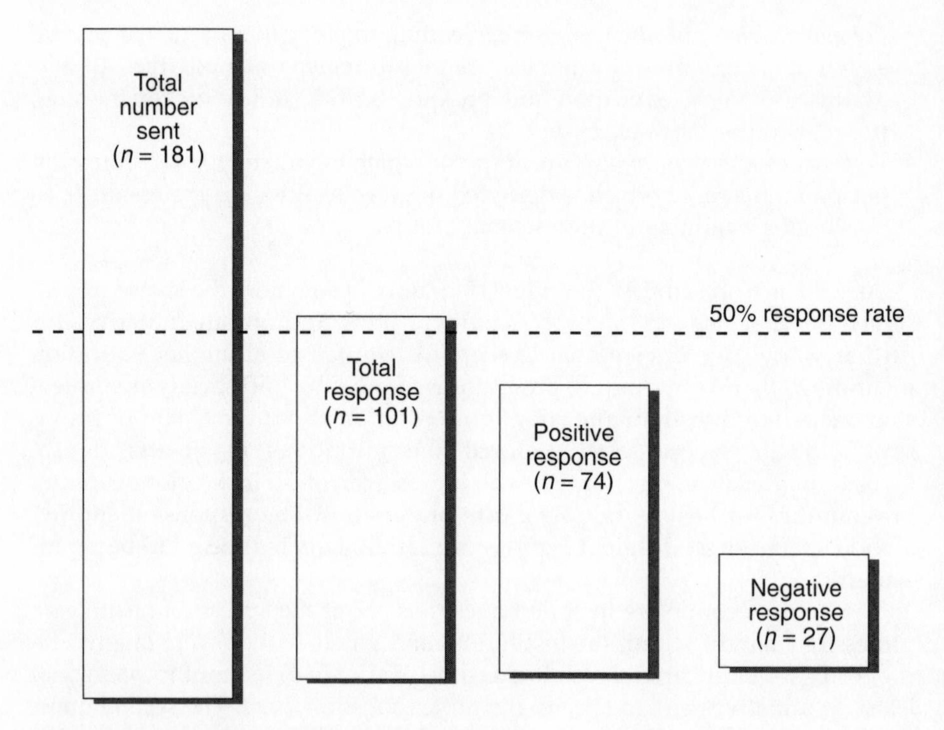

Figure 7.1 Response to the first postal survey.

Academic level of programmes

The second questionnaire revealed a considerable emphasis on degree-level learning, particularly in pre-qualification education. Figure 7.2 (opposite) compares the results obtained for the two categories.

Who instigated the initiative?

The overwhelming majority of initiatives were instigated by higher education alone, with small numbers being instigated by health care providers/purchasers alone, or jointly with higher education institutions (see Table 7.1 opposite). Three respondents did not provide this information.

Breadth of professional involvement

A broad spectrum of professions is involved in multiprofessional education. Most initiatives (85) included nurses, and of the remainder, eight involved different professions allied to medicine (PAMs) and two involved PAMs and social workers. Although the questionnaire was not designed to capture initiatives which only involved nurses, midwives and/or health visitors,

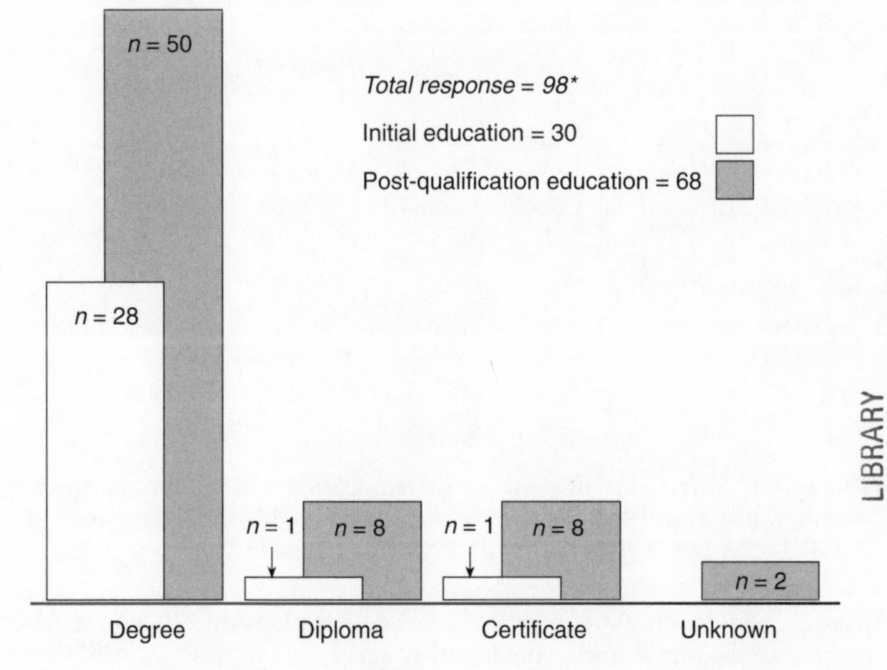

Figure 7.2 Academic level of initiatives in initial and post-qualification. *Initiatives relating to both initial and continuing education have been included in both categories, increasing the identified response from 95 to 98.

seven of the 85 initiatives involving nursing were of this type, leaving 78 initiatives involving nurses or nursing students with other professions. Figure 7.3 shows the balance of different combinations.

The nature of the initiatives

Of the 78 initiatives involving nursing, midwifery and/or health visiting plus other professional groups, six post-qualification and three initial education programmes were too broad to categorise in terms of learning focus. For the remainder, the main categories of learning focus are shown in Figure 7.4

Table 7.1 The instigation of initiatives

	Higher education instigated	Jointly instigated	Health service instigated
Initial education	22	6	1
Post-qualification	40	17	6

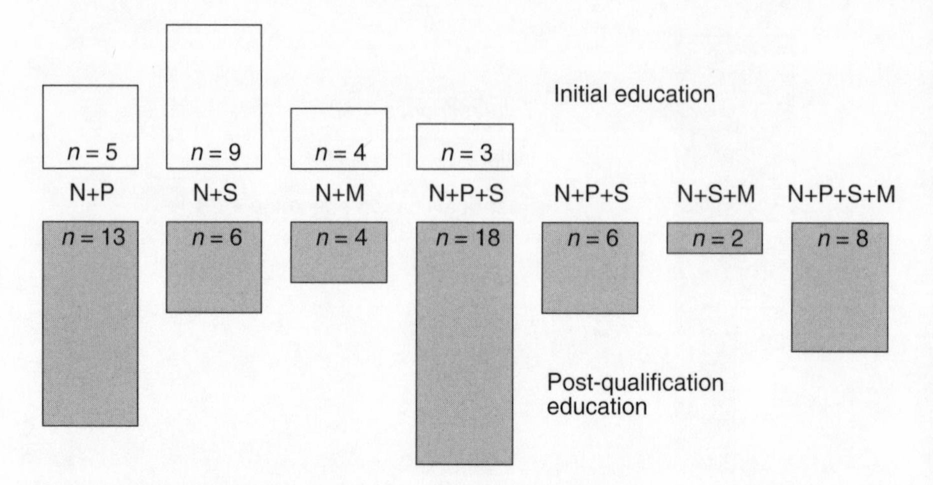

Figure 7.3 Professions involved in shared learning. N = nursing (nursing, midwifery, health visiting); P = PAMs (therapists, podiatrists, radiographers, etc.); S = social work (social workers, youth workers); M = medicine (all doctors).

(page 187), illustrating the emphasis in pre-registration education on common learning in biological and behavioural science, compared to a broader role-based agenda in post-registration education. The figure shows the proportion of identified initiatives that fall into each of four broad categories:

- *common theory* – programmes offering learning which was considered to be part of a theoretical knowledge base shared by all of the professions involved;
- *clinical roles* – programmes offering learning in relation to clinical skills required by all of the professions concerned, whether in terms of shared health care interventions or of communication and counselling skills;
- *broader roles* – programmes offering learning about aspects of professional working falling outside those core roles that involve direct interaction with patients, and which are therefore considered to be common to all of the professions concerned;
- *professional issues* – programmes offering learning which was explicitly concerned with professional issues considered to be common to the professions involved or the relationship between those professions.

In each case, these categories are further subdivided.

THE MISMATCH OF TEAMWORKING AND CURRENT EDUCATION

The survey highlighted major differences in the nature of the interactions expected between students in multiprofessional groups. Many of the initiatives, especially in pre-qualification education, did not require any interaction between professions, and can be typified as bringing students together because they were considered to have common learning needs, rather than learning that they could share. Such 'common learning' is particularly prevalent as part

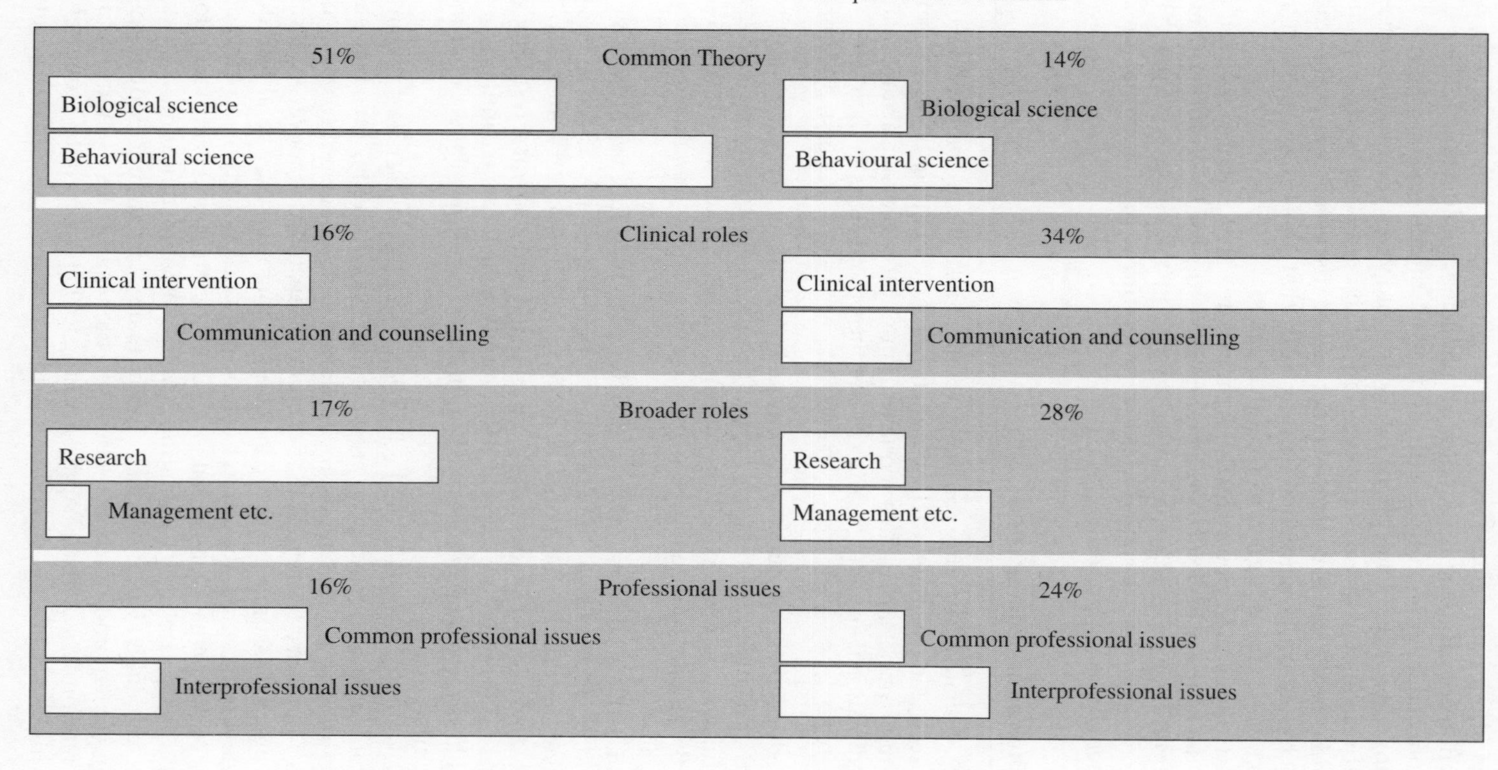

Figure 7.4 A comparison of the profile of subject matter of initiatives in initial and post-qualification education.

of foundation studies. By contrast, initiatives encouraging students to learn from and about each other ('shared learning') tended to occur later in pre-qualification education or as part of post-qualification education. Little multi-professional education in universities addressed interprofessional issues. The survey, together with the telephone interviews and visits, identified a range of potential reasons for this mismatch. Many of these related to the organisational and other practical constraints that will be discussed later in this chapter, but the most fundamental reason was that most higher education provision was never designed to meet that agenda.

The telephone interviews clearly demonstrated that initiatives which *did* address the teamwork agenda were invariably instigated by one or more individual professionals with a particular interest in the clinical outcome. The majority of them were designed to meet the legitimate organisational aims of the higher education provider.

The higher education agenda

> A lot of shared learning you hear about is just about the sharing of resources using a single teacher. Sometimes the economics of scale seem to be more important in the rationale for multiprofessional learning than any educational advantage. You can see the pound signs in their eyes.
>
> (Course director)

Higher education institutions are as enthusiastic in their support of multiprofessional education as trusts are of multiprofessional teamwork. However, this enthusiasm is not focused on meeting a need for teamwork education. Rather, the university agenda is focused on the economics and flexibility of provision.

The majority of universities provide education for a number of health care professions. Professional health care programmes are affected by the manpower needs of educational consortia. Since these vary annually, the contracted number of places for each profession will also vary, resulting in a considerable incentive to provide programmes which can accommodate the changes in professional numbers without altering staff numbers, departmental structures, etc.

The economics of professional education also push universities towards a multiprofessional approach. In pre-qualification education, the data show that programme content tends to be dominated by scientific knowledge. There is a tendency to suggest that anatomy is anatomy, whoever is learning it (although the assumption of a common learning need may be ill-founded). If this view is accepted, the subject can be provided in lectures to all groups simultaneously. Whatever the subject, such universal provision tends to be seen as appropriate at a foundation level. In post-qualification education, there is an equivalent 'problem', with many programmes focusing on common content and outcomes. However, the result is less serious, because more senior professionals can apply learning to their own context themselves.

The higher education agenda therefore promotes a pattern of multiprofessional education which assumes commonality rather than utilising and valuing differences. It values large-group, didactic teaching rather than small-group interaction and, in pre-registration education, it pushes provision to the early part of the programme.

Health service and higher education agendas push multiprofessional education in opposite directions in pre-qualification education (the former towards small-group interactive learning and the latter towards didactic lectures). If the NHS regards the multiprofessional agenda as sufficiently important, consortia must be encouraged to specify it in contracts and allowed to pay the extra costs incurred by education providers.

OTHER BARRIERS TO MULTIPROFESSIONAL EDUCATION

Not all barriers to effective multiprofessional education are as intransigent as the mismatch between the higher education and NHS agendas. The following areas were identified by a number of respondents, but those respondents also identified solutions or part solutions. Those identified at the end of each section are an extrapolation from these responses.

Historical and current patterns of higher education provision for the health care professions vary considerably. These differences throw barriers in the way of multiprofessional initiatives at a number of levels, including organisation, logistics of timetabling, group size, and timing and appropriateness for students. These obstacles will be discussed below.

Organisational barriers

> The opportunity for the clinical skills laboratory and joint teaching arose because [institution] had both a medical school and a school of nursing . . .The medical school has now gone to one university . . . and we've gone to another. I don't think the same initiative would have arisen in those circumstances.
>
> (Course director)

Medicine has a long history in higher education, and education is largely provided by long-established universities. In contrast, the recent entry of nurse education into higher education has most commonly been through institutions that have only recently been awarded university status. These newer universities are also the home of other health and social care professions, which preceded nursing into higher education. Schools of nursing often joined universities with existing health and social care programmes, including some nursing provision. However, the scale of the newcomer and its perceived potential to change the culture of pre-existing provision irrevocably has often meant that such schools maintain a semi-independent status.

Some of the initiatives studied in this project were *working across organisational boundaries*. Sometimes this was an accident of history, relating to organisational links which had since been severed. In other cases the links were intentional and were set up simply to enable the initiative. Although multiprofessional education can involve students in different faculties and, on rarer occasions, different universities, respondents identified that such divisions affect the ease and sometimes the quality of co-operation. The potential reasons for this include the following:

- *incompatibility* – all faculties work within university guidelines, but their interpretation of those guidelines may differ;
- *lack of leadership* – because faculties retain a high degree of autonomy, there may be no one person in a position to encourage co-operation;
- *complex accounting* – changes in accounting procedures have replaced the informality of reciprocal arrangements with formal identification of cross-faculty teaching time;
- *lack of knowledge* – initiatives may flounder because staff in one faculty are not familiar with the staff, programme organisation or student profile in another faculty.

Many respondents identified *timetabling difficulties* as a major barrier. Finding a point at which two or more groups can embark on a joint programme requires the identification of either:

- a common learning need which can be appropriately met for both groups at the same time;
- a time at which each group can satisfy its educational needs by learning from the other.

Even where common needs were identified, the appropriate timing for each group might differ. Issues cited included differences in educational background of the cohorts, the way in which the educational content slotted into the overall structure for individual programmes or the conceptual framework for the individual profession, and the level of practice experience at any given point in the programme.

At the 'whole-programme' level, especially in pre-qualification education, the overall length of the timetable could relate to the requirements of professional bodies and legislation. Pre-qualification education for medicine and dentistry involves 5-year programmes, whereas that for the majority of health care professions takes 3 years. The fact that this is the same duration as a standard university degree is coincidental since, for example, nursing programmes were the same length at certificate level. This suggests that there is a logic to the differences in terms of the learning required.

The organisation of programme components for each profession may also be constrained by nationally determined criteria (e.g. the common foundation/branch split in nursing education), but is equally likely to be shaped by tradition. Whereas nursing programmes have traditionally introduced practice experience early in the first year, PAMs students may have their first practice experience at the end of the first year, and medical students after 2 years. Although these patterns of organisation may be changing, the differences are still marked.

At the level of detailed timetabling, respondents reported difficulties in managing multiprofessional learning which were analogous to co-ordinating diaries in order to find an appropriate time for a meeting. Everyone may have 'signed up' to the initiative and agreed on the learning agenda, but getting professional cohorts together may be difficult.

As with any problem relating to programme organisation and timetabling, the level of difficulty will be proportional to the number of programmes which an initiative aims to serve.

The majority of the timetabling problems that were identified related to the historical context. Most initiatives are 'bolted on' to pre-existing monoprofessional programmes, and must work round existing elements. Even where shared or common learning is implemented as part of a new programme, the institution will normally have provided education for the professions concerned through previous monoprofessional programmes, and custom and practice may slow down the change processes.

Possible solutions

Respondents suggested a number of ways to overcome the barriers created by organisational division. The simplest of these might be described as the 'barrier, what barrier?' response.

The initiative for programmes involving shared interprofessional learning almost always came from highly motivated members of health care professions, who often maintained clinical links, including cross-professional links. Finding an interested colleague in another faculty or university was relatively easy, and the growing number of cross-professional organisations helped.

Where proven common learning is required by different groups at different times, there may be little potential for an effective solution unless groups can be mixed across years (e.g. second-year nurses with third-year medical students). This works in terms of shared learning, where equivalent rather than common learning is expected. One initiative involved shared learning between senior medical students and recently qualified nurses; each group felt that they had something to learn from and to teach to the other. Other respondents suggested strategies which could ease timetabling problems and organisational divisions through the use of information technology. One suggested that a virtual group working across universities could undertake problem-based learning by computer conferencing. Another initiative utilised the Internet to allow students to log on to a central computer, download a 'problem' and file their responses. Other students who subsequently logged on would then obtain both the problem and their colleague's responses, and could respond to both. With this type of solution, interprofessional work is timetable-free. However, there was general agreement that computer-mediated interaction could never completely replace face-to-face group work.

Cohort size: majority and minority problems

> Because of the student mix and the large number of nurses involved, there is a danger of nursing issues dominating. It only happens some of

the time. It depends on the module . . . on what subject we're teaching. (Course director)

As with any other university programme, the size of the cohort in health and social care programmes is partly subject to the whim of applicants. No one can produce a cohort if there are no candidates, and there is considerable risk involved when institutions reduce standards of entry to fill places.

Pre-qualification programmes for health and social care professions must contend with a further problem in relation to contractual arrangements with education purchasing consortia. These groups of NHS trusts determine their manpower requirements annually, and then use these figures to calculate how many higher education places they are willing to fund. The number of places which universities can offer is also affected by the professional bodies, who may determine the number of students that local care environments can support. In post-qualification education, the representation of any profession in a programme cohort may depend on different funding arrangements and the willingness (or requirements) of managers to free staff to attend.

Faced with these factors, it is not surprising that respondents identified considerable differences in the size of professional cohorts taking part in multiprofessional programmes. In one case, the smallest group consisted of 16 students, and the largest of 160 students. Considerable efforts were made by some interviewees to 'flatten' this differential by suggesting that the large cohort (often nurses) could be divided into specialties or branches. Although their end qualification might be different, the fact that all of them were currently members of a common foundation programme or community pathway suggests that this division was a little contrived. There were equal efforts to group the smaller therapy cohorts, although this link often appeared to be little more than semantic.

The intended benefit of 'massaging' cohort figures was clarified by the problems identified with regard to differences in professional group size. Problems could be experienced by both majority and minority groups.

The problems for minority professional groups related mainly to didactic teaching. A number of respondents identified that students regarded lectures as being tailored for the majority group, and several of them suggested that, even where lectures were specifically aimed at a multiprofessional audience, there was a tendency for minority groups to regard themselves as being less well served than the majority. Since the respondents were often members of the majority profession, such a contention might benefit from further scrutiny.

The use of practice-based examples was common in lecture programmes. Sometimes these reinforced students' perceptions of bias, focusing solely on the largest audience. In other cases, genuine efforts had been made to provide a range of examples to match the professions involved, but there was a resulting tendency for each group to consider only part of each lecture relevant to them. One interviewee stressed the importance of finding issues of relevance to all of the groups involved in order to avoid any perception of bias. This may be difficult because the mix of students is determined by programmes in the faculty. At a concrete level, there may be no common issues for those professions present, and abstractions cannot help students to apply learning.

The position of the majority professional group was not without problems. These difficulties related to small-group learning initiatives and especially to situations where shared learning between professions was a requirement. Some respondents reported that there were insufficient members of the smaller professional cohort to distribute round all of the small groups.

Where each professional cohort was expected to contribute specific knowledge or a specific perspective, the reduced spread of professions available to a particular group was regarded as impoverishing the learning opportunity. The problem of spread was exacerbated because students were typically distributed between small groups in pairs in order to avoid any sense of isolation or students from poorly represented professions being overwhelmed by the other group members and not putting forward their views.

Possible solutions

Didactic multiprofessional learning has inherent problems related to the varying learning needs of a mixed audience. Even if clinical relevance and exemplification were equivalent for all, it is difficult to see how multiprofessional learning could offer *added* value in such essentially non-interactive initiatives. However, a forum – in which clinicians from each profession would offer perspectives on a case and discuss their rationale for action – would develop shared knowledge of professional roles and a model of interaction. If the professional spread within the whole cohort is based on manpower requirements, it is likely to reflect the real situation in the clinical area. There may be only one OT attached to a ward with 10 or more nurses. However, that OT will also be a member of a monoprofessional team covering a wider area, with whom she can discuss issues, share ideas and seek corroboration.

This monoprofessional back-up is mirrored in a number of small-group teaching initiatives in which students from a single profession will discuss a problem and agree a response before offering it in a multiprofessional forum. One problem-based initiative took this a step further. After the monoprofessional groups had met to discuss the problem and multiprofessional groups had been formed, members of smaller professions were asked to act as 'consultants' to a number of groups, rather than as members of one. Varying roles in this way would appear to offer a solution.

Timing and professional socialisation

> When the students come into the lecture theatre they sit in blocks of the same profession. You feel like asking them to move around and mix up but. . . . They are very partisan when they come in, but that's all part of their socialisation. They have come to train to be physios, nurses, etc. and they're not interested in the multiprofessional side.
>
> (Course director)

The previously identified difficulties with regard to the timing of common or shared learning related to compatibility between professional programmes (and cohorts). Where these difficulties have been overcome and an appropriate slot identified, a further timing issue arises. This relates to the effect of multiprofessional learning on an individual programme, and specifically on the process of professional socialisation.

A number of respondents felt that multiprofessional learning at an early point in pre-qualification education would interfere with professional socialisation, resulting in students and qualifiers with a less clear sense of their own identity. The perception was that students had a natural monoprofessional focus during their early education, which they maintained until they had sufficient confidence to move into the multiprofessional arena.

The survey demonstrated that the predominant type of multiprofessional initiative during early pre-qualification education is didactic common learning. Therefore, although the concerns of respondents were not explicitly dependent on the nature of the learning proposed, it is appropriate to consider this type of initiative as the context for the comments that were made.

The respondents who expressed the strongest concern about early multiprofessional learning were often from the smaller professional groups, whose students felt disadvantaged in terms of content, focus and exemplification. Respondents from the majority groups also expressed reservations, especially where common learning was delivered by professionals with no background in health care. In both cases, the fundamental difficulty relates to the application of theory to practice. During early pre-qualification education, students lack practice experience, and such application processes are difficult for them to achieve for themselves.

Although socialisation may be affected by this lack of facilitated application of general theory to the practice of a specific profession, another common factor must be considered. Exposure to members of one's own profession is a key factor in the socialisation process, and was lacking in both of the situations identified above. If theory was to be provided wholly by teachers who were not from a student's profession, and professional contact was restricted to clinical practice, patterns of socialisation might be threatened. However, such initiatives almost always constitute a minor component of the overall programme, and it seems likely that multiprofessional learning is made less effective by students' natural monoprofessional focus, rather than by multiprofessional learning in some way threatening monoprofessional development.

A further factor in the responses about socialisation in multiprofessional education deserves mention. The tendency for concern to be expressed by small professions about their larger 'neighbours' appeared to be exacerbated in situations where a profession was fighting to establish or protect its independence. Other types of boundary dispute (e.g. where a profession was felt to be involved in 'territorial incursion' or 'role dumping') did not appear to raise the same concerns.

A small number of respondents took a more positive view of multiprofessional education, suggesting that current patterns of monoprofessional socialisation carried negative stereotypes of other professions which could bedevil teamwork. It was felt that multiprofessional education at an early stage provided an opportunity to ameliorate these prejudices. In this context, two problems needed to be considered.

First, it was impossible for multiprofessional education to begin before monoprofessional socialisation was under way, since socialisation started long before students entered professional education, beginning (however inaccurately) with the media and continuing through career selection and application. By the time students entered the programme they already had an image of their chosen profession and of other professions in the field, and the relationship between them. Clearly, this does not mean that early exposure to students from other professions might not modify their views, but it does mean that the monoprofessional focus (which was felt to blinker them to early multiprofessional learning) was already in place.

The second problem identified by respondents related to the process by which effective exposure to students from other professions might be managed. If multiprofessional learning was to enrich a programme, students must be in a position to take a profession-specific perspective. Although the process of professional socialisation might already be under way when students enter a programme, it is unlikely to have advanced to the point where they feel confident that they are taking an appropriate professional stance. In addition, case-based work of any kind requires students to share professional knowledge and practice experience. In early pre-registration education, both of these were recognised as being in short supply.

The problems identified above might suggest that, even if those who advocated early multiprofessional socialisation were correct, practicalities would continue to favour the placing of multiprofessional education late in both pre- and post-qualification education.

Possible solutions

This is an intractable problem. Socialisation into an individual profession is a vital component of education, and the timing of multiprofessional initiatives must utilise the flow of this natural development process, rather than trying to counter it. The major concerns (about the disruption of the socialisation process or the effect of socialisation on possible learning) relate to the early part of the programme.

The view of early multiprofessional learning may be inextricably bound up with perceptions of what type of learning is possible. There appears to be a danger that negative perceptions of these early processes may colour the views of both teachers and students about any multiprofessional learning. If this is the case, and the effectiveness of shared case-based learning later in the education process is being damaged, one solution may be to avoid multiprofessional education until a point in the programme where such effective processes are possible. However, another solution is suggested in Chapter 8.

The balance sheet: profit and loss

Numerous respondents appeared genuinely to welcome multiprofessional education and what it might achieve, but to mourn what was being lost from monoprofessional provision. Multiprofessional education was regarded as offering invaluable opportunities for students from different professions to interact, learn about each other's roles and develop into effective team players. However, the more focused nature of monoprofessional teaching, combined with the relevance of *all* clinical examples and the taught application to the single professional role, was viewed as too important to lose. The question that was being asked was whether the profit of the former was worth the loss of the latter.

A number of respondents felt that the loss outweighed the profit. Many of those who were antagonistic towards multiprofessional learning insisted that, if it could be incorporated without the loss of focused monoprofessional learning, they would be satisfied. However, because the curriculum was not elastic, they would continue to resist its inclusion. Respondents considered two aspects of the equation of profit and loss. The first related to a change in process. The majority of the multiprofessional programmes covered content which would previously have been delivered on a monoprofessional basis. Since making the programme multiprofessional did not increase its length, the only possible loss over previous provision was in the quality of coverage. A number of respondents felt that this was the case, citing the loss of focus and difficulty in identifying appropriate examples. Although institutions identified a profit in relation to economy of provision, the majority of the respondents perceived no educational benefit. For those who perceived a loss of focus or application, the equation was therefore simple. Many who regarded the equation for this type of initiative as positive agreed that the economy of provision (and therefore the security of jobs) outweighed concerns about loss of quality. Others came from a scientific discipline, rather than a health profession, and were often dismissive of differences in professional learning needs.

The second profit-and-loss equation relates to multiprofessional initiatives which introduce new areas of learning, displacing previous curriculum content. In pre-qualification education, such new initiatives would commonly include learning aimed specifically at multiprofessional communication and teamwork (i.e. areas which appear to best meet the identified clinical agenda). Although many respondents saw the potential profit of this pattern of multiprofessional learning as being considerable, they reported that others still felt it was outweighed by the loss of the displaced content.

Possible solutions

Unless a way can be found to demonstrate real educational benefit achieved through didactic teaching of 'common' learning, the equation for this type of initiative is bound to remain negative for many teachers.

To some extent, the profit-and-loss equation as it relates to shared learning is falsely expressed or perceived, since learning about interprofessional teamwork and communication is largely mediated by the nature of the teaching process, rather than by specific content. During the later stages of pre-qualification and throughout post-qualification education, much of the focus of learning is on clinical problems. This learning could be enhanced if it is managed, in part, through interprofessional case-/problem-based learning.

While the appropriate cases/problems for teaching and learning in a multiprofessional forum may be limited by the range of students involved, there is no reason why a strand of multiprofessional problem-solving should be viewed as taking students away from more relevant cases. If such a strand was to be a component of a larger, case-based programme, students would be able to gain confidence in problem-solving in the monoprofessional setting, before embarking on multiprofessional exercises. This would follow the previously identified pattern of socialisation.

Buying in: tailored and off-the-peg learning

> The communication course started as part of the nursing course. When the physiotherapy course started, they looked to see what was already extant in other courses, rather than taking on new staff themselves.
>
> (Course director)

A number of the initiatives identified were the result of a move by one profession to take on subject matter which was already part of a programme for other professions. This might have been part of a programme or, in post-qualification education, an entire programme. Many of the problems encountered were previously identified as those relating to any common learning programme, but they were exacerbated by the fact that such programmes were often taken 'off-the-peg' by the new professional cohort, with no tailoring to their specific needs or involvement of their professional teachers.

A number of respondents pointed out that tailoring was not simply about content, but also about the approach to a given subject. Some professions were viewed as approaching a particular subject from a scientific perspective, while others approached the same subject from the direction of general concepts.

Even when some tailoring had taken place, or the programme had been redesigned for a multiprofessional audience, respondents suggested that there could be considerable problems with regard to it being seen as belonging to and provided by another professional group, resulting in a devaluing of the programme. One respondent reported that the effect on students of having no professional role models involved in teaching one programme was exacerbated by members of their own professional faculty devaluing the subject matter and the move by their professional body to include it. Although this particular case cannot be generalised, the overall impression of multiprofessional learning as something rather avant-garde and peripheral to the professional agenda has considerable implications.

In terms of the more interactive patterns of shared learning, an equivalent set of problems can occur. A number of respondents pointed out the importance of careful selection of scenarios, so that the professions involved had something to offer and – where possible – the opportunity to lead the multiprofessional group. One respondent spoke of the difficulties which had arisen when a new profession joined the programme and the existing scenarios did not offer appropriate problem-solving roles.

Possible solutions

Respondents identified that the problems associated with 'taking someone else's programme' can be ameliorated, but not negated, by involving members of the new profession in programme delivery and planning. However, such a move may not overcome problems related to the new group's need for a different approach.

Where the programme relates to shared as opposed to common learning, the process is partly defined by the nature of the professional mix. With appropriate facilitation, it will adapt to the new situation. One respondent identified the importance of adapting the cases/problems to allow new students to take on appropriate roles.

Visibility: front door and back door learning

> There is no way that the medical students would agree to spend some time just on learning about teamwork. It had to happen as part of something else.
>
> (Course director)

As was suggested earlier, multiprofessional learning is felt to be particularly effective when it is focused on skills such as interprofessional communication and teamworking. Such shared learning can most readily meet the clinical agenda of multiprofessional teamwork through simulating and facilitating reflection on the practice situation.

However, the respondents suggested that this aspect of the curriculum in pre-qualification education is not popular with students, whether it is provided monoprofessionally or multiprofessionally. Although students do not necessarily underestimate the importance of such skills, there is a perception that they are 'common sense', develop naturally and do not require specific teaching and learning – a perception that is shared by a number of teachers. However, the clinical case studies suggest otherwise.

Although the majority of professional bodies require such skills of new members, they are under-represented in most pre-qualification programmes. This reflects the position of communication and teamworking skills as a relatively new component of many curricula, which may take time to displace more traditional content. As was identified previously, new educational outcomes required by professional bodies may not immediately receive the support of the professional faculty. As the same may be true of multiprofessional education in general, multiprofessional learning about teamwork may face a double resistance. Professional teachers who do value teamwork/communication as a focus of formal learning and shared learning as a process are unlikely to offer initiatives in this area. When enthusiasts for multiprofessional education are drawn towards this area of provision, they must take account of student reluctance when they frame the learning.

The strategies of the respondents varied. Some of them met student reluctance 'head on' and provided learning experiences specifically focused on communication and teamwork. These often focused on the use of clinical scenarios as a means of placing the skills in a more concrete context. Another respondent took a very different approach, concealing an agenda of teaching and learning about multiprofessional teamwork/communication behind a facade of equally valuable but apparently more attractive learning about advanced clinical skills. The danger of this strategy was that the clinical skills became the focus, tending to subvert rather than camouflage the communication/teamwork agenda. A number of issues relevant to interprofessional interaction were uncovered during the session, but they were not addressed. The respondent reported that, in evaluation, students were still negative about the communication/teamwork elements of the session, although they appeared to develop skills and ease in this area.

Possible solutions

By attempting to conceal the communication/teamwork agenda, teachers are likely to reinforce the student view that it is simply not 'headline material', and is better acquired as a natural by-product of learning about 'important' topics. If it is intended that students should recognise the worth of such learning, there would appear to be advantages in making the agenda explicit from the beginning. Students' concern for learning that they perceive to be clinically relevant is important.

The respondents were positive about strategies that employed clinical scenarios which demonstrated the value of multiprofessional perspectives and teamwork. As with the 'hidden agenda' model, the development of skills of interaction accompanied more concrete learning. Whereas the hidden agenda model uses clinical skills learning to develop multiprofessional team skills, the problem-based strategy requires the use of communication/teamwork skills for problem-solving. In the former, communication and teamwork remain an optional extra, whereas in the latter their centrality to clinical activity is demonstrated. Students from different professions are not expected to demonstrate or acquire the same knowledge, but are required to bring their own perspectives and expertise to bear. Co-operation therefore becomes paramount.

THE EFFECT OF THE HIGHER EDUCATION AGENDA AND ORGANISATIONAL BARRIERS ON THE EDUCATIONAL PROCESS

The research identified a whole spectrum of educational strategies (see Figure 7.5), with the type of interactive multiprofessional group-work process

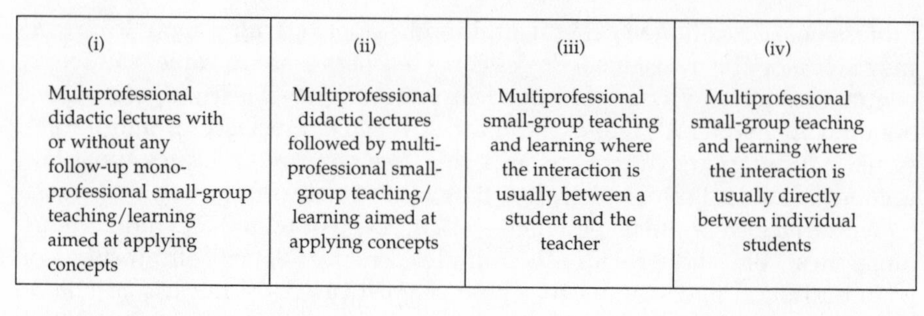

(i)	(ii)	(iii)	(iv)
Multiprofessional didactic lectures with or without any follow-up mono-professional small-group teaching/learning aimed at applying concepts	Multiprofessional didactic lectures followed by multi-professional small-group teaching/learning aimed at applying concepts	Multiprofessional small-group teaching and learning where the interaction is usually between a student and the teacher	Multiprofessional small-group teaching and learning where the interaction is usually directly between individual students

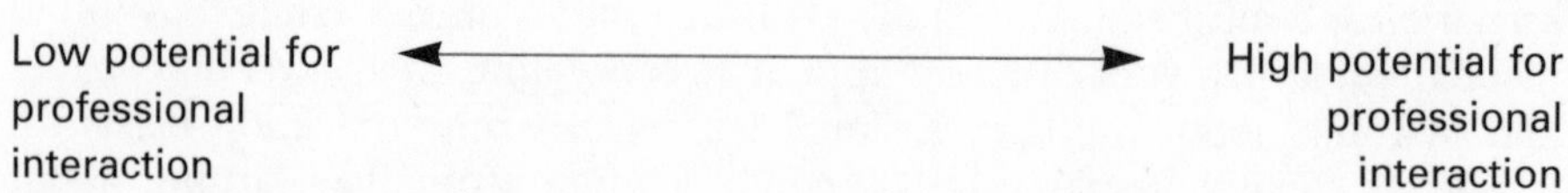

Figure 7.5 Potential of educational processes to facilitate interaction between students of different professions.

suggested by the case studies at one end, and a pure diet of didactic lectures at the other – that is, ranging from strategies which demand purposive interaction between students to strategies where any interaction between students is incidental.

If didactic lectures are followed by monoprofessional small-group teaching, there is no additional interprofessional learning and no opportunity for students to learn from each other. Some potential for interaction is added if didactic lectures are followed by multiprofessional small-group teaching but, having been given the basic concepts in the lecture, students will already be considering their application in the context of their own role, and may therefore fail to focus on its application to other professions. A further step towards interprofessional shared learning is the multiprofessional small-group session in which interaction takes place between students and the facilitator. Although this has many of the benefits of the fully interactive small group, the process does not mirror interaction within a team, and process-mediated learning about interprofessional communication and teamworking will be limited.

The survey clearly demonstrated that the majority of the multiprofessional learning initiatives were not aimed at meeting the teamworking agenda either in their content or their process. The potential economies of scale promised by multiprofessional education can only be realised through the type of didactic teaching which minimises students' interaction. In post-qualification education, the cohorts tend to be smaller and educational processes are naturally more interactive, but the driving force behind the opening of programmes to a multiprofessional audience is the need to maintain or increase numbers to ensure economic viability, rather than to encourage the sharing of experience.

Where programmes did aim to utilise a more interactive, multiprofessional approach, practical difficulties often hobbled the original ambition. Many of the initiatives captured in the survey:

- were relatively new – with the same potential for teething problems as any innovative programme;
- were built on to existing programmes – with the inherent problems of trying not to disrupt other parts of the programme;
- faced resistance from some members of staff – either because they felt that their part of the programme had been disrupted, or because of a more general mistrust of multiprofessional approaches;
- had to work within existing levels of human, physical and financial resources (or were expected to demonstrate a saving);
- were brought in rapidly, under pressure from the academic organisation, with limited time for consultation and the development of ownership.

Such factors, in addition to the barriers identified earlier, tended to exacerbate each other. The result was clear when data from the survey and follow-up interviews were compared. In a significant number of cases, the curriculum as planned promised something that was not delivered by the curriculum as implemented. The general effect was of a movement from a more interactive process to a less interactive one. Thus facilitated interaction between students from different professions might be replaced by tutor-student interaction, the multiprofessional small-group work planned to follow a lecture might be replaced by monoprofessional working, and in one case lectures that were to be delivered to a multiprofessional group were replaced by the same lectures being delivered to each professional group separately.

For many interviewees, this process of monoprofessional shift appeared to be a response to the difficulty in overcoming organisational inertia or particular structural problems. Others took a more proactive role and saw themselves as protecting their students and profession by taming the organisation's wilder fantasies.

The difficulties identified in this chapter in relation to structure, content and process and the response of staff to (or responsibility for) those difficulties are not solely confined to multiprofessional education. Indeed, they may be a feature of any curriculum development. The pre-registration problems may therefore be overcome as programmes mature.

As specific initiatives bed down and multiprofessional learning gains wider acceptance, what criteria may help us to judge whether any new initiative is likely to be beneficial, neutral or negative? Some pointers will be discussed in Chapter 8, in which evidence from both higher education and the case studies is drawn together in a model of shared learning.

8 Where we need to be: a model for multiprofessional education

INTRODUCTION

In this chapter we shall consider how the analysis of the data on team functioning and the implications of the teamwork agenda for multiprofessional learning might be reflected in higher education provision, and how the barriers to shared learning that were identified in the previous chapter could be overcome.

The survey data, together with the information from telephone interviews and visits, leave no doubt that the current multiprofessional provision in higher education is the result of a drive for economy and flexibility. These findings are supported by those of Mhaolrúnaigh *et al.* (1996). Their study of teacher preparation for shared learning concluded that higher education institutions had often adopted shared learning as a response to demands for financial stringency, rather than in an attempt to enhance educational quality. However, the selection of content and teaching method determined by the drive towards educational economy and flexibility appears to offer little of value in preparing students for multiprofessional teamwork.

Although we would hold that the potential for shared learning to add quality to a professional education rests largely in the teamworking agenda, it is undeniable that moves by higher education to enhance economy and flexibility are equally legitimate. Shared learning might not be able to provide improved economy and added quality at the same time, but both may have their place. This chapter therefore starts by examining the general design criteria to be met by multiprofessional initiatives which seek to present common learning to a varied group of students. These criteria often have their equivalent in shared, small-group learning but, in addition, specific criteria are offered for shared learning that aims to develop the qualities required for effective multiprofessional teamworking. The chapter goes on to propose a model that fulfils all of these criteria.

GENERAL DESIGN CRITERIA FOR MULTIPROFESSIONAL EDUCATION

Some criteria are common to all multiprofessional learning, whether it is aimed at promoting effective teamworking or at enhancing the economy and flexibility of education. These criteria relate to the overall quality, content and process of the educational provision.

Overall quality

In the previous chapter, considerable difficulties were recognised in bringing together a multiprofessional cohort of students. Even within a single faculty, timetabling problems are multiplied by trying to serve two or more courses with a single module. Often health care professionals (who work alongside each other in a single practice context) are not taught within the same institution, let alone the same faculty.

The effort required to overcome these difficulties suggests that a legitimate criterion for multiprofessional education might be that it should offer demonstrable benefit over its monoprofessional alternative. However, this fails to take account of the economic imperative in higher education. A more appropriate first criterion for multiprofessional education should be that *economy and flexibility for the institution should not be enhanced at the cost of a reduction in the quality of provision for any one of the individual professions concerned.*

Content

As was identified in the previous chapter, the assessment of learning as being common to a number of professions is often flawed. A major assumption that underpins many of the multiprofessional developments in initial education is that, because a discipline (e.g. anatomy, physiology, sociology) is a required component of the knowledge base for a number of professions, it necessarily constitutes appropriate common learning. This may be the case, but it may mask the truth that, in order to fulfil their roles, each profession needs to draw differently from the discipline in terms of both focus and depth of knowledge. In anatomy, this may relate to whole systems or to the more detailed selection of concepts.

With regard to systems, physiotherapists need a more detailed knowledge of the musculoskeletal system than do doctors or nurses, but doctors need the most detailed knowledge of the gastrointestinal system. In terms of selection of concepts, an understanding of the blood supply of bone may be particularly important for medical students, whereas the piezo-electric effect in bone is of particular importance to nurses' understanding of the value of passive limb exercise in long-term bed rest. Even where a system or concept is of equal importance for different professions, each profession may require different examples in order to grasp the relevance of the knowledge.

However, there are clearly areas in which the roles of individual professions overlap – a phenomenon that is likely to increase with the growing pressure to break down traditional demarcations. As some professional groups seek to devolve some of their traditional tasks (e.g. as a result of the reduction in working hours for junior doctors), others take on those tasks as part of an extended role which (history suggests) will often become incorporated into a professional core. Equally, pressure on professional demarcation may come from health care provider organisations seeking to implement multi-skilling initiatives or even to explore training of generic health workers. Wherever the pressure comes from, *where roles are actually common, it may be legitimately assumed that the knowledge required by each profession to support the role is also common.*

This does not necessarily mean that the required learning is the same. The different educational background and mind-set of cohorts of students may also have to be taken into account. Students who are intending to train for different professions may have to meet entry criteria that vary enormously in academic level of qualifications, or the specification of subjects. *Common learning requires students to be starting from a comparable point in terms of their specific knowledge and general educational background.*

Equally, individuals from two groups of degree-level students (e.g. nursing and radiography) might quite reasonably be assumed to require a common knowledge of certain psychological concepts relating to anxiety or patient compliance. The two groups may also have a similar general educational background and equivalent prior learning with regard to the subject, but their mind-set – their bent towards science or the humanities – may require the content to be organised in a different way.

> The groups of students are entirely different. The radiographers are hooked on technology . . . the nurses and occupational therapists on the other hand are far more interested in people. The knowledge base they need is similar, but the examples and the ways you have to use to get it over to them is different.
>
> (Course leader)

In order for common learning to be justified, *the way in which the subject matter is structured should appeal to and involve each of the represented professions.*

As has been suggested in previous chapters, there is an alternative to the fraught process of trying to identify real common learning. Institutions may provide multiprofessional initiatives in which the intention is equivalent or mutual rather than common learning. In this case:

- students from a number of professions should have equivalent opportunities to meet their own differing learning needs through interaction;
- the strategies used should enable each group to meet these needs effectively by building on their differing prior learning;
- recognising and valuing their different approaches to the subject matter is part of the richness of the learning experience, rather than a hurdle to be overcome.

These criteria form the basis of content selection for the team-focused learning which will be discussed later in this chapter. Although the selection of appropriate content is vitally important if multiprofessional education is to add (or at least not to subtract) value, it is clear from the above discussion that the selection of process is equally important.

	Factual knowledge	Professional wisdom
Didactic teaching	Traditional lectures or other didactic teaching aimed at presenting students with a series of 'incontrovertible' facts required for their professional function Cell 1	Cell 3 The 'expert lecture', through which a senior professional seeks to make explicit their experiential learning and the basis of their professional judgement
Exploratory learning	Cell 2 Interactive strategies providing students with the opportunity to discover 'incontrovertible' facts for themselves	Cell 4 Case/problem-based work providing students with an opportunity to mimic experiential learning and practise professional judgement

Figure 8.1 The relationship of factual knowledge and professional wisdom to didactic and exploratory teaching/learning.

Process

The selection of educational process has to be tailored to the students involved, taking into account their educational background, their professional experience and development and their mind-set, but it is primarily determined by the nature of the subject matter and the intended outcome of the learning experience. Figure 8.1 shows a matrix relating factual knowledge and professional wisdom to didactic and exploratory teaching/learning.

Eraut (1994) differentiates between the factual or 'propositional knowledge' required by members of a profession, and professional wisdom. The former can be readily codified and passed on to students as relatively stable and incontrovertible facts. Professional wisdom relates to what Schon (1991) describes as the 'marshy lowlands' where there may be no single right answer, and where individual practitioners have to use their own professional judgement. Eraut makes the point that the knowledge which underpins such judgement is often tacit, and that the way in which the judgement is reached may be unclear, even to the professional concerned.

In reality, there is no such stark division between propositional knowledge and professional wisdom. In many fields, 'factual' knowledge may be open to dispute by different scientists. Although professional wisdom might not be amenable to expression as a series of propositions, some aspects of the thinking that underpins judgements are perfectly capable of clear expression. However, the identification of these two ends of the knowledge spectrum does enable consideration of the appropriateness of different methodologies.

Where a real common learning need has been established, the delivery of factual knowledge to a multiprofessional audience may be effectively and economically managed through didactic approaches such as the lecture (cell 1 in Figure 8.1). Such teaching does not enable or encourage interaction between members of different professional groups, but when the focus is on a teacher providing information to meet a common need, interaction offers no particular advantage. However, if the aims of the learning include the development of interprofessional understanding as well as the acquiring of knowledge, such large-scale lectures would be inappropriate.

Learning the same factual knowledge through active small-group processes (cell 2 in Figure 8.1) is a well-tried alternative. A number of additional benefits will naturally accrue from the active nature of the learning process (e.g. development of students' independent learning skills, general communication skills, group working skills, etc.), but these are unlikely to be greatly enhanced if the small group consists of a number of professions. In anatomy, for example, facts are facts and opinions and perspectives are irrelevant (or at least not differentiated by profession). If the session is purely factual, then the only potential advantage to be gained from multiprofessional working would be the sharing of information about useful learning resources.

The occasions on which professional wisdom may be transmitted through didactic teaching (cell 3 in Figure 8.1) are limited. However, there is still a recognised place for what has been described as the 'master lecture', in which an expert is called upon to share the fruits of his or her experience – to illuminate his or her professional judgement. Often such lectures are designed as much to inspire students, to encourage their own professional explorations and to provide insights into expert practice, as to provide something specific which the audience can take away and slot into their own practice. As such, the lecture may well work effectively on a multiprofessional basis, and an alternative professional perspective on a problem may provide a valuable key to its solution.

Our research has suggested that the greatest 'value added' from multiprofessional education will be in the facilitation of learning about topics where perspectives, clinical opinions and interventions may vary from one profession to another (cell 4 in Figure 8.1). Such learning is likely to be focused on increasingly realistic clinical scenarios, mirroring the practice reality in which professional judgement and professional wisdom become important and the simple dualism of 'right' and 'wrong' answers is left behind. As has been identified by Perry (1968), this is part of the expected development of students during 'the college years'.

Where the aim is to improve multiprofessional understanding and to develop the skills of teamworking, multiprofessional small groups can offer the most effective approach.

Any such initiative should still take account of the professional mix of the students who are going to be involved. There is no advantage to be gained from utilising a realistic scenario if, to one or more of the professions to be taught, that reality has no apparent bearing on their own clinical field. Having identified a scenario from a relevant clinical field, it is still necessary to ensure that it provides the students of each profession with roles which will enable the desired learning. Usually this will mean that all professions need an active part to play, although one of the students interviewed as part of the survey recounted the valuable lesson she had learned from a scenario in which her professional role was to recognise that she had nothing to offer.

These broad criteria underpin the development of a number of suggestions as to how both initial and continuing education could be used to prepare for or enhance multiprofessional teamworking. We shall begin by developing a model for multiprofessional learning in initial education which meets the needs of the preclinical student, the clinical novice, the probationer and the newly qualified practitioner, as identified in Chapter 6. It also takes into account the difficulty of engaging students in the teamworking agenda (and the possible solutions to this problem) identified in Chapter 7.

MULTIPROFESSIONAL LEARNING IN INITIAL EDUCATION

The previous section proposed broad criteria against which the feasibility or advisability of any multiprofessional initiative might be judged, identifying how different teaching and learning strategies might be appropriate to the delivery of different content and could enable the achievement of intended learning outcomes. Whilst it recognises that every type of initiative may have its place, this research has suggested that the 'value added' to the student learning experience is maximised by multiprofessional initiatives which focus on shared learning (students learning from each other) rather than common learning and which exhibit the following key characteristics.

The learning should develop the prerequisites for teamwork. As demonstrated by the clinical case studies, teamwork is vitally important to the delivery of health and social care. This is equally true of monoprofessional and multiprofessional teamworking. As was identified in the previous chapter, students appeared to be reluctant to be taught about teamworking, but there is clearly a difference between *talking about* the principles of teamworking and *participating in* learning strategies that naturally build teamworking skills.

There seems to be little value in lecturing to students about what makes for good teamwork, certainly during the early stages of their education. Learning activities which progressively foster the skills that underpin teamworking are more likely to be successful. The clinical case studies indicate that the main skills required for effective teamworking are enabling team entry, communication, understanding of roles, team awareness and strategies for collaborative action. The learning programme should therefore provide experiences which build up these skills.

The learning should be patient/client focused. Students in every health care profession are, quite rightly, concentrating on developing the competence to provide effective treatment and/or care for patients. Any course content which cannot demonstrate legitimacy within this frame of reference is immediately devalued by the students. One of the difficulties in persuading students to consider the teamworking agenda is trying to demonstrate its relevance when the student learning focus is on their own role and the development of their personal competence. If multiprofessional education is focused on working co-operatively for the good of the patient/client in a particular situation, then the relevance of learning about the situation and the relevance of teamworking are immediately apparent and mutually reinforcing.

One of the points that has been made to us, and which is discussed in the literature (e.g. Tope, 1998), is that the patient and *all* of his or her health needs are the proper focus of the *whole* team. Although each profession may have a different focus and different expertise to offer, patient-centred working provides the appropriate holistic context for all professional activity. Once this is accepted, it becomes easier to see how the professions can act together to meet those needs, rather than the needs being compartmentalised to fit in with different professional roles. To start students off with this orientation will help them later when they are working at the boundaries of roles.

The status of the patient in relation to the health and social care team is changing. For example, in some fields, an attitude of paternalism from the medical profession is being replaced by a patient-centred approach that involves much more even power relationships. This relates partly to increasing access to information (e.g. via the Internet, Bader and Braude, 1998) and partly to changes in health and health care expectations (Greenhow *et al.*, 1998). As the patient becomes not only the focus of action for the team, but also an active member of the team, the benefit of patient- or client-focused education for teamworking becomes clear.

There has also been an increasing awareness of the role of the family or other non-professional carer in the patient or client's well-being, of the knowledge that carers have about the patient or client, and of the value of involving carers in decision-making. Alongside this has come a recognition that the carer's views about needs are not always the same as those of the patient or client, or of the health and social care professionals. Students need to learn about the value of the carer insights and about the caveats that apply to them. Since carers' insights may be important to team decision-making, they are a legitimate part of the education process.

The learning should be interactive. Didactic teaching aimed at enabling common learning offers no opportunity for students to find out how others have assimilated the same information, unless there are built-in opportunities for discussion. In the same way that practitioners need to *interact* with other members of the clinical team, rather than work *alongside* them, students need to engage with others if they are to dispel stereotypes and develop their understanding of how others think.

A passive or insufficiently assertive stance has been recognised as characterising some professionals' behaviour in relation to others in the team. Students need to develop skills of interaction, including constructive questioning, opinion-seeking and challenging others. Educational strategies which enable interaction between students provide a context in which students can develop these skills effectively. This interaction requires a focus, and it seems appropriate to utilise the reality of clinical interaction to provide it.

The learning should be case- or scenario-based. There are many general advantages to case- or scenario-based learning as a strategy for managing patient-focused education. So long as the cases are selected appropriately, the relevance of the learning to professional function is axiomatic, because it mimics the real-life situation. The exploratory, deductive nature of the learning process also mimics (and enables students to practise) the type of self-directive strategy which will be key to their continuing professional development. Students learn concepts in the professional context and, combined with the active nature of the learning process, this facilitates recall (Dolmans and Schmidt, 1996). It has the added advantage of being highly attractive to students. Tope (1996), in her survey of a large number of students from a wide range of health and social care professions, found that patient-centred learning using a case-study approach was their favoured learning method.

There are specific advantages to case or scenario-based learning when the focus is on teamworking. Students from different backgrounds who are tackling the problem collectively will recognise and learn to value different professional perspectives on the problem and the resulting differences in the identification and interpretation of key factors. Thus the exploratory nature of the learning provides the opportunity for insight into others' ways of thinking. As a strategy for learning about the teamwork agenda it is very flexible, and can be tailored to the stage of development. It is equally appropriate for considering the interactions of the monoprofessional team, for developing an early understanding of collaborative multiprofessional working, for considering areas of professional conflict and strategies for resolving them, and for considering organisational/management issues relating to the support of teamwork.

Learning should be built on a model of student development. Students will not assimilate knowledge that does not articulate with the stage of development they have reached. At one level this is relatively simple and relates to issues such as the complexity of concepts that students can deal with at different stages. In some shared learning, however, the problems can be greater. The focus on finding a 'generalisable' topic of 'relevance' to several professions has sometimes blinded educational planners to the equal importance of matching students' natural learning focus at each stage of a particular course. Students may fail to grasp such material because it does not appear to be relevant at that time – not because it is too complex or because it is irrelevant to the profession. The curriculum content must be realistically matched to a model of how students are expected to develop, stage by stage. This includes their general intellectual development – for example, their ability to work with relative rather than absolute truths (Perry, 1968) – but it also relates to the nature of their educational programme.

For students who are following a professional course, their development relates in part to how much exposure they have had to practice. This varies between professions, with some students having been in clinical areas much earlier than others. The programme of shared learning has to take into account the variety of clinical exposure, and matching this 'exposure time' is often more important than matching the overall length of time for which students have been in training.

Learning should be ongoing throughout the course. There is no single point during an initial programme of education that is most auspicious for multiprofessional education although, as was identified above, the agenda for such learning needs to move on. The programme of shared learning should be a strand running through the course if it is to be seen by students as a significant contribution to their professional development. An isolated multiprofessional module is likely to remain just that in the students' minds – as something separate from the real work of developing competence. The contribution of each shared component needs to build upon skills and attitudes that were previously developed in both monoprofessional and multiprofessional contexts.

A MODEL OF MULTIPROFESSIONAL LEARNING

Using the above six key criteria, we developed a model of learning which could usefully promote the development of enhanced multiprofessional working.

- The model proposed involves a shared learning approach in which multiprofessional groups of students use specific patient- or client-based scenarios to learn about the fundamental requirements of professional interaction and teamworking. In specific scenarios, teamworking is a requirement in order to achieve the best outcome for the patient, and is therefore immediately perceived as relevant. By generalising from the specific scenario, students can learn the principles of professional interaction, which they can then transfer to the clinical arena. These scenarios could be managed as sophisticated computer-mediated exercises using video clips and other images, but they could equally be run as 'traditional' paper-based exercises. Students will explore the working of the team in a specific clinical situation.
- As suggested previously, the selection of scenarios would have to acknowledge the general aspects of students' ethical and intellectual development and the growth of their professional perspectives. It should also take account of student concerns such as the need for topic salience and the requisite skills and knowledge that each profession would need for qualification. There is a fundamental requirement for the scenario to be relevant to all of the students in terms of their current clinical work and their future roles.
- Since we are proposing that the teamworking agenda is of relevance from the very beginning of initial education, it would initially focus on scenarios which did not require professional or clinical knowledge, to which students can bring a lay perspective or an understanding of the general principles of human interaction. Later on (i.e. as the student amasses clinical experience), the process could be based on clinical scenarios to which students bring their own relevant experiences.

THE FOCUS OF MULTIPROFESSIONAL LEARNING

One of the criteria for multiprofessional learning proposed earlier in this chapter was that the agenda had to take into account the developmental stage of the students (i.e. the aim of effective multiprofessional working will best be achieved if it is pursued in an incremental fashion throughout the course). Clearly, different aspects of the learning that underpins teamworking will be appropriate for initial introduction at different points in the professional development of the students and, once introduced, will assume greater or lesser importance at different times. Thus an initial focus might be on general principles of effective communication between professions. Only later (once students had clinical experience to call on) would it become possible to consider complex communication (e.g. in relation to conflict resolution). In contrast, there would be little point in even introducing learning aimed at enabling the development of effective teamworking strategies (e.g. shared philosophies and joint record-keeping) until quite late in training.

In Chapter 6 this incremental development was specified in terms of learning outcomes for each stage of professional development. How might these be achieved through the type of learning process that is suggested by the criteria identified earlier in this chapter? The framework on the following pages suggest how these outcomes might be achieved through the use of various types of case- or scenario-based learning strategies with small groups of students, and they identify where this would mesh with other aspects of the health care education agenda.

THE PRECLINICAL STAGE

By the end of the preclinical stage, students will:	**Issues relating to scenario-based learning:**
• have a more realistic perception of their own profession and of the way in which professional approaches differ;	At the preclinical stage, media representations of clinical scenarios offer a fertile base for discussion of the *roles fulfilled by members of their own profession*. They provide an opportunity for students to air their own perception of the profession and recognise both its truths and its falsehoods.
• have started to develop skills of assertive and facilitative communication which can be applied in the clinical arena;	Many of these students will be spending some time focusing on the development of basic communication skills. Although this will be primarily aimed at preparing the student to listen to and engage with the patients, multiprofessional group work could widen the learning opportunities. Using a video of a patient and/or carer talking about their experience of illness, students could practise listening and observation skills. Mixed group discussion of what they had 'heard' from the

	patient and the priority/value of the information would allow them to explore their different priorities, whilst the experience of *listening to and challenging other students* would begin the development of interprofessional communication skills.
• have developed skills of group working which will facilitate team entry;	At this stage, much of the preparation for teamworking can be inherent in the group process. With group continuity, students function as members of 'learning teams'. The *skills developed through becoming an effective member of a mixed learning team* will be transferable to the clinical arena.
• be able to communicate easily on a social level with students from other professions;	If the strand of multiprofessional learning forms a sufficient component of each course, and the component is structured in such a way as to include coffee breaks, etc., *students from the different groups will socialise automatically*.
• have been given positive role models of interprofessional interaction.	Such group learning should ideally be facilitated by teachers representing all of the professions involved in the scenario. The *interaction of teachers from different professions* provides a valuable role model for students.

THE CLINICAL NOVICE STAGE

By the end of the clinical novice stage, students will:	**Issues relating to scenario-based learning:**
• have an outline understanding of the roles fulfilled by each profession and the ways in which these roles abut/overlap;	During the 'clinical novice' phase, scenarios need to provide a *focus for each profession on what they do, as well as an opportunity to explore the roles fulfilled by others* and role boundaries.
• demonstrate a clearer understanding of the solid core and fluid	As students are still seeking monoprofessional credibility at this stage, a

periphery of the role of their own profession;

scenario needs to provide the opportunity for them to confirm their understanding of their core role. However, scenarios should be designed to identify that *the roles of individual professions are mutually dependent, that roles are often shared, and that responsibilities vary depending on the setting.*

- respond to members of other professions with confidence, communicating formally within parameters and using channels determined or defined by the professions involved;

Clinical scenarios which require students to explore standard types of interprofessional communication (e.g. selection of information for referral; negotiation regarding given interventions) offer the opportunity to *practise communication skills in a relatively safe environment*. In the 'classroom setting' the difference in status between various professions is not complicated by the differences in status within each profession, and the fear of communication which might endanger a patient is removed.

- have reflected on the ways in which the health care professions view each other, and recognise the truths and fictions underpinning these views;

Some learning is best tackled initially from a multiprofessional standpoint. Clinical scenarios can be tackled by monoprofessional groups who identify their own profession's reaction to a situation and their expectation of the reaction of others. *These stereotypes held by each group of their own and other professions can then be discussed* in a multiprofessional group.

- recognise that each profession consists of a heterogeneous collection of individuals, and that individual members of a profession should be treated as such;

There is some advantage to having a group that consists of more than one representative of each of the professions needed to tackle a particular clinical situation. Within each profession, it provides verification/correction/refinement of ideas through a sharing of still limited experience. That discussion is of itself enlightening to other members of the group, because it can illuminate the professional thought processes. Equally, *the face of the profession that is presented to others is of a group of individuals, rather than a stereotype.*

- be able to identify effective strategies for securing entry to and support from the monoprofessional team;

Strategies for gaining entry to a team are not necessarily dependent on whether it is mono- or multiprofessional. Students' concern at this stage is about acceptance in the monoprofessional team. Although any strategies which they learn are likely to stand them in good stead when they are ready to seek membership of the multiprofessional team, there are considerable differences in the structure of teams in the different professions. *Where the intended learning from a scenario is related to strategies for gaining entry/support, there may be a positive advantage in using monoprofessional groups.* Later in training, when the focus moves towards the multiprofessional team, there is value in learning from other professional groups and sharing best practice.

- observe different teamworking strategies within the monoprofessional teams to which they are exposed, identifying the factors that shape those strategies and their consequences;

At this stage of clinical training, a monoprofessional group may also be the appropriate context for *initial learning about teamworking strategies.* Scenarios provide the opportunity to bring back and share observations of strategies within the monoprofessional teams of which students have been a temporary part. The definition of a team and the strategies employed for teamworking may differ so widely from one profession to another that there is little benefit to be derived from students comparing their lot.

- apply their initial assertiveness training when dealing with members of their own and other professions.

It is important to recognise that once students have entered the clinical arena, the teamworking agenda in the 'classroom' can only be an adjunct to a process that is, at its roots, clinically based. Scenario-based learning in the classroom provides students with the opportunity to practise skills in a safe environment. The scenario may demonstrate the relevance of what is being learned, *but those skills are not of actual value until they are applied in the clinical context.* Scenario-based learning in the classroom also provides students with a vehicle to reflect on and draw from their real clinical experience – to undertake the type of in-depth exploration of professional activity that is often impossible in the pressured clinical environment. However (as with their skills), the understanding and insight that students develop in the classroom are not of value unless they are taken back into practice.

THE PROBATIONER STAGE

By the end of the probationer stage, students will:

- have an understanding of how the roles of the various professions translate into required action and interaction in a given clinical situation;

Issues relating to scenario-based learning:

At this stage in professional development, scenario-based learning comes increasingly into its own. By the end of the probationary period, students have sufficient experience of real clinical situations to be able *to identify with considerable clarity what they would do in a given situation, and what they would expect of others.* At this stage, specific clinical problems can be powerful classroom learning tools, providing a framework within which students can share opinions (both mono- and multiprofessionally) about appropriate actions. Drawn from their various clinical experiences, these opinions are bound to reflect differences in practice. Both intellectually (Perry, 1968) and professionally (Eraut, 1994) these students have moved on from the belief that there is a single right answer. Being presented with a number of different options provides an opportunity for comparison that is often impossible within the hierarchical structure of a clinical situation, and a chance to practise judgement in safety.

- demonstrate a growing understanding of the thought process underpinning clinical decisions made by members of other professions and what that process demands of them in terms of sharing information;

Discussion is further enriched if it takes place within a multiprofessional forum. Here *each profession gets an opportunity to listen to the thinking behind the professional judgement of the others*. This in turn provides students with an opportunity to identify how they can influence decisions through the sharing of information, or how their own decisions might be improved through inviting the perspectives of other professions.

- start to engage effectively in dialogue with members of other professions in the clinical area, in both unstructured situations (e.g. bedside planning) and structured situations (e.g multiprofessional team meetings);

To some extent, students could acquire this clinical knowledge, insight and expertise through a detached discussion of alternative courses of action. Equally, they could valuably discuss negotiation strategies that they have encountered in practice.

- be able to lead for their profession in negotiating an effective, co-ordinated multiprofessional response to a specific clinical situation.

However, it can be more effective for students to move into 'role-play mode', so that they are *acting as members of a team trying to influence each other – to reach a concerted view of the appropriate action*. If this type of exercise is to be perceived by students as a safe learning environment, a degree of trust must be developed. Once again this highlights the importance of reaching a critical mass in the extent of multiprofessional learning.

SHARED LEARNING IN CONTINUING EDUCATION

Professional development as lifelong learning would include learning to work effectively with colleagues from other professions in a context of sustained development of the skills that were fostered during initial education. The situation with regard to shared learning in continuing education differs from that in initial education in a number of ways, not least in the heterogeneity of the courses on offer. The vast range (from Masters programmes to weekend workshops, and from programmes designed to develop skills in the use of a highly specialised piece of equipment to courses aimed at developing ethical reasoning) makes it impossible to generalise about how the teamwork agenda might impinge. Although adequate numbers of students are still important for the viability of groups (hence the advantage of a larger potential catchment population offered by multiprofessional courses), continuing education never approaches the 'mass production' processes of initial education. Because the groups are smaller and less didactic, adult education strategies are employed and there is always opportunity for exchange between group members, making 'common learning' without discussion far less likely.

We found that the professional mix of students on a course may appear far more varied on paper than it is in reality; for while courses may be *open* to a number of professions, they may *actually* recruit predominantly from one or two, with annual fluctuations. Even with a mix of two professions, there may be the imbalance of numbers that is observed in initial education courses. The difference between *recruiting* a course from a range of health and social care professions, and *explicitly aiming* to provide shared learning experiences is important. A course which uses a multiprofessional approach simply to maintain viability cannot claim to be making use of shared learning as a core strategy, as it will not always be possible. If a course is to take on board the multiprofessional teamworking agenda, then its viability is as dependent on the mix of professions as it is on total numbers.

From the very wide spectrum of courses that are offered in continuing higher education, there are some that are multiprofessional, and may be valued as such, but which have no explicit shared learning strategies other than the 'obvious' benefit of bringing together different professions. It could be argued that there are some neglected opportunities here for *interprofessional* development which could be taken up, without changing the focus of the course, by making better use of the advantages of having a multiprofessional group. Case-focused scenarios can again prove of great benefit in developing a richer appreciation of the roles of others, and allowing practice in negotiating differences between roles. For example, our survey identified an example of a group of professionals who spent a day working on a complex family case scenario, which brought about interaction in a way that talking about each issue would not have done.

To some extent, the agenda for scenario-based learning during the early part of the practitioner stage (see framework below) is a continuation of that identified previously for the probationer phase. However, it has to be recognised that, until recently, there has been very little general professional development at this career stage, and that the majority of early continuing education was aimed at the development of particular expertise required within a specialist clinical area. That situation is now changing. The development in nursing of initiatives such as the ENB Higher Award has promoted a much broader pattern of continuing generic development. In medicine, there is a similar recognition of the value of continuing generic as well as specialist teaching through the pre-registration and senior house officer phases.

THE PRACTITIONER STAGE

As practitioners, qualified staff will:	Issues relating to scenario-based learning:
• apply appropriate strategies to gain entry to the multiprofessional team, including the selection of an appropriate mentor from their own or another profession;	It is at this point that the developing professional finally gets the opportunity to become a full (as opposed to an affiliated) member of the multiprofessional team. In moving into a new clinical area, the first aim of the newly qualified professional will still be acceptance into the monoprofessional team but, once accepted, they will rapidly *expect to take an active role in multiprofessional teamworking*. If the strategies described earlier in this chapter had been followed during initial training, the development of appropriate strategies might rest largely on prior scenario-based learning. However, this will not be the case for most current practitioners.
• demonstrate attitudes which facilitate the development and maintenance of effective multiprofessional teamworking;	Now that full membership of the multiprofessional team is a possibility, there will be real value in examining scenarios about gaining team entry and support in a multiprofessional context. As each professional needs to gain the acceptance of all the other professions, an understanding of those strategies that have been found to be effective by the other professions is likely to be of value.
• be able to respond to change processes in a multiprofessional	When the developing professional reaches the practitioner stage, they

context, especially in relation to professional boundaries, in a way that balances professional and whole-team considerations;	are making a longer-term commitment to a team than has been possible previously. This means that they are likely to experience change within the team for the first time, as opposed to experiencing change as an effect of moving from one team to another. *Practitioners need to develop comfort with the change process* and to respond to change in a manner which enables them to maintain an appropriate degree of influence over alteration in role boundaries.
• demonstrate assertive and facilitative communication styles as appropriate in multiprofessional negotiation;	Scenarios involving changes in role boundaries can *enable practitioners to practise appropriate patterns of negotiation*.
• select appropriate joint working practices from those with which they are familiar, and propose their adoption by the multiprofessional team.	This might build on learning undertaken during the probationer phase. The selection of joint strategies appropriate to the team cannot be part of scenario-based learning for practitioners who come from a range of teams. However, newly qualified practitioners may still be glad of a role-play scenario that allows them to *practise the skills involved in proposing new practices to an existing team*, or to play the role of an existing team member receiving the 'advice' of a newcomer.

None of the initiatives identified in the survey offered whole-team teaching. This was not unexpected in view of the fact that higher education relies on individuals making a personal commitment to programmes of academic study. It is much more likely that whole-team development would be provided internally by the health care system. Interviews with trust managers confirmed that their training officers include team *training* as part of their brief, and there are regional authority training programmes for primary health care teams (e.g. Spratley, 1989; Dark, 1994). The sample of trust managers to whom we spoke were concerned to improve teamwork alongside the development of professional roles. As was discussed in Chapter 1, their particular concern with role boundaries has to be understood in the context of the shortage of manpower. With vacancies in nursing teams being the norm, and the therapy professions spread very thinly, the need to have a flexible work-force becomes increasingly important. For services to survive, team members have to pull together and be able to share across the gaps. There is a place for the use of examples of researched case studies of teamwork to act as a focus for a team in order to help them to explore interpretations of teamwork, and to consider the issues surrounding roles and communication. The following framework suggests strategies that might be useful for enabling teams to achieve the learning outcomes that were first identified in Chapter 6.

WHOLE-TEAM LEARNING

Through whole-team learning, practitioners will work together to:	**Issues relating to scenario-based learning:**
• develop a shared team philosophy and culture which supports individual and collective responsibilities;	In terms of whole-team learning, all scenarios should be based on the real context, structure and organisation of the team concerned, unless there is a specific need to take team members away from the real setting (e.g. in order to circumvent the barricades of hidebound attitudes and behaviours).
• develop a multiprofessional team structure that will enable the team philosophy to be enacted in patient care;	The purpose of scenario-based learning as part of whole-team development is therefore normally *to run a series of 'what if' exercises about new philosophies and structures*. Working through the 'what ifs' requires an exploration of their effect in real situations.
• develop shared strategies for clinical intervention in given circumstances, identifying the roles of each profession and the means of ensuring effective interactivity;	There is therefore a need to examine 'concrete' examples (e.g. how the *shared strategies and identified roles* might affect the care of a particular client group or the running of a theatre list, or might have avoided that nasty incident with 'Patient X').
• develop strategies for inclusion of new members which allow sharing of team culture and philosophy whilst at the same time promoting openness to the new ideas and ways of working they bring with them;	Once a team philosophy and structure is starting to gel, it is equally possible to run 'what if' scenarios focusing on the involvement of new members: considering how *different structures or communication strategies*

can facilitate or block input from newcomers. Such scenarios can also help existing members to see the pitfalls that lie ahead if the agreed common philosophy/structure becomes fossilised.

- develop patterns of communication which facilitate efficient interaction between existing team members, but which do not exclude new members.

By the use of 'what if' scenarios it is possible to *identify the best communication strategies / channels for facilitating efficient interaction.* However, the problems may relate to the communication styles of individuals, and this can be a far more difficult situation to tackle. Senior professionals may be unable to recognise that their own communication styles may not facilitate teamworking.

There is one further category to be considered, and that is the senior professional. At this stage any scenario-based learning is likely to be part of a strategic planning process within a specific health-provider organisation, or part of a broader initiative by the regional health authority, rather than a higher education initiative.

THE PROFESSIONAL LEADER STAGE

As professional leaders, senior staff will:

- develop an understanding of multiprofessional working which will enable them to provide a fertile environment for the development of a shared culture and joint practices;

Issues relating to scenario-based learning:

In essence, the issues relating to scenario-based learning for professional leaders are similar to those discussed previously and therefore do not need to be rehearsed here.

- use their professional expertise to respond constructively and critically to multiprofessional initiatives coming from the clinical area;

The obvious difference is that the scenarios paint a broader picture, examining the organisation as a whole and as the context which it provides for multiprofessional working. It may also involve scenarios in which the organisational aims

- have a clear understanding of the context created for each profession by the organisation and their management structures;
- balance their role as champions of their own professions with their organisational role in the promotion of effective health care in a multiprofessional environment;
- Develop effective strategies for multiprofessional leadership within the organisation.

conflict with those of a professional body, or in which the aims of professional bodies are mismatched.

FACILITATING MULTIPROFESSIONAL LEARNING

Classroom-based teaching

The skills required to facilitate multiprofessional groups in scenario-based problem-solving are not the easiest to acquire. In a collection of papers which brought together some European experiences of multiprofessional courses, Linköping University, one of the first and most committed institutions to introduce shared learning, compiled a set of a dozen difficulties and constraints for teachers which had arisen in their experience (Areskog, 1995). The need for time for planning, consultation, evaluation and training, plus support and cross-departmental funding was cited, as was a lack of multiprofessional teaching materials. At Maastricht, staff felt de-skilled and de-motivated when they perceived themselves as 'minders' of mixed groups of students where their special professional expertise was not called upon. The move from the model of teaching in which specialist knowledge is *transmitted*, to the role of *facilitator*, is a difficult one to achieve even in monoprofessional groups.

In this country, Mhaolrúnaigh and colleagues (1996) evaluated educational programmes that prepare nurse, midwife and health visitor teachers for shared learning. Their findings indicated that teachers had few opportunities to put into practice the small-group work skills they had learned, and which they associated with positive experiences of shared learning. After completing their programme, they found that they were expected to teach in large lectures in the 'common learning' environments which characterised multiprofessional higher education provision. Many nurse and midwife teachers have been acquiring facilitative skills over the past few years, with the emphasis on reflective practice in Project 2000 Diploma courses. The next step would be to move from developing reflection in monoprofessional groups to multiprofessional groups. As students developed their clinical experience, reflection about the roles of other professionals in the team could be developed.

Clinically based teaching

It would be valuable to have a process that would facilitate reflection on multiprofessional clinical experience carried out by clinicians in the clinical areas. The challenges of training preceptors and the recognition of the competing demands on their time would seem to be considerable obstacles. A small number of institutions have tried to overcome this problem by establishing specific clinical environments for multiprofessional education. One example is an eight-bedded orthopaedic ward in Linköping, Sweden. In the UK, a London hospital has designated part of a ward as a multiprofessional learning environment. In Finland, a nurse training institution has bought and converted part of a hospital as a multiprofessional learning environment. The dilemma in creating 'special' environments is whether students are being sufficiently prepared for the reality of some of the quite different clinical areas they will find in practice. The argument is that, once understandings of other professions have been gained within a clinical framework centred on multiprofessional learning, these will never be lost, and the confidence to forge positive working relationships with other professionals will persist.

CONCLUSION

In the model we have proposed ideas for both classroom-based and clinically based learning. However, we would maintain that, in order to give students a compatible educational experience across both, higher education and trusts need to work together to produce constructive interprofessional learning environments. In the final chapter we shall highlight some of the persistent gaps between intentions and reality, and we shall discuss where efforts could be made to bring them together.

9 Closing the gaps

RHETORIC AND REALITY

We began by exploring the issues and processes involved in multiprofessional teamworking so that we could identify whether students and practitioners in the health and social care professions were being prepared to work together effectively. The evidence has illuminated the gaps between the rhetoric and the reality. Some of the gaps are very difficult to deal with, embedded in seemingly intractable problems, whereas others could be closed by stakeholders tackling them collectively.

A lack of congruence between policy and practice is nothing unusual. In evaluating working practices and curricula it is usually the case that what is written down as policy differs from what is translated into action by the various individuals involved in implementation. At the next level, the actions that people say they take are not necessarily what they *actually* do. Finally, what they are perceived to have done by their patients or clients or by their students may be different again. This is not because people are inevitably devious, but because the context and reality in which policy is put in place, coupled with different individuals' aims and understandings, lead to different interpretations. Moreover, achieving congruence between these different levels is not necessarily seen as desirable by individuals if, for example, policies about integration and multi-skilling conflict with their concerns about maintaining their professional autonomy. Even where people do wish to achieve more integrated teamworking, their actual practice under the pressure of everyday working may not reflect their aims. 'Gaps' between policies and practice are therefore to be expected; the interesting questions are concerned with illuminating their extent and the reasons behind them. This informs the debate about whether such gaps need attention, whether they can realistically be dealt with and, if so, how this can be done.

The practice/education gap

We have highlighted the *lack of congruence between the issues involved in multiprofessional working and the majority of shared learning education*, which is not directed at these issues but is centred on the economics and flexibility of provision in higher education. This is a gap which we have argued needs to be addressed by a radical change in emphasis in education programmes, and we presented one model for doing this in the previous chapter.

However, curriculum change is rarely easy and straightforward. The data from curriculum managers and programme leaders have indicated many barriers to introducing multiprofessional education, including concerns about 'loss' of monoprofessional time, organisational problems, and difficulties with timetabling, logistics and group sizes. These barriers will still have to be overcome even if there is a shift in purpose and content towards shared learning as team-focused care. Nor will universities' concerns about economies of scale, which have driven the 'common learning' agenda, disappear. In other words, no single model or approach will meet all agendas. However, the apparent gulf between multiprofessional work in practice and what is undertaken in shared learning in higher education brings the imperative for change, if the evidence of the value of collaborative teamwork to patients or clients is believed. Given the effort that staff in higher education must put into organising shared learning initiatives, it could be argued that directing them specifically towards preparation for interprofessional teamwork would provide a better long-term pay-off for students, patients or clients and carers.

Teamworking: The ideal/reality gap

Nevertheless, we need to remember that it is in the clinical areas where students experience multiprofessional working. If they are not involved in collaborative teamworking and have no role models from which to learn, then their preparation in higher education falls on barren ground. Our research suggests that *there is a further gap here – between NHS trusts' concern to achieve effective teamworking, and achieving it in practice*. No matter how supportive of multiprofessional teamworking professional education becomes, it would be dealing with only half of the equation if students were then faced with a culture that is hostile to the pursuit of such practice.

The problems involved in creating good practice environments for teamwork and fostering a culture for *inter*professionalism are considerable. In the acute sector, organisational policies have driven working practices towards greater patient throughput by filling as many beds as possible, and staff turnover rates are high. Despite good intentions, therefore, the development of highly collaborative working practices may be practically impossible. The 'reality' of the stable team in relatively predictable environments may be the exception. Where more stable and predictable environments do exist, as was seen for example in the teams where core and periphery working was prevalent, other factors have combined to make collaboration of the whole team difficult to achieve. For instance, putting individuals together and calling them a team does not necessarily lead to collaborative teamworking, as evidence from the case studies showed. Trust managers and clinicians need to develop a culture in which teams are set up as coherent, interdependent units and are sustained as such.

We also saw that having no whole-team focus with regard to patient care, being subject to other prioritisation for work outside the team by some members, and having separate management structures which were not in communication with each other, all served to divide team members. Furthermore, teams working across more than one trust and with outside agencies experience problems with mismatching policies and procedures. In the community, cross-agency working has its own problems in terms of dealing with different practices and philosophies.

The reality of managing trusts with limited financial and manpower resources has created a situation that would appear to undermine initiatives to enhance collaborative multiprofessional working. However, several of the managers in our research, and some trusts, have made attempts to redress the negative outcomes of earlier changes in structure and process. Moves such as a return to *ward-based* professionals and *multiprofessional practice boards* are in their infancy, and are patchy in terms of spread across the trusts. If multiprofessional teamworking is high on trusts' agendas, then scrutiny and modification of structure and process would appear to be fundamental to the success of such a drive.

The strategic policy/chalk-face opportunities gap

Clinical governance has concentrated minds at the strategic level on the need for better communication between those who care for patients, and therefore the need for better 'team development' (Department of Health, 1998c). However, even brief amounts of time away from patients to achieve this are rendered almost impossible in many cases because of staff shortages. There is frequently no slack in the system to provide cover.

There is therefore a gap between senior management's advocacy of teamwork development and its failure to take place at 'grass-roots' level. Dedicated persistence and forward planning by middle managers are needed to create such time, amidst all of the other initiatives they are required to implement. Some would argue that the political rhetoric encouraging better multiprofessional working, both within and between health and social care providers, to forge 'joined-up' services, will not be possible unless it is backed by sufficient resources.

Status, training and pay gaps

Even with larger resources, it can also be argued that *there is another serious and persistent gap in terms of the inequalities in status, pay and training opportunities between members of the different professions, and that this will always militate against the best intentions for developing the equal partnerships that are valued in teamworking*. In our research, some clinicians in positions of power operated in a democratic fashion, recognising the expertise that others had to offer, listening to advice and acting on it, despite the perceived intransigence of structural inequalities. Others used their position to ignore or dismiss the input of colleagues, to whom they appeared arrogant and sometimes unaware of the negative reactions they were causing. The importance of doctors engaging in interprofessional working has been highlighted throughout our research. In cases where their leadership style has marginalised others, addressing team development may not be a 'quick fix'. Although a trained and independent facilitator (which again has resource implications) can do much to help to integrate a team, this will not alter differences in remuneration or status between its members. However, some research does show that it may reduce team members' stress and increase their motivation to remain in the service.

CAN EDUCATION CONSORTIA NARROW THE GAPS?

> The gap between education and service has widened since nursing and midwifery education have moved into HEIs, and this is a cause for great concern. Evidence to the Commission suggests that pre-registration education should place greater emphasis on the development of practice skills, which will require improved links between education and service and new ways of working.
>
> (Department of Health, 1999, *Integrating theory and practice*, Professional Letter from the Chief Nursing Officer for England, PL/CNO(99) 1, cited in United Kingdom Central Council for Nursing, Midwifery and Health Visiting, 1999, p. 40)

What of the gap between education and service for other professions besides nursing and midwifery, whose students have been educated in universities for many years? If meeting of minds is to take place, *the education consortia are the linchpins* linking trusts' policies (including those via clinical governance) on multiprofessional working with *relevant* education to support it.

Since education consortia now have the role of purchasing, their actions are vital in steering the evolution of future programmes towards team-oriented activities which feed directly into multiprofessional working. However, to be effective, consortia need to include a range of professionals who are representative of common clinical team formation, rather than the limited range reported currently.

As shared learning becomes accepted as 'a good thing', and is endorsed in education by professional bodies (as was described in Chapter 1), there is a tendency for the *nature* of the shared learning to be left to the universities. As long as 'it' is being done, then obligations have been met. Consortia need to create criteria for *appropriate* shared learning which will ensure that programmes meet the agenda of *inter*professional teamworking, and are not there solely to provide a flexible and economic means of managing large groups of students. Paradoxically, it is of course the consortia's fluctuating demands with regard to numbers of different professionals to be trained that have encouraged the pooling of student numbers in classes in the first place, as was discussed in Chapter 7.

There is an argument for consortia collaborating to create national programmes for commissioning relevant multiprofessional education. This does not imply that such programmes would all be the same.There would be local differences reflecting the locations where professional groups are taught (e.g. whether there is a medical school, or which PAMs students were catered for in the different universities).

At the same time, consortia need to consider students' practice placements. Are there initiatives in place in the consortia's trusts to foster a positive interprofessional culture? What kind of role models will students see? If the 'reality' is too fraught for collaborative practices to flourish, then changes to educational preparation will be in vain unless some of the problems are addressed by trusts. Within their remit, consortia can exercise their influence to keep teamwork development on trusts' agendas.

WHY ATTACK THE GAPS?

Before people embark on attempts to close gaps in order to sustain and enhance multiprofessional teamworking and the underpinning education, they need to be convinced that this is worth the effort. Much of the evidence in the past has concerned the problems which arise when teamwork fails (e.g. in high-profile child protection cases). Similarly, a lack of communication between team members and/or between a team and patients and carers is one of the most frequent causes of complaints to trusts. Our study of clinical teams adds to a growing body of evidence of the value of integrated teamworking. Although we had not set out to examine outcomes for patients, the findings in the case studies were clear. In teams where there was more collaborative working, there were identifiable benefits for patients, carers and the team itself. The higher the level of collaboration across the whole team, the greater was the number of incidents observed which showed continuity and consistency of care from professional to professional, a reduction in ambiguous messages between team members and between them and their patients or clients and carers, appropriate referral (in terms of both profession and timing), a wide range of knowledge being used as a basis for team decisions, and a problem-solving approach being used across the team to determine care programmes. It was equally clear that the more fragmented patterns of working compromised patient care on a regular basis.

Many of the individuals whom we have met during the course of our research emphasised that collaborative working should start with the patient or client and their problems and needs – these are the driving factors for interprofessional working and learning. Although economic and flexible programmes in higher education are key considerations, they should not be driving the content and process of shared education. In the NHS trusts, taking time out to review and improve the way in which a team works with and around the patient or client is time well spent if it helps to reduce the frustrations of fragmented practice, and prevents patients and clients from falling through the 'gaps'.

Appendix: the methodological approach

THE CASE STUDIES OF CLINICAL TEAMS

Case study shares many similarities with *illuminative evaluation and research* (Miller and Parlett, 1974; Parlett and Dearden, 1977; Miller, 1983). Both have five main principles, these being that the approach is

- *problem-centred*: beginning with issues and concerns as defined in real life settings. The 'problem' does not necessarily mean a puzzle or difficulty – it may be a general interest in particular aspects of the context, such as how a particular role is seen and enacted;
- *practitioner-orientated*: concerned with questions relevant to individuals involved in practice, as opposed to generating questions of interest only to other researchers. The language used must be accessible to practitioners from different professions if the findings are genuinely to communicate with them;
- *cross-disciplinary*: methods should be determined by the problem, not by the methodology of a particular discipline, such as psychological testing;
- *adaptive in terms of methods*: the problem determines the choice of methods, and depends on the setting and practitioners. The methods are accordingly responsive and flexible. Triangulation of methods is used (Webb *et al.*, 1966), in which accuracy is enhanced at the intersection of the data 'sight-lines' produced by each method. Interviews and observations take a central place because of the importance of individuals' experiences and perceptions;
- *flexible*: the researcher does not pre-specify how the research will develop, because the concerns, interests and perspectives of those being researched shape the direction as the study proceeds. This is consistent with responding to the concerns of the practitioner rather than to the needs of the researcher with a predetermined plan. Being flexible does not mean losing sight of the goals of the research, and the researcher maintains a degree of independence in order to remain in control of the research.

Three propositions underlie both *case study* and the *illuminative approach*. First, there is a difference between intention and actual behaviour, and therefore a need to study both. Furthermore, those on the receiving end of a particular action may see neither the intention nor the behaviour in the way that those carrying out the action would expect. Secondly, the links between aspects of the studied setting need to be explored – a single act cannot be understood unless it is seen both in relationship to and within a pattern of events. Thirdly, historical and evolutionary differences affect the judgements of people within different settings and must be accounted for. One characteristic which differentiates *case study* from the *illuminative approach* is that the former gives greater prominence to the nature of the case itself, and what makes it different from the other cases of a similar kind.

However, *case study* is faced with a particularly difficult ethical problem. This concerns the contextually bounded nature of the research and the issues that are raised within that context with regard to more public dissemination of the findings. How to balance obligations towards individuals and/or teams with obligations to publish the case study findings needs to be considered carefully. In our study this was particularly relevant, both for individuals with regard to feedback of the research findings to the team, and for the teams with regard to subsequent publications, which may be accessed by senior management of the organisations within which the teams worked.

One way of attempting to overcome difficulties in releasing potentially sensitive information to a wider audience is by negotiation with the participants about the collection, interpretation and feedback of the data at different levels. However, this has to be achieved without undermining the impact of the research findings – a tension that is difficult to resolve. In this research, all of the teams that took part in the case studies were visited on several occasions to discuss the research process and feedback, either by talking to all team members, or by talking to a senior representative of the team (who would then discuss these issues with other team members). The aim of these meetings was to ensure that all potential participants were aware of what the research process would entail both for the individuals and for the team. Where negotiation took place with a senior representative, all team members were given an information sheet for their approval. In either case, understanding was reached on the following issues.

- Involvement in the process would be voluntary.
- Access to meetings would be negotiated in the case of sensitive issues.
- Confidentiality and anonymity of information were assured for all individuals and teams as a whole.
- All participants would have access to their interview transcripts in order to agree their inclusion as data.
- Negotiation should be possible if participants were particularly worried about certain responses made at interview.
- In order to safeguard the confidentiality of individual team members' input, they were assured that sufficiently abstracted information in the form of a summary report would be fed back to the team as a whole.
- Further agreement on this summary of interpretations of the data would be sought from the team before the findings were incorporated into the wider data set.

This negotiation process was continued at a later stage in the research process, where a case study was selected for complete representation within the final report. The relevant team was given access to an unabridged but anonymised version of the case study for their consultation and agreement.

Methods of gathering case study data

One member of our research team carried out all the fieldwork for the case studies. This allowed her to make constant comparisons across the six sites as well as within single sites, thereby enabling similarities and differences to be identified and compared. The other two members of our team provided a critical forum for discussion of the findings from each case, and for considering the nature of the variations between sites. The irony of being 'a team' studying 'teams' was not lost on us, and our own processes as a group were discussed at points throughout the research.

All of the case study sites were visited intensively for a period of up to 3 months, and similar methods were used to gather evidence, namely *non-participant observation, semi-structured interviews* and *document analysis.* For the purposes of the observation, teams were visited each day of the working week for several hours at a time (and at some weekends where appropriate to observe differences in patterns of working). All aspects of team function were observed. This included both formal and informal meetings between the various professionals, sessions where they were working together with patients or clients, and telephone calls that they made to other team members. Some professionals in each team were 'shadowed' for part of the day, enabling us to explore patterns of individual practice and how these linked with other team members.

All of the interviewees were formally interviewed at least once, for about 40–50 minutes. Follow-up interviews were conducted where necessary in order to clarify certain points. Consistent with our research approach, all interviewees received a copy of their interview transcript, thus allowing them to correct misheard or misunderstood information, and to give their agreement to the inclusion of the information supplied by them in the analysis. We interviewed all members of smaller teams, and for large teams we used purposive sampling of all professional groups. Documents such as relevant case-notes, promotional literature, policies and guidelines were then used to reinforce our understanding of teamworking in each case study.

METHODS OF EXAMINING SHARED LEARNING PROVISION IN HIGHER EDUCATION

The aim was to review and explore the stage reached and the direction taken for programmes in shared learning across the country at pre- and post-qualifying levels, in order to document what had taken place and what curriculum developments were planned, analyse the driving forces behind different developments, and explore the implications for students and the relationship with clinical needs.

A funnelling system of information gathering was used, starting with a two-part national survey (Youngman, 1984; Oppenheim, 1992), followed-by telephone interviews (Cassiani *et al.*, 1992) with a sample of respondents, and finally visits to a smaller sample.

Surveys

Information was sought from all higher education institutions in the UK that were running or planning initial or continuing programmes of education for health and social care professionals. Copies of a first questionnaire seeking information about the extent of shared learning provision were sent to a named person in each of 181 faculties/departments. The survey was not restricted to institutions offering nursing education. There were 74 respondents who identified a total of 206 multiprofessional initiatives running or under development. A second questionnaire designed to explore the nature and purpose of shared learning initiatives in greater depth was sent to these respondents, which resulted in details of 95 programmes being completed and returned.

Telephone interviews

The main purpose of the telephone interviews was to follow up a sample of the questionnaires in order to clarify and explore issues raised by the initial responses. These interviews were rich sources of data because respondents were open in discussing the challenges faced by those involved in the initiatives, and the resulting differences between the curricula as planned and as implemented.

Selection of subjects for telephone interview began with a categorisation of the multiprofessional initiatives identified in the questionnaires as follows: pre- and post-qualification; long and short programmes; initiatives initiated by higher education and those initiated by service providers; shared learning early and late in the programme; different modes of shared learning; and institutions with a large number of multiprofessional initiatives.

Some initiatives involved both pre- and post-qualification students, and all of them included nurses. Shared learning which only involved nurses, and programmes leading to qualification in more than one profession were excluded. This left 78 initiatives. Difficulties in contacting some of those who had completed the questionnaires, and the reluctance of a few individuals to give a telephone interview, meant that some initiatives could not be pursued. The following factors also affected the follow-up of initiatives in the original categories:

- as initiatives were explored, the picture presented in the questionnaire was altered by the respondent's perception and it no longer fitted the category;
- issues arose in the interview which suggested alternative initiatives to follow up;
- additional initiatives came to light which appeared to merit follow-up.

By the end of the telephone interview process the research team had:

- conducted interviews in each of the original categories where programmes were available and respondents were willing;
- followed up the major issues raised in the early interviews by looking for other examples where the same strategies were used or problems identified;
- examined additional initiatives where these appeared to have something new to contribute.

This process covered 23 initiatives in 21 interviews. In most cases the interview was with the programme co-ordinator, who was therefore involved in both planning and implementation. All of the respondents were assured of complete confidentiality. The interviews lasted an average of 35 minutes. They were not taped, but detailed notes were taken and typed up.

The questions that were asked in each telephone interview were not standardised, although they had common elements. This was because a number of questionnaires had information gaps or responses which were open to more than one interpretation, which meant there was a need to clarify the situation through the interviews. The questionnaires also raised different issues concerning the nature of the student cohort, the expected learning outcome, perceived advantages and problems, etc. Although issues raised by one respondent can influence the questions that were asked of others, the focus for each interview had to be individualised. However, the following core areas were open to limited exploration within the questionnaire format, but respondents could be asked to expand upon them verbally:

- the relationship between health care providers and higher education providers in relation to the initiative;
- the rationale for the initiative and expected learning outcomes;
- the expected benefit of multiprofessional education and the degree to which it had been realised;
- the nature of the teaching/facilitation processes and the response of students;
- barriers and enablers in the development of multiprofessional education.

Visits to initiatives

A sample of seven programmes was chosen to be visited in order to obtain more detailed information about their planning, organisation and delivery. Each was different with regard to its aims and participants, and it was not the intention to evaluate their success. In selecting the sample, it was found that many programmes were open to a range of professionals but did not in fact recruit from that range. The reasons for selection of the sample and the data collected are given below.

A 1-day workshop on advanced clinical skills for final-year medical students and recently-qualified nurses

Why selected Although programmes involving doctors and nurses have a particular importance because of their interaction in the clinical area, the survey identified few examples. This programme also had an explicit intention to facilitate teamworking.

Data gathered Observation of the day; interview with medical and nurse teachers leading the workshop; informal discussion with the seven nurses and six medical students about their perceptions of the day.

A programme of education for qualified staff, open to a variety of professions and aiming to facilitate the development of clinical effectiveness

Why selected Clinical effectiveness is an important issue in education and practice. The team expected to gain insight into how multiprofessional education would promote multiprofessional working.

Data gathered Interviews with three staff managing and/or implementing the programme; discussion with two students (a nurse and a PT) about the programme and their projects.

A faculty of health providing shared modules for students in the first year of initial training (study and research skills – the social context of professional health/social care)

Why selected This was an example of initial education involving students from a broad range of professions (radiographers, SWs, OTs, PTs, SLTs, nurses and midwives).

Data gathered Interviews with the dean and seven other staff involved with the programme; review of outline documentation; interview with two students.

An advanced life support course

Why selected This was an example of a knowledge/skills-based programme involving doctors and nurses with a broad range of experience, which runs in numerous centres throughout the UK. (The programme was open to paramedics, but none were included on this occasion.)

Data gathered Review of programme documentation; observation of the 2-day programme; interview with the organiser; informal discussions with 12 of the 30 students and four of the 12 teaching staff. Both groups included doctors and nurses.

A healthy alliances workshop

Why selected This was one of the few initiatives in which teamworking was the explicit focus for the whole event. The case study/role play methodology was also of particular interest.

Data gathered Discussion with the manager as follow-up to a detailed telephone interview; interviews with four students at different stages on the programme.

A combined department of obstetrics, gynaecology and midwifery

Why selected This was a successful amalgamation of educational provision for two professional groups offering an opportunity to explore the relationships both between midwifery and nursing and between midwifery and their medical colleagues.

Data gathered Interviews with the lead midwife and two other members of staff, one of whom volunteered a student perspective because she was undertaking a multiprofessional programme run by the department.

A palliative care workshop for GPs and community nurses

Why selected This was an example of community-focused education involving these important professional groups.

Data gathered A whole-day observation of teaching and learning; interviews with the lead nurse teacher and medical teacher; informal discussion with five of the 20 students. Staff were open in discussing the challenges they faced as well as the positive aspects of their initiatives. They provided documentary information about the university context as well as the particular initiatives discussed.

METHODS OF DATA COLLECTION FROM TRUST MANAGERS

The aim was to elicit the perspectives of a sample of trust managers and appropriate senior NHS executives about multiprofessional practice. Representation from nursing, medicine, physiotherapy, occupational therapy, diatetics and radiography was sought. Of those invited to take part, only two managers from physiotherapy and 12 managers from nursing responded, providing a rather uneven picture of the management perspective.

All of the managers were interviewed face to face except one, who was interviewed over the telephone. The semi-structured interviews lasted for approximately 1 hour and were taped and transcribed. Managers were asked to comment on the following areas:

- the external agenda for multiprofessional education;
- the trust's perception of the purpose of a multiprofessional approach;

- how financial constraints shape the development of a multiprofessional approach;
- whether changes were being made to facilitate a multiprofessional approach;
- the form and function of multi-skilling within the trusts;
- the barriers to multiprofessional learning – both external and internal to the organisations.

OBTAINING THE VIEWS OF PROFESSIONAL BODIES

The aim was to gain an understanding of the views of different professional bodies about the problems and potential for developing multiprofessional education.

Over 40 bodies represent the health and social care professions. Representatives of a sample were interviewed, selected from the professions that were seen most frequently in the clinical case studies. Some of the bodies that were approached for an interview preferred to provide documents setting out their position on multiprofessional education:

- Chartered Institute of physiotherapists – interview;
- College of Occupational Therapists – interview;
- Dietetics Board – interview;
- Clinical Psychology – provided a position paper;
- Professions Supplementary to Medicine – the Deputy Registrar (CPSM) provided and discussed explanatory papers relating to the nine professions covered by the Council;
- Council for the Education and Training of Social Workers (CETSW) – provided papers on joint CETSW/ENB programmes;
- Standing Committee on Postgraduate Medical and Dental Education – provided a consultative document on multiprofessional education;
- General Medical Council – provided several papers.

SYNTHESIS OF THE DATA

The synthesis of the data was the final element of the research. Data from the clinical teams about the processes involved in multiprofessional working were examined for their implications for education. The results of the higher education surveys, interviews and visits were analysed to give a national picture of shared learning provision. The key implications for learning arising from the case studies were then compared with what was offered in shared learning programmes of education. This comparison was set within the context of the organisational and managerial challenges for multiprofessional working and for programme development, using information derived from interviews with NHS managers and programme leaders.

The last stage of the synthesis was to consider models of education which would meet the needs of pre- and post-qualification students, based on analysis of the contexts of multiprofessional working and existing educational provision.

BIBLIOGRAPHY FOR THE METHODOLOGICAL APPROACH AND METHODS

Cassiani, S.B., Zanetti, M.L. and Pela, N.R. (1992) The telephone survey: a methodological strategy for obtaining information. *Journal of Advanced Nursing* **17**, 576–81.

Glaser, B. (1965) *Awareness of dying*. Chicago: Aldine.

Glaser, B. and Strauss, A. (1967) *The discovery of grounded theory: strategies for qualitative research*. New York: Aldine.

Guba, E.G. and Lincoln, Y.S. (1981) *Effective evaluation*. San Francisco, CA: Jossey Bass.

Miller, C. (1983) Evaluation research methods: a guide. In *Research in practice teaching*. London: Central Council for Education and Training in Social Work, 18–26.

Miller, C. and Parlett, M. (1974) *Up to the mark*. London: Society for Research in Higher Education (reprinted (1983) Slough: NFER-Nelson).

Oppenheim, A.N. (1992) *Questionnaire design, interviewing and attitude measurement*. London: Pinter.

Parlett, M. and Hamilton, D. (1977) Evaluation as illumination. In Hamilton, D., Jenkins, D., King, C., MacDonald, B. and Parlett, M. (eds), *Beyond the number game*. London: Macmillan Education, 6–22.

Parlett, M. and Dearden, G. (eds) (1977) *Introduction to illuminative evaluation*. Cardiff-by-the-sea, CA: Pacific Soundings Press (republished in 1981 by Society for Research in Higher Education, Guildford, Surrey).

Strauss, A. and Corbin, J. (1992) *Basics of qualitative research: grounded theory procedures and techniques*. Newbury Park, CA: Sage.

Webb, E.J., Campbell, D.T., Schwarz, R.D. and Sechrest, L. (1996) *Unobtrusive measures: non-reactive research in the social sciences*. Chicago: Rand McNally.

Youngman, M.B. (1984) Designing questionnaires. In Bell, J., Bush, T., Goodey, J. *et al.* (eds), *Small-scale investigations in education management*. London: Harper Row, 157–76.

References

Abramson, J. (1990) Making teams work. In Schopler, J. and Galinsky, M. (eds), *Groups in health care settings*. New York: Haworth Press, 45–63.

Adshead, G. and Dickenson, D. (1993) Why do doctors and nurses disagree? In Dickenson, D. and Johnson, J. (eds) *Death, dying and bereavement*. London: Sage, 161–8.

Areskog, N. (1995) Multiprofessional education at the undergraduate level. In Soothill, K., Mackay, L. and Webb, C. (eds), *Interprofessional relations in health care*. London: Edward Arnold, 125–39.

Bader, S.A. and Braude, R.M. (1998) Patient informatics: creating new partnerships in medical decision-making. *Academic Medicine* **73**, 408–11.

Barr, H. and Waterton, S. (1996) *Interprofessional Education in Health and Social Care. Report of a United Kingdom Survey*. London: Centre for the Advancement of Interprofessional Education.

Bass, B.M., Avolio, B.J. and Atwater, L. (1996) The transformational and transactional leadership of men and women. *Applied Psychology: an International Review* **45**, 15–34.

Brown, R. (1988) *Group processes: dynamics within and between groups*. Oxford: Basil Blackwell.

Busby, A. and Gilchrist, B. (1992) The role of the nurse in the medical ward round. *Journal of Advanced Nursing* **17**, 339–46.

Cambell-Heider, N. and Pollock, D. (1987) Barriers to physician/nurse collegiality: an anthropological perspective. *Social Science and Medicine* **25**, 421–5.

Cerinus, M. and Furguson, C. (1994) Preparing nurses for preceptorship. *Nursing Standard* **836**, 34–8.

Clark, P.G., Spence, D.L. and Sheehan, J.L. (1986) A service/learning model for interdisciplinary teamwork in health and ageing. *Gerontology and Geriatrics Education* **6**, 3–15.

Colliere, M.F. (1986) Invisible care and invisible women. *International Journal of Nursing Studies* **23**, 95–112.

Corner, J. (1997) Beyond survival rates and side-effects. *Cancer Nursing* **20**, 3–11.

Dark, P. (1994) *The Primary Health Care Team Workshop Programme: report on the development and progress of Local Organising Teams in SWTRHA*, 1989–1994. London: NHSE and South Thames Regional Health Authority.

Delaney, F. (1994) Making connections: research into intersectoral collaboration. *Health Education Journal* **53**, 474–85.

Department of Health (1989) *Caring for people: community care in the next decade and beyond*. London: HMSO.

Department of Health (1990a) *National Health Service and Community Care Act* London: HMSO.

Department of Health (1990b) *The Care Programme Approach for people with* mental illness. London: HMSO.

Department of Health (1998a) *A first class service: quality in the NHS*. London: HMSO.

Department of Health (1998b) *The new NHS charter – a different approach.* London: HMSO.

Department of Health (1998c) *The new NHS: modern, dependable.* London: HMSO.

Dolmans, D. and Schmidt, H. (1996) The advantages of problem-based curricula. *Postgraduate Medical Journal* **72**, 535–8.

Embling, S. (1995) Exploring multidisciplinary teamwork. *British Journal of Therapy and Rehabilitation*, **2**, 142–4.

English National Board for Nursing, Midwifery and Health Visiting and Central Council for Education and Training in Social Work (1994) *Shared learning: a good practice guide.* London: ENB and CCETSW.

English National Board for Nursing, Midwifery and Health Visiting (2000) *Education in focus: strengthening pre-registration nursing and midwifery education. Section 1. General curriculum guidance and requirements for pre-registration nursing and midwifery programmes. Section 2. Specific curriculum guidance and requirements for pre-registration nursing and midwifery programmes.* London: ENB.

Eraut, M. (1994) *Developing professional knowledge and competence.* London: Falmer Press.

Fewtrell, W.D. and Toms, D.A. (1985) Pattern of discussion in traditional and novel ward-round procedures. *British Journal of Medical Psychology* **58**, 57–62.

Field, R. and West, M. (1995) Teamwork in primary health care 2. Perspectives from practice. *Journal of Interprofessional Care* **9**, 123–9.

Fokke, C. (1994) Role of the nurse in rehabilitating patients with head injury. *British Journal of Therapy and Rehabilitation* **1**, 82–5.

Funnell, P., Gill, J. and Ling, J. (1992) Competence through interprofessional shared learning. Saunders, D. and Race, P. (eds) *Aspects of educational and training technology, XXV. Developing and measuring competence.* London: Kogan Page, 3–7.

Furnell, J., Flett, S. and Clark, D. (1987) Multidisciplinary clinical teams: some issues in Establishment and function. *Hospital and Health Services Review* **83**, 15–18.

Garside, P. (1993) *Patient-focused care: a review of seven sites in England.* Leeds: NHS Management Executive.

General Medical Council (1993) *Tomorrow's doctors.* London: General Medical Council.

General Medical Council (1995) *Good medical practice.* London: General Medical Council.

General Medical Council (1997) *The new doctor.* London: General Medical Council.

General Medical Council (1998) *Maintaining good medical practice.* London: General Medical Council.

Gibbon, B. (1992) The role of the nurse in Rehabilitation. *Nursing Standard* **6**, 32–5.

Gill, J. and Ling, J. (1995) Interprofessional shared learning: a curriculum for collaboration. Soothill, K., Mackay, L. and Webb, C. (eds) *Interprofessional relations in health care.* London: Edward Arnold, 172–94.

Goldenberg, D. (1990) Nursing education leadership: the effect of situational and constraint variables on leadership style. *Journal of Advanced Nursing* **15**, 1326–34.

Greenhow, D. Hewitt, A.J. and Kinnersley, P. (1998) Patient satisfaction with referral to hospital: relationship to expectations, involvement, and information giving in the consultation. *British Journal of General Practice* **48**, 911–12.

Griffiths, R. (1988) *Community care: agenda for action*. London: HMSO.

Harrison, R.G. and Roberts, M.J. (1985) Organisational Development: an alternative strategy for organisational renewal in the NHS. *Hospital and Health Services Review* **81**, 125–9.

Hersey, P. and Blanchard, K. (1982) *The management of organisational behaviour: utilising human resources*, 3rd edn. Englewood Cliffs, NJ: Prentice Hall.

Hewstone, M. and Stroebe, W. (1994) Revision and change of stereotypic beliefs: in search of the elusive subtyping model. In Hewstone, M. and Stroebe, W. (eds), *European review of social psychology*. Vol. 5. Chichester: John Wiley & Sons, 69–109.

Hilton, R. (1995) Fragmentation within interprofessional work. A result of isolationism in health care professional education programmes and the preparation of students to function only in the confines of their own disciplines. *Journal of Interprofessional Care* **9**, 33–40.

Iles, P. and Auluck, R. (1990) From organisational to interorganisational development in nursing practice: improving the effectiveness of interdisciplinary teamwork and interagency collaboration. *Journal of Advanced Nursing* **15**, 50–58.

Jarvis, P. (1988) *Adult and continuing education: Theory and Practice*. London: Routledge.

Johnson, J. and Fokke, J. (1995) Achieving effective rehabilitation outcomes: does the nurse have a role? *British Journal of Therapy and Rehabilitation* **2**, 113–18.

Katz, D. and Kahn, R. (1978) *The social psychology of organisations*. New York: Wiley & Sons.

Knowles, M. (1984) *The adult learner: a neglected species*, 3rd edn. Houston, TX: Gulf Publishing Co.

Leathard, A. (1994) (ed.) *Going inter-professional: working together for health and welfare*. London: Routledge.

Lennon, S. (1996) The Bobath concept: a critical review of the theoretical assumptions that guide physiotherapy practice in stroke rehabilitation. *Physiotherapy Review* **1**, 35–45.

Lippett, R. and White, R.K. (1958) An experimental study of leadership and group life. In Macoby, E.E., Newcomb, T.M. and Hartley, E.L. (eds) *Readings in social psychology*, 3rd edn. New York: Holt, 496–510.

Long, S. (1996) Primary health care team workshop: team members' perspectives. *Journal of Advanced Nursing* **23**, 935–41.

Lucas, J. (1990) *Towards shared learning*. Salford: Salford College of Technology.

Luszki, M. (1958) *International team research methods and problems*. New York: National Training Laboratories.

McGrath, M. (1991) *Multidisciplinary teamwork*. Aldershot: Avebury.

MacKay, L. (1993) *Conflicts in Care. Medicine and Nursing*. London: Chapman and Hall.

McKenna, P.M. (1981) Role negotiation. *Nursing Leadership* **4**, 23–8.

Mallik, M. (1992) The role of the nurse on the consultant's ward round. *Nursing Times* **88**, 49–52.

Mandy, P. (1996) Interdisciplinary rather than multidisciplinary or generic practice. *British Journal of Therapy and Rehabilitation* **3**, 110–12.

Merriam, S.B. (1988) *Case study research in education: a qualitative approach*. London: Jossey Bass.

Mhaolrúnaigh, S., Clifford, C. and Hicks, C. (1996) *An evaluation of share learning in educational programmes of preparation for nurse, midwife and health visitor teachers*: London: English National Board for Nursing, Midwifery and Health Visiting.

Miller, C. (1983) Evaluation research methods: a guide. *Research in practice teaching*. London: Central Council for Education and Training in Social Work, 18–26.

Miller, C. and Parlett, M. (1974) *Up to the mark*. London: Society for Research in Higher Education (reprinted (1983) Slough: NFER-Nelson).

Miller, C., Alderton, J., Ross, N. and Procter-Childs, T. (1997) *The nurse's role in the health care team: implications for multiprofessional education*. Bovington: General Nursing Council Trust.

Miller, C., Ross, N. and Alderton, J. (1998) Becoming a member of the diabetes ward team. *Journal of Diabetes Nursing* **2**, 59–62.

Newcomb, T.M. (1965) Attitude formation as a function of reference groups. Proshansky, H. and Seidenberg, B. (eds), *Basic studies in social psychology*. New York: Holt, Rinehart and Winston, 215–24.

NHS Executive (1995) *Education and planning guidance*. Leeds: NHS Executive.

NHS Executive (1996) *Education and planning guidance*. Leeds: NHS Executive.

NHS Executive (1997) *Education and planning guidance*. Leeds: NHS Executive.

Nolan, M., Booth, A. and Nolan, J. (1997) *New directions in rehabilitation: exploring the nursing contribution*. ENB Research Report Series No. 6. London: ENB.

Onyett, S. (1997) *Pulling together: the future roles and training of mental health staff*. London: Sainsbury Centre for Mental Health.

Onyett, S., Pillinger, T. and Muijen, M. (1996) *Making community mental health teams work*. London: Sainsbury Centre for Mental Health.

Øvretveit, J. (1990) Making the team work. *Professional Nurse* **5**, 284–8.

Øvretveit, J. (1993) *Co-ordinating community care: multidisciplinary teams and care management in health and social services*. Milton Keynes: Open University Press.

Øvretveit, J. (1995) Team decision-making. *Journal of Interprofessional Care* **9**, 41–51.

Palmer, A.M., Burns, S. and Bulman, C. (1994) *Reflective practice in nursing: the growth of the reflective practitioner*. Oxford: Blackwell Science.

Pearson, P. and Spencer, J. (1995) Pointers to effective teamwork: exploring primary care. *Journal of Interprofessional Care* **9**, 131–8.

Perry, W. (1968) *Forms of intellectual and ethical development in the college years: a scheme*. New York: Holt, Rhinehart and Winston.

Petrie, H.G. (1976) Do you see what I see? The epistemology of interdisciplinary inquiry. *Journal of Aesthetic Education* **10**, 29–43.

Pettigrew, A., Ferlie, E. and McKee, L. (1992) *Shaping strategic change*. London: Sage.

Pietroni, P.C. (1991) Stereotypes or archetypes – a study of perceptions among health care students. *Journal of Social Work Practice* **5**, 61–9.

Porter, S. (1991) A participant observation study of power relations between nurses and doctors in a general hospital. *Journal of Advanced Nursing* **16**, 728–35.

Poulton, B. and West, M. (1993) Effective multidisciplinary teamwork in primary health care. *Journal of Advanced Nursing* **18**, 918–25.

Pritchard, P. and Pritchard, J. (1994) *Teamwork for primary and shared care*. Oxford: Oxford Medical Publications.

Quilitch, H. (1978) Using a single feedback procedure to reinforce the submission of written suggestions by mental health employees. *Journal of Organisational Behaviour Management* **1**, 155–63.

Randolph, W. and Dess, G. (1984) The congruence perspectives of organisational design: a conceptual model and multivariate research approach. *Academy of Management Review* **9**, 114–27.

Sands, R.G., Stafford, J. and McClelland, M. (1990) I beg to differ: conflict in the interdisciplinary team. *Social Work in Health Care* **14**, 55–72.

Sanson-Fisher, J., Poole R.W., and Harker A.D. (1979) Behavioural analysis of ward rounds within a general hospital psychiatric unit. *Behavioural Research and Therapy* **17**, 333–48.

Schatzman, L. and Strauss, A.L. (1973) *Field research: strategies for a natural sociology*. Englewood Cliffs, NJ: Prentice Hall.

Schein, E. (1985) *Organisational culture and leadership*. San Francisco, CA: Jossey-Bass.

Scholes, J. (1998) Advance practice and innovation: implications for practitioners. Conference paper given at *Chances, changes and choices: a view towards 2000*, Heriot Watt University, Ricarton, Edinburgh, 23 September 1998.

Schon, D. (1987) *Educating the reflective practitioner*. San Francisco, CA: Jossey Bass.

Schon, D. (1991) *The reflective practitioner*, 2nd edn. London: Temple Smith.

Sharp, K. (1998) The case for case studies in nursing research: the problem of generalisation. *Journal of Advanced Nursing* **27**, 785–9.

Shaw, I. (1995) *Locally based shared learning*. London: Centre for the Advancement of Interprofessional Education.

Silver, S. (1998) A multidisciplinary health faculty team: formation and first-year production of problem-based learning in gerontology/geriatrics. *Journal of Allied Health* **272**: 83–8.

Simons, H. (ed) (1980) *Towards a science of the singular*. Norwich: Centre for Applied Research in Education, University of East Anglia.

Simpson, A. (1998) *Creating alliances: the development of the community mental health nurse to support people with severe and enduring mental illnesses in the community*. Brighton: The Sussex Consortium Mental Health Development Project.

Sinclair, S. (1997) *Making doctors: an institutional apprenticeship*. Oxford: Berg.

Snyder, B.R. (1971) *The hidden curriculum*. New York: Knopf.

Soothill, K., Mackay, L. and Webb, D. (1995) (eds) *Interprofessional relations in health care*. London: Arnold Press.

Spratley, J. (1989) *Disease prevention and health promotion in primary health care: team workshops organised by the Health Education Authority*. London: Health Education Authority.

Spurgeon, P. (1999) Organisational development: from a reactive to a proactive process. Mark, A. and Dopson, S. (eds) *Organisational behaviour in health care*. London: Macmillan Press Ltd, 25–34.

Stacey, M. (1992) *Regulating British Medicine: the General Medical Council*, Chichester: John Wiley & Sons.

Standing Committee on Postgraduate Medical and Dental Education (1997) *Multiprofessional working and learning: sharing the educational challenge*. London: Standing Committee on Postgraduate Medical and Dental Education.

Standing Committee on Postgraduate Medical and Dental Education (1999) *Equity and interchange: multi-professional work and learning*. London: The Stationery Office.

Stein, L. (1967) The doctor–nurse game. *Archives of General Psychiatry* **16**, 699–703.

Stein, L., Watts, D. and Howell,T. (1990) The doctor–nurse game revisited. *New England Journal of Medicine* **322**, 546–9.

Svensson, R. (1996) The interplay between doctors and nurses – a negotiated order perspective. *Sociology of Health and Illness* **18**, 379–98.

Tappen, R. and Touhy, T. (1983) Group leader, are you a controller? *Journal of Gerontological Nursing* **91**, 34–8.

Tellis-Nayak, M. and Tellis-Nayak, V. (1984) Games that professionals play: the social psychology of physician/nurse interaction. *Social Science in Medicine* **18**, 1063–9.

Temkin-Greener, H. (1983) Interprofessional perspectives on teamwork in health care: a case study. *Milbank Memorial Fund Quarterly/Health and Society* **61**, 641–58.

Tope, R. (1996) *Integrated interdisciplinary learning between the health and social care professions*. Aldershot: Avebury.

Tope, R. (1998) *The impact of interprofessional education in the South West region: a critical analysis. The literature Review*. London: Department of Health.

United Kingdom Central Council for Nursing Midwifery and Health Visiting (1992) *Registrar's letter*. London: UKCC.

United Kingdom Central Council for Nursing, Midwifery and Health Visiting (1999) *Fitness for practice*. London: UKCC.

Van den Ven, A. (1976) A framework for organisational assessment. *Academy of Management Review* **1**, 64–78.

Walby, S. and Greenwell, J. (1994) Medicine and nursing: professions in a changing health service. London: Sage Publications.

Webb, E.J., Campbell, D.T., Schwarz, R.D. and Sechrest, L. (1966) *Unobtrusive measures: non-reactive research in the social sciences*. Chicago: Rand McNally.

West, M. and Pillinger, T. (1996) *Team building in primary health care: an evaluation*. London: Health Education Authority.

West, M.A. and Slater J. (1996) *Teamworking in primary health care: a review of its effectiveness*. London: Health Education Authority.

Whale, Z. (1993) The participation of hospital nurses in the multidisciplinary ward round on a cancer therapy ward. *Journal of Clinical Nursing* **2**, 155–63.

Wicks, D. (1998) *Nurses and doctors at work: rethinking professional boundaries*. Milton Keynes: Open University Press.

Wilmot, S. (1995) Professional values and interprofessional dialogue. *Journal of Interprofessional Care* **9**, 257–65.

Index